THE ANCIENTS AND THE POSTMODERNS

THE ANCIENTS AND THE POSTMODERNS

FREDRIC JAMESON

VERSO
London • New York

First published by Verso Books 2015

Author and publisher would like to acknowledge the prior appearance of earlier
versions of certain chapters in the following publications: Chapter 2, *Modernist
Cultures* 8: 11 (2013); Chapter 4, Andrew Horton, ed., *The Last Modernist: The Films
of Theo Angelopolous* (Trowbridge: Flicks Books, 1997); Chapter 5, *Critical Inquiry*
1: 33 (2006); Chapter 6, D. Kellner and S. Homer, eds., *Fredric Jameson: A Critical
Reader* (London: Palgrave, 2004); Chapter 7, *New Left Review* 64 (July–Aug. 2010);
Chapter 10, *Criticism* 52: 3–4 (Summer/Fall 2010); Chapter 11, *New Left Review* 71
(Sept.–Oct. 2011); Chapter 12, *New Left Review* 75 (May–June 2012); Chapter 13,
London Review of Books 34: 22 (22 November 2012)

1 3 5 7 9 10 8 6 4 2

Verso
UK: 6 Meard Street, London W1F 0EG
US: 20 Jay Street, Suite 1010, Brooklyn, NY 11201
www.versobooks.com

Verso is the imprint of New Left Books

ISBN-13: 978-1-78168-593-8 (HC)
eISBN-13: 978-1-78168-594-5 (US)
eISBN-13: 978-1-78168-744-4 (UK)

British Library Cataloguing in Publication Data
A catalogue record for this book is available from the British Library

Library of Congress Cataloging-in-Publication Data

Jameson, Fredric.
The ancients and the postmoderns / Frederic Jameson.
   pages cm
Includes bibliographical references and index.
ISBN 978-1-78168-593-8 (hardback : alk. paper)
1. Modernism (Aesthetics) 2. Art, Modern. I. Title.
BH301.M54J36 2015
700.9—dc23
                    2014048484

Typeset in Garamond by MJ & N Gavan, Truro, Cornwall
Printed in the US by Maple Press

for Ranjana Khanna and Srinivas Aravamudan

Contents

PART ONE

OUR CLASSICISM

Mercy Altar, Basilica of the Fourteen Holy Helpers (also Basilika Vierzehnheiligen), 1743–1772. Bad Staffelstein, Germany

Chapter I

Narrative Bodies: Rubens and History

Modernism, Alexander Kluge observed somewhere, is our classicism, our classical antiquity. That presumes that it is over; but if so, when did it begin? It is a question, or perhaps a pseudo-question, that leads to deeper ones about modernity itself, when not about historical storytelling. I will myself begin (as one must) with an outrageous assertion, namely that modernity begins with the Council of Trent (ending in 1563)—in which case the Baroque becomes the first secular age. I'm sorry to say that this may not be as perverse a claim as it sounds at first: for if we inevitably associate the Baroque with the building of extraordinary churches all over the Christian world, and with an unparalleled efflorescence of religious art, there is an explanation ready to hand.

With modernity and secularization, religion falls into the realm of the social, the realm of differentiation. It becomes one worldview among others, one specialization among many: an activity to be promoted and sold on the market. In the face of Protestantism, the Church decides to advertise and to launch the first great publicity campaign on behalf of its product. After Luther, religion comes in competing brands; and Rome enters the contest practicing the usual dual strategy of carrot and stick, culture and repression, painters and architects on the one hand and generals and the Inquisition on the other. Maravall's thesis—that the Baroque is the first great deployment of a public sphere and of mass culture—thereby finds its corroboration and confirmation.[1]

But we may well want to augment this periodizing hypothesis with another, of a rather different kind. Hegel thought there

---

[1] José Antonio Maravall, *Culture of the Baroque* (Minneapolis: University of Minnesota Press, 1986).

was a moment in which, after religion, art assumed the vocation of expressing the Absolute: a moment then rapidly superseded by philosophy.[2] It is a theory of history we may want to complete by suggesting that, even as he saw it, the various arts will have chances at this vocation unevenly and in distinct chronological periods (I'll come back to music in a moment). We do not meanwhile need to mount any head-on assault on the concept of the Absolute at this time, but can certainly deduce something from the odd implication that at a certain moment religion is no longer able to assume its vocation. That moment is surely the moment of "the end of religion," a profoundly Hegelian idea we can forge on the model of the famous "end of art" also implicit in these formulations (but having nothing to do with Kojève's infamous "end of history").[3]

It is then plausible to assume that "the end of religion" is on us with secularization, and probably with Luther's revolution, which transformed a culture organized by religion into a space in which what is still called religion has become an essentially private matter and a form of subjectivity (among many others). In that case, it would follow that the apogee of art as a vehicle for the Absolute arrives in the Renaissance/Reformation period and finds its most extraordinary flowering in that century normally characterized as the Baroque, which opens with Shakespearean drama and concludes (stretching the notion of a century somewhat) with the building of Vierzehnheiligen (or maybe even with Bach's elaboration of the tonal system).[4] The Baroque is the supreme moment of theatricality, the Elizabethans only serving as the prelude to Spanish theater (Calderón) and French classicism (not excluding the somewhat less than illustrious German playbooks cited in Walter Benjamin's *Trauerspiel* book): but drama also includes the emergence of opera (and perhaps it will not be extravagant already to glimpse the proleptic shadow of Wagnerian music drama in those early forms).

This is an age which is poor in many of the things and experiences we take for granted; poor in images, before technical reproduction, not to speak of advertising; no radio, no newspapers, not even a bourgeoisie; poor in instrumental sounds, save for that rudimentary

---

[2] G. W. F. Hegel, *Aesthetics*, trans. T. M. Knox, 2 vols (Oxford: Clarendon, 1998).

[3] Alexandre Kojève, *Introduction to the Reading of Hegel* (Ithaca: Cornell University Press, 1980).

[4] Wylie Sypher is perhaps the first in English to posit these periodizations for literature. See his *Four Stages of Renaissance Style* (New York: Doubleday, 1955).

instrument called the human voice; poor in that rich background of continuous aesthetic sensation which makes it so hard to define art in our own society of images and spectacles, but which here is limited to the specialized and discontinuous moments of performance, of festival, of chorale, and even of sumptuous space, which in that period was still limited to churches and palaces. We have to try to imagine a time before film (and before television); a world without the novel; a world which is therefore also poor in narrative. Theatricality is thus the punctual eruption of the aesthetic in this newly secularized world whose principal excitement is the unexpected arrival of foreign mercenaries in unprotected peasant villages, which they sack most cruelly—it being remembered that for Nietzsche as for Artaud long after him cruelty was an essential feature of aesthetic pleasure.

Otherwise, art in the small towns and fields of this world whose dazzling epithet—*barroco*—causes us today to see transcendent sunbursts and an excess of richness in physical ornament and language alike—aesthetic pleasure is limited to the shock of an unexpected encounter—the abrupt flash of the vision of Caravaggio's *Crucifixion of St. Peter* in a dim side chapel of Santa Maria del Popolo, say. We have to imagine that shock today; it will have to be an accident, the boredom of a London afternoon in the National Gallery suddenly transfixed by Rubens's immense *Samson and Delilah*. And indeed the whole century, the long seventeenth century is here, in the forcefield between Caravaggio and Rubens, the immensity of the struggle of these narrative bodies suspended in blinding oil paint before our disbelieving eyes.

I want to examine the historical conditions of possibility of such works; but first I will read into the record a famous, or indeed, notorious aesthetic generalization by Nietzsche, which may not on the face of it seem the most obvious reference here, and indeed on the face of it would seem to result from the crossing of the wires of quite distinct interests. Indeed, this Nietzsche reference documents what I have been trying to theorize as the emergence of affect in nineteenth-century literature, an emergence of which I see him both as theorist and a symptom. His characterization of aesthetics as a physiological matter will have to suffice at this point, and the relevance of this typically nineteenth-century (or "decadent") view to the seventeenth century is what will have to be defended in a moment. At any rate here is the passage I wanted to recall:

For art to exist, for any sort of aesthetic activity or perception to exist, a certain physiological precondition is indispensable: intoxication. Intoxication must first have heightened the excitability of the entire machine: no art results before that happens. All kinds of intoxication, however different their origin, have the power to do this; above all, the intoxication of sexual excitement, the oldest and most primitive form of intoxication. Likewise the intoxication which comes in the train of all great desires, all strong emotions; the intoxication of feasting, of contest, of the brave deed, of victory, of all extreme agitation; the intoxication of cruelty; intoxication in destruction; intoxication under certain meteorological influences, for example the intoxication of spring; or under the influence of narcotics; finally the intoxication of the will, the intoxication of an overloaded and distended will.—The essence of intoxication is the feeling of plenitude and increased energy. From out of this feeling one gives to things, one *compels* them to take, one rapes them—one calls this procedure idealizing.[5]

By spiritualization Nietzsche means that "path of distance," that "formidable erosion of contours" evoked by Gide, and not any spiritualization or intellectualizing dilution. Now the word *Rausch* is here untranslatable; Kaufman gives us "frenzy," David Crell "rapture"— the one seems to me too kinetic, if not excessive, the other too prim and religiose. Heidegger of course does not need to translate, but he interprets this state as the primal form of the will to power, thus stressing that "feeling of plenitude and increased energy" of which Nietzsche speaks, without really coming to terms with the outright physiological drunkenness Nietzsche's whole description wishes to convey.

I therefore think that Hollingdale's forthright "intoxication" best preserves the ambiguities and multiple connotations of the German Rausch. Meanwhile, if we attempt to sanitize this term by reconfining it to the Nietzschean canon and simply identifying it with the Dionysian, it should be added that in the second paragraph after this one, Nietzsche evokes a properly Apollinian "intoxication" which is above all active in the eyes, in the visual (just as the heightened form of the Dionysian overwhelms the ear, and finds its heightened form in music).

Still, Apollinian Rausch remains more enigmatic: it is not clear what form an "intoxication of the eyes" might take; all we have along those lines in the way of a concept is voyeurism, which may or may

---

[5] Friedrich Nietzsche, *Twilight of the Idols*, trans. R. J. Hollingdale (London: Penguin, 1968), pp. 82–3.

not be relevant here; but anyone committed to the experience of paintings will feel the lack of a name for what is certainly a distinctive experience. As far as Nietzsche himself is concerned, it is worth pointing out, not only that his eyes were bad and that his sight suffered chronically, complicated by almost permanent headaches, but that in general his reference to painting and the visual arts is virtually absent, a curious silence for someone willing to talk endlessly about his taste in the other arts. He was in short not an *Augenmensch* and very much an *Ohrenmensch*; and therefore, apart from stereotypical evocations of Greek statuary, not particularly inclined to speculate or theorize on the matter—even though he very emphatically wishes to distance his aesthetic concepts, and in particular the Apollinian, from standard (German) views of the classical. So there is a conceptual gap to be filled, which I cannot hope to remedy here.

I am myself currently interested in making a historical distinction between affect and emotion, and am therefore motivated to understand Nietzschean Rausch or intoxication in terms of an explosion of affect rather than the expression or sympathetic reception of this or that named emotion. (Nietzsche also serves to authorize a theory of affect that formulates it as an unnamable scale of bodily states, ranging from melancholy to euphoria, and in strict counterdistinction to the reified conscious objects tabulated in the various historical and traditional "theories of the passions.")[6] Affects are bodily feelings, emotions conscious states; and one line of my interrogation of these various Baroque works presupposes that affect enters painting at the moment of modernism, the moment of Manet and impressionism, the moment in which bodily feeling becomes inscribed in oil paint. In that case, what is it that we find happening in Caravaggio or Rubens, unless it is simply the representation of an emotion in the content, if not the rhetorical call for emotional reaction along the lines of Aristotelian psychology? In other words, I also want to refuse the facile solution which would grasp Caravaggian chiaroscuro or Rubens's brush-strokes simply as anticipations of some modern foregrounding of the medium as such.

But just as clearly the history of the medium and of technique will have its role to play in any approach to these works. That history will then have to be grasped in its intersection with the history of

---

[6] The discussion of affect (in my *Antinomies of Realism*) is meant to stand in binary or structural opposition to what I call named emotion, whose allegorical systems I plan to study in a forthcoming work on allegory.

the social, that is, the history of human relations and the historical subjectivities they produce; and it will also have to take account of the relationship of the specific art itself to narrativity and to the availability of narrative vehicles in which both levels—that of the advanced technology of the medium, that of the variety of human relations and interactions developed in the social realm—can be more fully exercised. We might also want to make a separate place here for the accumulation of precedents, of stories and legends in the case of the narrative arts, of precursors in the visual realm, of generations of musical exercises in the auditory: a level which can then either be identified with or distinguished from the social evolution of the status of the craftsman and of the economic demand for his products, which is to say, the evolution of his public.

The individual work stands at the confluence of all these levels or conditions; and music may once again be taken as the example of what happens when some are missing; before tonality, nothing like the emergence of a musical absolute—for example, of the extraordinary multidimensionality of Beethoven—is yet possible. The withdrawal of some of these same conditions also results in an interesting historical question: such as the gradual end of tragic drama after the seventeenth century, let alone the extinction of epic as such.

In any case our topic here is rather the efflorescence, the unique combination of possibilities that alone can explain, in that first great secular age which is the Baroque, the artistic achievements I have mentioned earlier and which I now want to begin to approach in terms of an accumulation of stories and of precedents. Let's speak then of that peculiar historical and cultural heritage which is the concept of Christ's body. The development of the visual arts in the West is unthinkable without the resources of this body, from its birth to its agony and death (and even including sexuality, as Leo Steinberg has shown in a notorious essay).[7]

Christ's body has therefore served as the laboratory for innumerable experiments in the representation of the body in all its postures and potentialities; and these will then enable the theatrical staging of equally innumerable dramatic—which is to say narrative—scenes, in a far more dynamic and cinematographic way than the various stills or freeze-frames of the High Renaissance. I hope it is not too

---

[7] Leo Steinberg, *The Sexuality of Christ* (New York: Pantheon, 1983).

Peter Paul Rubens, *Christ on the Cross* (1627),
Rockoxhuis Museum, Antwerp

outrageous to claim that the body in this sense—I will call it the
narrative body, rather than the three-dimensional one—the body in
this sense only truly emerges in the Baroque period in Caravaggio's
oil paint.

But let's talk more particularly about Christ's crucifixion, a rich
and unusual resource for Western painters. Leaving aside the various
theological acrobatics (themselves unusual resources for Western
philosophy), what uniquely characterizes this subject is its dialectical identification of success and failure, of transcendence and
extinction, of life and death.

We may conjecture that before this these opposites are separate
and distinct; the victorious, the healthy, the living, on the one hand,
the dying, the wounded, the maimed and suffering on the other.
Now perhaps for the first time these opposites are united; mortality
can express resurrection, physical suffering and agony can stand for
life transfigured, defeat and execution for triumph and victory. In
representational terms, then, the crucifixion enables a revolution in
what the representation of the organic human body can mean and

do, and it is a conceptual revolution as well as an artistic one, a transformation in ideology as well as in perception. I suppose that some interpretive approximation can be made here to the equally unique possibility of the theatrical genre of tragedy in this same period, but I won't speculate on that here.

Matthias Grünewald, *Isenheim Altarpiece: The Crucifixion* (1512–1516), Musée d'Unterlinden, Colmar, France

Such is then the peculiar ideological opening the crucifixion offers for the affirmative content of even the most unnoble bodies and bodily states. But it also offers some uniquely physical openings and new possibilities as well. Consider how complicated a matter it is to lower a dead body from a cross. This might certainly be a comic matter, as when, in Sokurov's *Second Circle*, all kinds of desperate gymnastics are required to get the coffin down a narrow staircase; and one might well imagine ferociously atheistic cartoonists doing the same for the corpse of the Redeemer. But

Michelangelo Buonarotti, *Pietà* (1498–1499), St. Peter's Basilica, Vatican City

this hypothesis only helps us to a keener sense in what the great narrative painters had to face, and wanted to face, in elaborating all the possibilities of this physical subject, as rare as it is complex.

The suppleness of the body could already be dramatized in the Pietà, which would, however, seem to be more an occasion for representing the maternal, as we shall see shortly. The crucial property of the new narrative body, however—one perhaps hitherto mainly achieved in sculpture—is sheer weight and mass. It will be understood that the Pietà only conveys an inert feeling for load, while the nailing of Christ to wooden boards lying on the ground is in this respect simply cheating, although one wouldn't want to say

Michelangelo Merisi da Caravaggio, *The Crucifixion of Saint Peter* (1601), Santa Maria del Popolo, Rome

that about Caravaggio's *Crucifixion of St. Peter* for all kinds of different reasons. As for the elevation, it is certainly sublime (as witness its afterlife in the famous Iwo Jima photograph), but the heroic straining that stages the earthly gravity it conveys redounds to the bodies of Christ's executioners rather than to the divine form itself; it might, to be sure, convey something far more peculiar physiologically, namely the dizziness of the movement aloft, as in the executions in Flaubert's *Salammbô*—clearly an affect more congenial to nineteenth-century decadence than to our people here.[8]

---

[8]   Gustave Flaubert, *Salammbô*, Chapter 14, "Le défilé de la Hache":

Quelques-uns, évanouis d'abord, venaient de se ranimer sous la fraîcheur du vent; mais ils restaient le menton sur la poitrine, et leur corps descendait un peu, malgré les clous de leurs bras fixés plus haut que leur tête; de leurs talons et de leurs mains, du sang tombait par grosses gouttes, lentement, comme des branches d'un arbre tombent des fruits mûrs, —et Carthage, le golfe, les montagnes et les plaines, tout leur paraissait tourner, tel qu'une immense roue; quelquefois, un nuage de poussière montant du sol les enveloppait dans ses tourbillons; ils étaient brûlés par une soif horrible, leur langue se retournait dans leur bouche, et ils sentaient sur eux une sueur glaciale couler, avec leur âme qui s'en allait …

Au milieu de leur défaillance, quelquefois ils tressaillaient à un frôlement de plumes, qui leur passait contre la bouche. De grandes ailes balançaient des ombres autour d'eux, des croassements claquaient dans l'air; et comme la croix de Spendius était la plus haute, ce fut sur la sienne que le premier vautour s'abattit.

Peter Paul Rubens, The Elevation of the Cross (1610), Cathedral of Our Lady, Antwerp

Peter Paul Rubens, Descent from the Cross (1612–1614), Cathedral of Our Lady, Antwerp

So only the descent from the cross suits the purpose: the multiple articulation of the body's joints are here dramatized in a variety of ways one would be hard put to represent in any other posture. We may hypothesize that it is only after this exercise that the human body is available for the immense variety of gestures and stances required for that properly narrative painting that concerns us. In other words, the body of the anatomy theaters was but the prerequisite for an anatomically correct representation of the body in a single static posture; only the anatomy of the body in motion as it is laboriously lowered from the cross demonstrates the multiple postures of which it is susceptible. Only this multiple pliancy then opens up the possibility for what we have called the narrative body to emerge.

To this first complex of possibilities, we must now add the matter of gravity, of weight and mass, and better still, of the dead weight of the dead body, which completes the abstract lessons of three-dimensionality developed in earlier painting. It is paradoxical that the weight of the dead body, as it can alone dramatically be experienced here, and not in the prone of supine figures of the anatomy theater, should be what adds the possibility of narrative life to the human form; and certainly one does not want to exploit this paradox in philosophically ingenious ways—the union of opposites, death or finitude alone making life possible, and so forth. Perhaps all we need to stress here is the way in which the potentiality of our bodies, not only to act and to move, but also to become the sheer mass of the inorganic object—perhaps this potentiality alone adds true materiality to our anthropomorphic illusions, and makes some truly materialist painting possible. For oddly enough it is this dead body weight that stuns and arrests us in front of these immense canvasses, that allows the new painterly lighting to become dramatically operative, and that opens the possibility of what Lyotard would have called libidinal investment in these forms, something not quite available in full intensity in Michelangelo or Mantegna, for example: the foreshortening of the legs of Christ being in my opinion a remarkable image, but not of the same order as the Madonna's dirty feet in death, which so scandalized its original patrons and allowed a young and enthusiastic Rubens to snap a priceless Caravaggio up for his own employers in Mantua.[9] I want to argue that libidinal investment—something a good deal more complicated than mere

---

[9]   Mark Lamster, *Master of Shadows* (New York: Doubleday, 2009), p. 34.

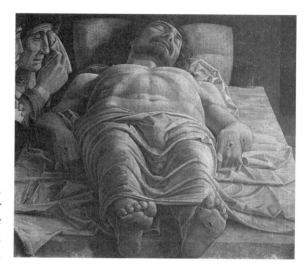

Andrea Mantegna,
*Lamentation over
the Dead Christ*
(c. 1480), Pinacoteca
di Brera, Milan

Michelangelo Merisi
da Caravaggio, *Death
of the Virgin* (c. 1606),
Musée du Louvre, Paris

sensual interest—is a radically different, a radically new experience, and perhaps begins to give us something of a clue as to the real nature of that visual or Apollinian Rausch, that intoxication or even frenzy of the gaze, which Nietzsche was only able to note in passing. This also seems to be something more than the mere further teleological exploration and development of perspective, although I don't have the technical knowledge to argue that feature adequately.

Gesturality, dead weight: now we need to add in a final property of the innumerable descents from the cross, and it is a property of another kind altogether. For the lone dead body in this particular situation has a very special quality which has not yet been mentioned: it demands many hands, it is impossible without a host of other living beings around it, the corpse is thus by necessity profoundly collective, as strange as that may seem. For here alone the individual object, even the individual body, cannot exist in isolation, cannot sit for its individual portrait so to speak: it demands manipulation, it is defined by the labor of any number of living individuals, some shouting warnings and commands, others seizing an unexpectedly dangling limb, counterbalancing effects of gravity that had not been taken into consideration, or bracing themselves for a direct yet well-nigh unbearable burden. It thus turns out that this repository of all the postures of which the human body is capable which is the corpse itself now calls into being around itself an immense variety of living postures and stances in its collective entourage—a variety of strained poses immensely more numerous than the struggle of one or two men to move a thing or indeed to raise a heavy cross in the air. So already, when we speak of the descent from the cross we necessarily invoke a social totality, a collectivity which is in its turn the condition for the closure of the painting as a whole world, and the completeness of what lies within the frame and fills our eye.

After this then, the painters are able to dispense with the immediate textual pretext, the crucifixion itself, and recreate these possibilities in a variety of other situations, as in those martyrdoms of Caravaggio which do not involve the act of lowering as such. Indeed, they no longer need involve the religious tradition at all, and so I come now to my main exhibit, biblical enough in its reference, but extraordinarily secular in its execution and implications, I mean Rubens's great *Samson and Delilah*.

Peter Paul Rubens, *Samson and Delilah* (1609–1610), National Gallery, London

Here also, we confront a dead weight, but it is the dead weight of a sleeping body; and yet it nonetheless partakes of what an older popular language called a kind of death:

Le sommeil d'amour dure toujours …

This is indeed the sleep of love, the most exhaustive gratification, in a painting that unlike anything in Caravaggio (or in Rubens himself either) virtually reeks of sex. The libidinal is here therefore not our standard poststructuralist concept of desire, but perhaps that very un- and anti-Freudian and un-Lacanian thing which is desire so fully satisfied that its sleep is itself a form of transcendence. This is a far better union of life and death than any crucifixion, in its sheer body weight—and Samson is surely more massive than any Christ, his hanging arm more materialist and carnal in its sheer strength as well as its abandon, than Christ's whole body.

The single hanging arm determines a position of the limbs and of the whole body comparable to the descents we have described, and yet which articulates its frame in a repose as electrifying as its death and transfigurtion in the competing schemes.

So here the dead weight of postcoital slumber is organic life itself, and Samson's legendary and heroic exploits are more fully and arrestingly rendered in this electrifying immobility than in any action painting or any individual exploit. Nor is this pornography either, for whatever putative sexual exploit might be thought to be documented here is, in my opinion, bypassed towards life itself in the slumbering narrative body. To be sure, Schama believes "the throes of sexual transport recapitulated in the liquid scarlet silk of Delilah's gown"; but he also describes Samson as "the pathetic brute, omnipotence made impotent,"[10] which is not at all the way I see things, unless the word brute here merely signifies a force that is somehow beyond the human and its categories

Peter Paul Rubens, *Saint Christopher Carrying the Christ Child* (1612–1614), Cathedral of Our Lady, Antwerp

and characterology (but see the *St. Christopher*). Samson here is certainly not genetically related to any of the other human figures in the painting, but that is because the hero, or the Nietzschean superman, is altogether beyond those categories. But so was Christ, and we have to grasp the way in which this kind of apotheosis of the narrative body must necessarily be larger and other than the viewers—just as the painting itself must be huge, and the very colors themselves superhuman: Baroque cloth is like nothing we have ever touched, the jewels (when there are any) more intense than normal human eyes, the actions themselves convulsed in earthquake proportions. Into this prodigious enlargement of our senses, the viewer

---

[10]   Simon Schama, *Rembrandt's Eyes* (New York: Random House, 1999), p. 142.

plunges in a Rausch or Apollinian intoxication of the eyes quite distinct from the Dionysian frenzies of music or perhaps of poetic language. This is, indeed, the sense in which Milton rather than Shakespeare is the more relevant equivalent in Baroque language:

> Now came still evening on, and twilight gray,
> Had in her sober livery all things clad;
> Silence accompanied, for beast and bird,
> They to their grassy couch, these to their nests,
> Were slunk, all but the wakeful nightingale;
> She all night long her amorous descant sung;
> Silence was pleased.
>
> (*Paradise Lost* IV, 598–605)

Not only does Milton's deliciously mute language embellish an Italianate, a painterly art; the spectator is himself not missing:

> Unspeakable desire to see, and know
> All these his wondrous works, but chiefly man,
> His chief delight and favor.
>
> (*Paradise Lost* III, 661–4)

One only needs to add the obvious, namely that Milton's Samson is not the sequel to this sensual triumph of Rubens, but rather the expression of the experience of political defeat, of the desolation that follows the collapse of superhuman revolutionary enthusiasm.

Besides the iconological level of Samson's sleep (as a variant of the Pietà), as well as what we may call the libidinal investment of this figure, we may also note its value on a formal or narrative level. The approach to this moment of narrative art has taken a route through and beyond the problematic Lessing dealt with in his *Laokoon*, namely that storytelling which consists in choosing the "optimal moment" in an action, the moment in which all the various individual actions and their distinct temporalities come together in one unique and uniquely visible crisis point.

"Objects which exist side by side (*Nebeneinander*) or whose parts exist side by side are called bodies. Accordingly bodies, with their visible properties are the proper object of painting. Objects which succeed each other in time, (*Nacheinander*) or whose parts succeed each other in time, are called actions (*Handlungen*). They

are accordingly the objects of poetry (literature here narrative) …
Painting can, in the coexistence of its compositions, only use a single
moment of action, and must therefore choose the most pregnant
moment, the one from which we can most clearly grasp (*am begrei-
flichsten*) what has preceded and what will follow that moment in
time."[11]

Clearly enough my thesis here wants to posit a synthesis of these
two dimensions—properly narrative bodies which transcend the
linearity of Lessing's Nacheinander, his moment-after-moment, his
before-and-after, in time. What is implied is that there exist two
kinds of time, an absolute present and a chronological or successive
temporality that moves from past to future; but I can't argue that
any further here.

For Lessing's emphasis on the moment then in a sense reifies it
and produces a kind of linear temporality, one which has its much
more obvious equivalents or reproductions in other media—the
freeze frame in film, for example, or the once very popular eight-
eenth tableau in theater, in which suddenly and unexpectedly all
the actors come together in the posing of a well-known painting
of the period. (The filmic equivalent of that would be the famous
moment in Bunuel's *Viridiana*, where the beggars' feast suddenly
is arrested in the attitudes of Leonardo's *Last Supper*.) Meanwhile
there are interesting contemporary works which, adapting the high
society salon spin-off of the charade, make of this formal device
a meditation on representation itself, and a profoundly modernist
turn—I think of Raoul Ruiz's *The Hypothesis of the Stolen Painting*
in film, or the video installations of James Coleman.

Behind these versions of the tableau, however, there lies not only a
specific construction of temporality around the "moment," but also
a specific mode of expression (which is to say, of acting and theatrical mimesis): namely the florid gesticulation and facial grimaces
which, become a table of codified styles, notoriously characterized
the worst of silent-movie acting (and of the opera of the period).
This is then the physiognomic style which threatens the aesthetic of
the optimal moment: a set of signs designed to be read by the viewer
and to convey the meaning of the actions or reactions of each of
the participants in the tableau. This then becomes the conventional
style of low-level Baroque narrative painting, and even Caravaggio

---

[11]   G. E. Lessing, *Laokoon* (Stuttgart: Reclam, 1964), pp. 114–15.

Michelangelo Merisi da Caravaggio, detail from *The Martyrdom of Saint Matthew* (1599–1600), San Luigi dei Francesi, Rome

himself is not exempt from its influence—as in the grimaces of horror or amazement with which he endows spectators within the paintings, thereby rhetorically asking us to share their reactions.

But Samson's sleep in the present work short-circuits this aesthetic altogether. It might well seem that the painting exposes itself to all the dangers of the aesthetic of the optimal moment: the old woman extending the lamp, the young man severing a lock of hair, the armed men waiting at the open door. Yet all these are temporal processes and not isolated moments in the temporality of an unfolding event. But it is above all Samson's drugged sleep which transforms the bodies assembled here and lifts their conjuncture out of normal additive or linear temporality: for sleep is not exactly an event which can be arrested photographically. Even in time it weighs on the action like a force of gravity; its immobile intensity draws everything into the temporality of a different world and different representation: a narrative body which transforms the very nature of narration as such.

On the other hand, it may be argued that from a narrative perspective the prehistory of Samson is less important than his subsequent destiny, and that for most people the narrative of which this episode—of the shearing of the hair and the loss of his superhuman strength—is only an prelude to the climax, namely, long after his blinding, Samson's miraculous recovery of his powers in order to bring down the heathen temple upon his enemies' heads (and his own): a feat—a kind of suicide bombing—which restores his glory and his status as a legendary hero. In other words, it is not the Delilah episode but rather this final heroic act of self-sacrifice that constitutes Samson's true destiny and thus makes this narrative memorable. If that were so, then the moment Rubens immortalizes here is itself secondary to a much larger absent narrative *chronology*.

But you could just as plausibly argue (that is to say: I will argue here) not only that Rubens's painting acknowledges that traditional narrative and somehow restructures it, but even more, that it denarrativizes it. In my own jargon, he repudiates chronological time—the past-present-future of destiny—for a kind of eternal present of

consciousness. It is a substitution which the content of the narrative
enables, by way of figuration. Figuration was the method whereby
Christianity adapted the stories of the Old Testament to the revelations of the New: thus Samson's blindness would prophetically
foreshadow Christ's death and descent into Hell, his final destruction of the Temple would figure Christ's resurrection. But in the
reversal of figuration that begins to take place in that secular age of
which Rubens is one of the masters, blindness is no longer the figure
which Milton still so powerfully expressed:

> O dark, dark, dark mid the blaze of noon ….
> The sun to me is dark
> and silent as the moon
> when she deserts the night,
> hid in her vacant interlunar cave …
>
> (*Samson Agonistes*, 80, 86–9)

In Rubens' version I believe that what happens is that the whole thematics of blindness and light has been appropriated and invested in
the new image of this libidinal slumber I have been describing, itself
a new synthesis between body and spirit, an immanence of life in
which sight is however dialectically projected outwards, becoming
the sight of the viewer, just as consciousness and sight are separated off from both spirit and light and becomes something else in
the figure of Delilah, to which we now turn, along with the other
players in this extraordinary scene.

Clearly Delilah will mark the place of multiple inquiries—not
only about Rubens's women in general—and a more feminist take
on this picture in particular, which does not I think really stage the
battle of the sexes, but also about Rubens's specific reading of the
biblical tale.

The latter is not, to be sure, very explicit on the subject of Delilah
(indeed, Milton adds the detail of their marriage, which is not
present in the biblical text); and even though the old crone with
the candle corresponds to the traditional iconography of the go-
between and brothel madame from *La Celestina* on, the biblical
narrative does not identify Delilah as a prostitute, or even infer that
she is not a Hebrew—although the historical Samson seems to have
had a weakness for alien women, despite the fact that he is a member
of a particularly ascetic and orthodox sect (the Nazarites)—whence

the ban on the cutting of the hair. It is therefore not clear whether Delilah is a patriot or merely a paid agent.

We have been only too ready to see Delilah in the light and perspective of the biblical story: although as I have already pointed out, not only is there nothing in the famous episode from Judges to confirm her participation in the oldest profession (one remembers of course that the second oldest one is espionage), there is also nothing to confirm her identification as a Philistine or Palestinian. It might be wondered therefore whether we could not view the story—very much including her own participation in it—from a different standpoint. Indeed, Susan Ackerman asks precisely this question in the title of her study of the matter: "What if Judges had been written by a Philistine?" Her conclusion is the surprising one, namely that "so bumbling is Samson in his role as an Israelite hero that it almost seems as if Judges 14:1–16:22 had been written by a Philistine."[12] In that case, the very focus of the story shifts and Delilah becomes its hero, a perspective which is then confirmed by comparing her, as Milton does, to the other great biblical (and Israelite) heroines Judith and Jael, who equally triumph over male and alien oppressors:

> I shall be named among the famousest
> Of women, sung at solemn festivals,
> Living and dead recorded, who, to save
> Her country from a fierce destroyer, chose
> Above the faith of wedlock bands …
> (*Samson Agonistes*, 982–6)

Still, this is not exactly the heroic figure we find in Caravaggio's Judith for example; nor, to locate it more specifically within the Rubens canon, does Delilah epitomize any of the characteristics of the notoriously voluptuous Rubens nude, which have alienated so many contemporary viewers and contributed no little to the sinking reputation of that artist who was once "the greatest painter in the world." Delilah's delicate features are indeed far more comparable to his great portraits of his own wives than to the various ecstatic or fearful goddesses, whose folds of flesh echo the excessive musculature of the standard Rubens male hero (an excess also diminished in

---

[12] Susan Ackerman, "What if Judges Had Been Written by a Philistine?," *Biblical Interpretation* 8: 1 (2000), pp. 33–41.

Michelangelo Merisi da Caravaggio, *Judith Beheading Holofernes* (1598–1599), Galleria Nazionale d'Arte Antica, Rome

this particular work by sleep itself); for denarrativization also means the virtualization of action as such, action that necessarily exists in a past-present-future continuum. And the neutralization of action then means flabby muscles, whether we are talking about males in struggle or the supine nudes ...

As for Delilah, we may similarly note that, apart from the hero, she is the one character in this scene who is doing nothing, who is not engaged in this or that project (for even Samson's sleep is here a form of action and jouissance). Nor is Delilah an observer precisely (privileged or not): hers is not in that sense our point of view, the spectator's—rather there disengages from her features that preternatural calm and lucidity which may be grasped as a different kind of post-coital effect than Samson's (without necessarily turning this into an allegory of gender) and which in many ways sets the atmosphere of the painting as a whole, suspending it in a serene moment beyond tragedy or drama (while still maintaining it firmly at the center of narrative as such).

Of most significance is the neutrality of her expression: we cannot here detect the hatred of the male common enough in such situations of subalternity; nor any great excitement about her ultimate victory. It might be simple indifference at this development, in which she was

Peter Paul Rubens, *The Disembarkation at Marseilles* (1621–1625), Musée du Louvre, Paris

Peter Paul Rubens, *Self-portrait with Isabella Brant* ('The Honeysuckle Bower'), 1609–1610, Alte Pinakothek, Munich

Peter Paul Rubens, *Portrait of Isabella Brant* (c. 1620–1625), Cleveland Museum of Art

a mere instrument (the presence of the figure who actually executes the fatal shearing might already seem to diminish her own centrality and importance). Or with a certain goodwill, we may even imagine we detect a note of sympathy here if not an almost maternal expression. This final interpretation might find some unlikely evidence in the statuary above the scene—it seems to be a mother and child—but it also returns us to the original text and perhaps the only detail of any real interest in it for Rubens in his composition: "And she made him sleep upon her knees" (Judg. 16:19), otherwise a rather unnecessary and perhaps even incomprehensible piece of information.

What the posture does in our present context, however, is to reactivate the whole tradition of the Pietà to which we have already referred, and not only to assimilate Samson figurally to Christ, but also to identify his sleep with the letter's death in a different way than in the conventional pun.

For all these alternative readings or interpretations of Rubens's Delilah, I prefer to substitute this one: Delilah's expression conveys some lucid and impersonal consciousness that corresponds to the sated slumber of Samson. This is not quite an allegory of mind and body, and yet if you projected it to a metaphysical level, that might just give us a hint at the intensity of the coexistence! No longer the relationship between two people or characters, it is an overlay of two whole incommensurable dimensions, in that closer to Spinoza's twin attributes of substance, thought and extension (the *Ethics* is of course yet another Baroque masterpiece). If so, then we have here a phenomenon which allows us a glimpse of what Hegel might have meant when he asserted that art could somehow, at the right historical moment, convey the Absolute; or what Deleuze meant when he claimed that painting also produces concepts, albeit of a painterly rather than an abstract-philosophical kind.

At any rate, I myself here argue that it is by reading what can only be called an utter stillness and universal lucid consciousness without content into our apprehension of Delilah that we can come close to sensing what is extraordinary about Rubens's vision. This is the relationship of the painting to temporal chronology as such: it is out of time, not even a present, let alone the freeze-frame of so much narrative painting, according to the Lessing formula of the optimal moment of drama or movement or action. This temporal peculiarity also accounts for the raw immediacy of the painting in its space of exhibition.

On the other hand, if some class differentiation seems desirable here, it must surely lie in the distance of the work from those late feudal or absolutist publics with which the grandest Rubens is conventionally associated, the courts which commissioned portraits and historical pageants from him, the counterreformation Church that gave him the chance at some remarkable altar-pieces. This particular painting was commissioned by the mayor of Antwerp, presumably, like Rubens himself, a Catholic. Still, the biblical overtones and the secularity of the work surely lend it a faint flavor of the Protestantism that triumphed in the neighboring Dutch bourgeoisie, thereby distancing it notionally from Rubens's other work. (Indeed it has been argued that it is not really by Rubens at all.)[13] The class dynamics suggested here however do not posit a bourgeois class affiliation as opposed to the aristocratic one, but rather that the class relations of the future position it in a classless space (before the bourgeois revolution redefines that class as one among others). In other words, the abolition of the feudal order which defines revolution here is still a

---

[13]   See Edward M. Gomez, "Is 'Samson and Delilah' a Fake?," December 19, 2005, at salon.com.

utopian perspective in which classes themselves disappear (unlike what happens when that revolution really comes to pass, in Holland as well as in France itself).

At any rate Delilah's strange imperturbability means, I think, all of that and unifies the work in another sense, makes of it a totality quite different from most dramatic scenes. But now we need to move on to what is perhaps the most peculiar detail of this painting, one also suggested by the biblical text, in the lines that immediately succeed those I have quoted: "and she called for a man, and she caused him to shave off the seven locks of his head" (Judg. 16:20). Yes, it does look in retrospect as though Delilah were contemplating an operation she herself dictated, and the young man himself as though he were a servant of some kind. Our own contemporary associations would probably tend to identify him as a young bureaucrat in the service of the state, a CIA agent in training or a dark-suited trainee of the great monopolies, banks, insurance companies, multinationals, all those who who have some vital stakes in the essentially political conspiracy. Yet I now think he is too menial a figure for even that status, and his rapt attention to the task at hand, his sheerly manual tact and proficiency, tend to make him, along with the crone who has also been pressed into service to light the operation, part of Delilah's own entourage—something which only increases her power and centrality and makes her into the protagonist of this work. There is then a movement from Samson to Delilah herself which organizes the shift in the viewer's attention and reorients us away from the first overwhelmingly libidinal focus towards a sense of the project more political in the sense of tactics and operations.

It also, on the other end of this shift from right to left, returns our gaze in a powerful rebound to the upper-righthand corner door, where the emissaries of state power wait for their denouement, and for the significant shift in power relations expected by the disarming and disabling of the hero. The civilian representative in the state is still an observer, in the darkness, but the military personnel are lit by their own distant light. History itself is here, about to break into the space of the painting and to transform everything, to sweep all in its path, and open the way for new narratives and new episodes, like the one Milton elaborated. The place of history is thus marked and included in this suspended totality; its presence makes the totality complete, while still withholding the arrival of the future. Waiting is then one of the most powerful elements of the whole, a kind of emotion in its own right, if not a passion. Waiting is the very presence of Time itself, now personified and arrested in a representational figure; overcome only by its incorporation.

So it is that past and future are drawn within this present: this is the temporality of destiny and its chronological succession—Samson's election and his subsequent redemption—retentions and protensions as Husserl would have called them, external dimensions of time external to the present—the temporal narratives of destiny all now drawn back within that painted present and interiorized or denarrativized in such a way that the painted bodies now include them. This is a perpetual present of the canvas, a kind of aesthetic autonomy, quite different from that selected and frozen moment as which Lessing could imagine the transfer of narrative to a visual art.

Its conditions of possibility are technical—the completion of perspectival representation in Caravaggio's great breakthrough—and historical—the fulfillment of a secular age: as well as the enrichment of narratives of destiny by the subjectivities of the Shakespearean age—a unique historical conjuncture that will not return, but which we can certainly characterize as some first distinctive moment of realism.

As for the meaning of the painting, perhaps the term is inappropriate. An old-fashioned allegorical reading might as I've already suggested translate our picture into an intersection of consciousness and body menaced by the twin external forces of bureaucratic technology and state power as those foreshadow the moment of absolutism. If such a reading makes us uncomfortable, it is because the painting may well think those thoughts or those meanings, but if so, it thinks them as Deleuze would say in a painterly way, it thinks in concepts of oil paint and not in those or abstract intellection. *Il n'y a pas de rapport sexuel*: through this breach or gap now stream all the ideological binaries piling up like pus or toxins in the naturalization of sex: the battle of the sexes, to be sure, their virtual transformation into two species; but also—mind or spirit versus body or matter; Israeli versus Palestinian (First versus Third World); beauty versus the sublime; the state versus terror (or the nomads); politics versus sexuality (public versus private); force versus power (unless it was violence); one even expects global versus local to arrive any minute, followed by the whole metaphysical bodyguard of space versus time to reinforce the land grab versus revolution itself. In these oppositions the ethical bouncing ball touches first on one then the other, passing back and forth from one term to the other (bound together as they are by History), now certifying one as good and the other evil until the inevitable alternation and reversal, thereby perpetuating the timeless Apollinian stillness of the two eternal figures.

The allegorical formula would only be useful if it helps us transform our visual contemplation of this image into an encounter of two dimensions of being which has all the impact of a physical collision and all the intensity of an event. It is this event which is received with Nietzschean or Dionysian intoxication. The narrative painting of the Baroque thus marks some first approach to immanence, to an aesthetic autonomy very different from that of the later modernist era as such. It thereby completes Hegel's notion of a situation in which for a time art constitutes a vehicle for the Absolute: for the Absolute emerges from just this immanence of the narrative body.

Chapter 2

Wagner as Dramatist and Allegorist

for Peter Fitting

Wagner's architectonic and metaphysical excess, particularly in the *Ring*, does not encourage modesty in the critic, who also ends up wanting to say everything, rather than one specific thing. If I had to do the latter, like a good scholar or philologist, an erudite commentator, I would probably try to say something about the magic potions in Wagner; and may still briefly touch on that. But as a specialized topic that would also require us to deal more centrally with *Tristan*; and here clearly it is the *Ring* that demands our full and complete attention, not least on account of the interpretive controversies it continues to cause.

So perhaps one guideline should be, not so much what Wagner really "meant," but rather what interpretation and meaning might actually be in the "case of Wagner." This is a dialectical problem that greatly transcends the traditional questions about the *Ring*: namely, whether it is about Wotan or Siegfried, and also what "the gods" can be said to mean (in order for them to undergo a twilight, indeed a wholesale conflagration and extinction). On a philosophical level, this problem traditionally confronts Feuerbach with Schopenhauer; and meanwhile, in another part of the forest, there lurks the question about the meaning of the ring itself and to what degree it may be said to represent capitalism, as Shaw famously argued.

What it is now dialectically important to do is to suspend all the alternatives such questions ask us to choose, and to step back in order to ask what such questions themselves mean. We need to ask what meaning means in this situation, and therefore what interpreting it might involve. And it is crucial to retain our specification "in this instance," and to remember that the discussion engages Wagner alone, or rather his historical situation, and not music in general, drama in general, interpretation in general, or reading in general (for it is about reading that we must focus on here). Still, it seems minimally fair to generalize Wagner's aesthetic situation to that of an early moment of artistic modernism as such, so I will venture a few tentative parallels in what follows.

The first problem interpretation faces in this historical situation of nascent modernism is a gap between what sociological jargon calls the macro and the micro: in other words between overall form, the action or plot as a whole, and individual detail, here not merely language but also musical scoring. It is suggestive, if not altogether correct, to think of this as an opposition between the project as a whole and its page-by-page execution. In fact, though, the gap here constitutes a more dialectical distinction, between totality and the individual or empirical phenomenon. Totality is necessarily always absent; the phenomenon is, as its name suggests, always perceptually present in one way or another. The two levels are both dialectically inseparable and at the same time incommensurable: no synthesis is possible between them, and interpretation always ends up choosing one or the other for its focus, as much as it would like to posit some ultimate unity, some organic form, in which detail and whole might be at one.

Now this dialectical opposition is no doubt a permanent dilemma for the human mind (otherwise it would not have been necessary to invent the dialectic). But I want to argue that it is exacerbated in the modern period, and very specifically in all the arts we characterize as modernist, and that it is exacerbated in the modernist period for a specific historical reason, namely the process of differentiation characterizing modernity in general. "Differentiation" is a useful term and concept invented by Niklas Luhmann, and it designates the tendency of reality in the modern period to differentiate itself into distinct semiautonomous levels which we come to think of as multiple and coexisting realities with their own specific intelligibilities, each semiautonomous and relatively distinct from the other.[1] Thus, to take an easy example, that of the academic disciplines: their differentiation from that initial, primordial magma which is theology can be documented and dated with some accuracy. The trajectory of this immense historical process—in which Philosophy separates itself out from Theology, and the Law and the Natural Sciences from

---

[1]   See Niklas Luhmann, *The Differentiation of Society*, trans. Stephen Holmes and Charles Larmore (New York: Columbia University Press, 1982).

Philosophy, only then to undergo further differentiation themselves, as when Chemistry and then Biology become separate disciplines in their own right—this process can stand as a kind of model of the kind of dynamic of differentiation that is seemingly reversed in our own postmodern period (where, for example, Biology folds back into Astronomy, and Linguistics and Anthropology back into the thing we now call Theory).

This last also happens in the arts. It will thus be an interesting question to determine whether the Wagnerian *Gesamtkunstwerk* is a premonition of such postmodern de-differentiation or whether on the other hand, like Baudelaire's poem "Correspondances," it is not simply (as I would be tempted to argue) an apparatus, a formal device, designed to intensify difference—either in the arts or the physical senses themselves—by way of their identification with one another. We can return to that too; and I should stress, in passing, that Luhmannian differentiation is only one philosophical language or code among others in which this historical process could be articulated.

At any rate, the Gesamtkunstwerk brings together any number of arts—poetry and music to be sure, but also theater and acting, plot and myth, set design, stage direction, opera as a form, and even architecture itself (Wagner was very close to Gottfried Semper, and while the latter did not design Bayreuth, its space and acoustics are virtually built into the music, particularly into *Parsifal*, first performed in 1882). To all these we must today add film and video, along with subtitles or supertitles, which alone make a truly international Wagnerian music drama possible in ways he could never have anticipated. My point in this obvious enumeration is twofold. Firstly, each of these levels, or arts, or media, has its specific history, and the event that was Wagner would have to find its unique position in each of them. This is to say that "Wagner" means multiple positions which are scarcely reducible to each other and which cannot really be synthesized into a single history. To position him in nascent modernism is not to invent a space in which they are all somehow combined, but to add yet another historical framework or story to the list.

Secondly, it may well be said that such multiple histories are still somehow teleological, in the old modernist fashion of the progress of the new, or even in the supposedly Hegelian or Marxian fashion of the progress of history itself. We have only displaced this more general teleology (associated with the so-called "philosophies of history") onto the various levels: so now we have a teleology of musical material, of acting, of set design, and so forth. I think some such historical scheme is essential, otherwise the movement of history becomes a random one from which the very notion of history evaporates (and of course sometimes this is exactly what the opponents of this view are seeking to achieve). But what such critics have conflated here is teleology and theodicy, the latter still visible in the bourgeois idea of progress or the Second International idea of inevitability. Adorno is a better guide, I think, for whom historical progression is not the movement from one victory to another, greater one: it is the movement of contradictions, which as they are worked on, dissolved, even forgotten or left to fester, themselves produce new contradictions and radically new situations (which may of course not be for the better but for the worse).[2] History is the temporality of the production of these new situations and new contradictions, and this is the sense in which the various levels I've evoked can be running at different speeds and different rhythms and tempos at one and the same time (the analogy with contemporary music, such as that of Pierre Boulez, is here irresistible). At certain moments, to be sure, these multiple histories and contradictions intersect: and so it is that today the moment of the history of contemporary theory crosses paths with the chronological changes in operatic staging and direction, and we get *Regietheater* and *Regieoper*, in which I happen to delight, itself however even now relatively distinct (or semiautonomous) from that history of Bayreuth with which any Wagner production anywhere must necessarily entertain a relationship of one kind or another.[3]

The further point to be made is that these levels can never coincide or completely fold back into each other. This is not to say that the ideal of the Gesamtkunstwerk is somehow fallacious or imperfect— odd words to use about an aesthetic or a style or artistic practice. Rather, we must speak of an essential distance between each level, however minimal and imperceptible. To use contemporary theoretical jargon, we must speak of an excess of one level over the other: an excess of the music over the words, and at one and the same time an

---

[2]   I have always appreciated Slavoj Žižek's remark: "Does not Hegel's *Phenomenology of Spirit* tell us again and again the same story of the repeated failure of the subject's endeavour to realize his project … ?' See *The Ticklish Subject: The Absent Centre of Political Ontology* (London: Verso, 1999), p. 76.

[3]   See Chapter 7, below.

excess of the words over the music; an excess of the visual over the sonorous, and vice versa; an excess of bodily representation or acting over the content to which it is supposed to refer or the emotion which it is supposed to express; and so on. To unify these incommensurable dimensions is to underscore their difference; to identify them with each other is to heighten our perception of their distance from each other.

I will try to come at all this from an angle that seems unaccountably to have been a relatively unexplored one. Wagner himself notoriously wavered back and forth in his attempt to characterize music drama: sometimes music is in the service of drama, then later on drama turns out to have been in the service of music. In fact, the alternatives—analysis of the music, analysis of the drama—turn out most often to be an alternative between the music and its meaning or philosophy (the reiterated mention of Feuerbach and Schopenhauer is obligatory here). The words prove embarrassing as poetry, save for their singability (Wagner has a theory about that as well, involving vowels and consonants). But the archaic style is relegated to the general nineteenth-century fantasy about the Middle Ages (comparable in English, perhaps, to William Morris's poetry). As for the drama, which also includes the words, but now as speeches and acts between characters on stage, that is left to directors like Patrice Chéreau who need to take it seriously in order to stage his singers and make them act. In what follows I want to make a beginning on taking Wagner's drama seriously, even to the point of respecting him as a great playwright (whatever else he was).

To be sure, instances can be found in which the interaction of music and words has a heightened significance. Ernst Bloch has singled out moments in which Beckmesser's ridiculous antics are underwritten by the most delicate and inappropriately exquisite music.[4] Deryck Cooke has pointed to the astonishing identity of the scoring of Siegmund's triumphant recovery of the sword from the tree with the Alberich leitmotif of the renunciation of love.[5] Here, as in the best *nouvelle vague* tradition the soundtrack contradicts the image and indicts synchrony as such as pure ideology. But the very possibility of such effects is dependent on the deeper structural rift

[4]   Ernst Bloch, "Paradoxa und Pastorale bei Wagner," in *Literarische Aufsätze* (Frankfurt am Main: Suhrkamp, 1965), pp. 294–332.

[5]   Deryck Cooke, *I Saw the World End: A Study of Wagner's* Ring (Oxford: Oxford University Press, 1991), pp. 2–5.

or gap here between the levels, however much traditional composers (for example) might have tried to paper it over, conceal it, resolve it, and so forth.

This is of course not to exclude moments in which the levels are not perceived in terms of contradiction or differentiation (something sometimes signaled by dissonance), but which actually do seem to generate some mysterious and incomprehensible harmony: that is, moments in which distance is expressed by way of identification. For example, such would be the moment, also cited by Bloch, in which the musical accompaniment to Siegfried's dying monologue is that motif identified as Brünnhilde's awakening (in *Die Walküre*).[6] What are we to make of this curious association, this seeming identification of an awakening to the world with a departure from it? And indeed, does this musical segment have a meaning at all in that extra-musical or philosophico-thematic sense? Is Siegfried simply remembering Brünnhilde as, waking, she was first revealed to him? Is this some *Tristan*-like association of love and death (the *Ring* being normally considered to be quite incompatible with *Tristan*'s love mysticism)? Or is the music itself, in some purely musical mode, producing a new and enlarged musical concept which will not fit under standard traditional philosophemes such as death, awakening, love, and the like?[7] In fact, this moment is truly sublime, one of the deliriously transcendent high points of the whole cycle and probably its climax, in which Siegfried reawakens to his love for Brünnhilde, thereby forgetting the present of dying itself. In any case, the unique event is virtually the opposite of Tristan's submersion in a love indistinguishable from death. Perhaps, indeed, we might dialectically propose the notion that the association in question sharpens both the sense of awakening and that of dying; or better still differentiates by way of identification the three musical concepts, awakening, love, and death. The listener will presumably have to decide all this, or perhaps ignore it on the grounds that musical meaning has nothing in common with such thematics. Yet there is still here the multiplicity of textual and narrative levels to be somehow taken into account.

---

[6] See Bloch, "Paradoxa und Pastorale bei Wagner."

[7] I am referring to Deleuze's insistence on the production of "new concepts" by the arts—concepts which are, however, not produced in the abstract language of philosophy but by way of their own specific medium: thus cinematographic concepts, painterly or sonorous concepts, and so on.

I want to situate these problems now in what I hope is a new or at least different light, and that involves my opening a parenthesis here, and talking about some other themes and problems that have preoccupied me lately and in which Wagner features only incidentally. These turn essentially around the current topic of affect, which I understand in an idiosyncratic way and which has mostly been drawn from two main sources, on the one hand Eve Kosofsky Sedgwick and queer theory, and on the other Deleuze.[8] It is a debate to which I don't particularly wish to contribute here, nor do I wish to challenge any of the varied and interesting work pursued under this rubric by younger scholars (some of them my own students). I do want to add that it is worth pointing to a third possible source for the discussion, namely phenomenology and in particular Heidegger's notion of Stimmung or mood, and Sartre's analysis of emotions. Meanwhile, my sense is that both Freudian and Lacanian psychoanalysis are very far from being direct inspirations for such theories; they are rather something like the trigger and the excuse for such new theorization.

The approach that has interested me is one which pits emotion against affect as two distinct systems or types of experience; and this proposition is incidentally also one that raises the question of a historical perspective on all this, but for the moment that can remain a secondary issue. This new binary dualism also involves temporal distinctions and perhaps an opposition between two systems of temporality, but that too can remain in the background for a moment.

First, let me address the matter of emotion as such. I think that historically emotions have been grasped as a kind of system, and one which has traditionally given rise to a number of systematic treatises: Aristotle's *Nicomachean Ethics*, the various theories of the humors, Aquinas's disquisition on emotions, Descartes's *Passions of the Soul* (completed in 1649), and sundry more recent and perhaps more partial contributions by this or that more modern school of academic psychology. To be sure, as in all systems, the emotions

---

8   See, for example, Eve Kosofsky Sedgwick and Adam Frank, eds, *Shame and Its Sisters: A Silvan Tomkins Reader* (Durham, NC: Duke University Press, 1995); Eve Kosofsky Sedgwick, *Touching Feeling: Affect, Pedagogy, Performativity* (Durham, NC: Duke University Press, 2003); Jonathan Flatley, *Affective Mapping: Melancholia and the Politics of Modernism* (Cambridge, MA: Harvard University Press, 2008); and Sianne Ngai, *Ugly Feelings* (Cambridge, MA: Harvard University Press, 2005).

tend here to be organized in pairs of binary oppositions, but what seems to me more significant is the nomenclature of the emotions or passions as such. These are named emotions, and it is the name which organizes and orders the psychic material for which it stands, the name which confers a kind of essence on each of the emotions so designated. This amounts to a kind of objectification of these various psychic states, or, to be more pointed about it, to a reification of whole zones of our subjectivity. It should come as no great surprise that it is language as such and in particular names which have the task of mapping out the inner landscape, or better still of making it appear for the first time; Lacan already taught us that names, and in particular proper names, were an alienation and indeed a trauma. Sing, Muse, the wrath of Achilles! If the word "love" comes up between them, I am lost! And I want to argue, additionally, that there comes into being, alongside this taxonomic and classificatory process, a whole aesthetic of expression as such: named emotions are there to be "expressed"; expressiveness is just a more general extension of their nominal and linguistic being.

All of which will be clarified by setting in place what I claim to be the very different logic of affect (in my acceptation of that term). Kant distinguished feelings from emotions as follows: feelings are bodily states; emotions are states of consciousness. If we change "feelings" to "affects," this will not be a bad starting point, provided we don't endorse the mind/body separation it perpetuates. But it will allow me to assert the following proposition about affect: as bodily states affects are nameless, in distinction from emotions. Affects run the gamut of nameless states from euphoria to depression, from vibrant health to stagnancy and ill humor (indeed, if any of the classic systems of emotions come closer than others to this new system I am trying to describe, it would be the system of the humors as it found its coordinates in the body and foresaw a whole scale of mixtures and combinations down through the ages). Indeed, the principal reproach I would have for contemporary affect theory is this neglect of the well-nigh infinite sliding scale of bodily states, from the high to the bad trip, with its adherents preferring to concentrate their descriptions on this or that allegedly fundamental affect, such as shame (for Silvan Tomkins) or in a more general way melancholia. On the contrary, affects are not essentializable in that way: they are multiple and perpetually variable; they shimmer like the orchestra itself in constant mutability.

Now let me use a historical narrative to convey what for me is the difference, quite absolute, between emotions and affects, a word which, as you will already have noted, I prefer to use in the plural. This will be a literary proposition this time, and a quite outrageous one at that: for I want to claim that before the middle of the nineteenth century and the bourgeois era, the body is scarcely registered in literature, and I mean registration in the sense in which a Geiger counter registers the degree of radiation in a given environment. Let Flaubert and Baudelaire be the markers for such a momentous event as the emergence of the bodily sensorium into literature and written language as such: I claim that before this moment the traditional literary apparatus is incapable of registering, or ill equipped to register, the kinds of sensations which I can only briefly illustrate here. We can adduce Baudelaire's description of a painted street sign: "a green so delicious it hurts"; or Flaubert's remark that all of *Salammbô* (1862) was written to convey a certain bilious shade of yellow (we might also want to remember his other remark about this novel, namely that few people can know how *triste*, how "sad," he had to be to want to resuscitate Carthage).

But let's also have some objections, some protests. What about Balzac? No writer is so replete with descriptions and physical sensations (and here you may add your own favorite page, but the *locus classicus* is of course the Pension Vauquer in *Le Père Goriot* [1835], with its musty odor and its worn fabrics and outdated furniture). It is an excellent riposte: for Balzac precisely proves my point, namely that these features of his description are not really affects at all but rather meanings (they mean decent misery, respectable poverty, a decaying past, etc.): they are allegorical of social and psychological states; they have none of the sensory singularity, the unclassifiable and indeed unnameable haecceitas or "this-ness," of the 1840s and '50s Baudelairean or Flaubertian sensations.

Now we must quickly underscore the consequences of all this for narrative. In fact, what we have been outlining is essentially a theory of two temporalities: the temporality of the named, that is the reified, emotion, will be that of past and future, of time as a destiny that can be narrated. The temporality of affect, on the other hand, will be that of a perpetual present, a kind of eternal present if you will—a temporal perspective calculated to destroy narrative as such. It is the passage from realism to modernism that will the most vividly illustrate this supersession of narrative time by the non-time of affect, their struggle—récit versus scene, telling versus showing, narrative versus lyric—constituting the very history of art (and of the arts in general) over the course of the nineteenth century, as we shall see.

Now perhaps we may return to Wagner and in particular rewrite that overfamiliar tale according to which the *Tristan* prelude (1857) is the very beginning of modernity as such, its theme song and national anthem as it were. Yes, *Tristan* and the Tristan chord are the beginnings of something, which certainly includes what people still call modernity; but Wagnerian chromaticism, in my framework, is to be grasped as one of an emergence of affect as such on the stage of world culture and art, as the emergence and expression of a new kind of content. But to understand this in terms of the opposition between affect and the older named emotions one has only to compare the Wagner ideal of the so-called endless melody with the traditional (Italian) practice of the aria, whose aesthetic function is clearly that of expressing emotion, and a given named emotion at that: Vengeance! Love! Jealousy! The extraordinary variability of the Wagnerian orchestra as it ceaselessly develops its musical language, like an endless Proustian or Faulknerian sentence, stands in stark distinction from the closure of the aria, which wishes to express one thing powerfully and completely, and then stop. There are, to be sure, breaks and silences in Wagner, but these are so extraordinarily momentous as to be part of the musical fabric itself, intense musical events in their own right.

But just as clearly, the Wagnerian endless melody will need to be extraordinarily varied in its mood swings, in its dramatic shifts from one kind of affect to another: shifts we tend to characterize in the older language of emotions simply because we do not have names for affects as such: so that we still anachronistically evoke these momentous shifts as those between Brünnhilde's love music, that of Siegfried's rage, that of Alberich's hatred, and so on and so forth. But it adds another dimension to this discussion to remember that one of the fairy-tale motifs is precisely that of the boy who could not learn to fear: fear is, of course, an emotion and not a feeling. What Siegfried comes to identify with fear—the anxiety of sexual differentiation, the hitherto unknown confusion of sexual desire—is in fact an affect. The fairy-tale motif can thus be taken virtually as an allegory of the overcoming of emotion by affect in Wagner.

At any rate the problem that emerges from this variability of affect across the arts of modernism is clearly the way in which the moments of an unstable and well-nigh neurotically variable subjectivity can be combined into the narrative fabric of the work of art. Musically, to be sure, they can be superimposed, and we have already touched on examples in which a single musical present can be woven out of the most disparate materials, which are then reflected in the instrumentation and its timbre, and in the composition of various tempos and temporalities. But in a temporal art like music or the novel it will be the succession of these moods or wildly alternating affects that poses the fundamental compositional problem. Nowhere is Tolstoy more astonishing, for example, than in the changeability of his characters' inner weather, their feelings, their impressions, their reactions, which on the same page can modulate from irritability to dreaminess, from curiosity to the distraction of a truly insignificant thought of some kind.

In music such interweaving of multiple affects demands what Wagner, in a famous letter (October 29, 1859), called "an art of transition," a fundamental phrase for all of modernism, ranging from the poets to Cézanne, and from Flaubertian crosscutting to Eisenstein's montage.[9] What is particularly fascinating about his letter, however, is the way in which Wagner uses everyday life and his own mood swings to characterize a technical musical problem he cannot otherwise convey to his destinatee (Mathilde Wesendonck). It corroborates our intuition that what were always loosely identified as passionate emotions in Wagner are in reality the stormy succession of the affects and intensities themselves, something he will even (rather comically) try to characterize in terms of the conduct of a conversation (but remember that it is also a dramatist who is here trying to "express himself").

Now if this is to be our basic topic here, we will need to disentangle our theme on at least two levels: how the pull of affect is registered in the musical fabric, and how it inflects the plot as such. These are two distinct discussions. For music, it would seem enough for the non-specialist to murmur "chromaticism" as the identification of the transformation of sonata logic and development into a vehicle for affect. But this at once confronts us with the central

---

9   Richard Wagner, *Selected Letters of Richard Wagner*, ed. and trans. Stewart Spencer and Barry Millington (New York: Norton, 1988), p. 475–6.

problem of the leitmotif, which Adorno has famously denounced as the image and symptom of swiftly spreading and intensifying commodification (but did Adorno himself not teach us that the modern artwork protects itself against commodification in its environment by commodifying or reifying itself?).[10] However, those who seek, like Deryck Cooke, to demonstrate the richness of scoring and the new complexities made possible by the practice of the leitmotif would surely not want to wish to describe it as a further development out of Beethoven, whose perfection of sonata form, variation, and development marks a climax and that end and fulfillment of something beyond which later composers are technically unable to go. Adorno would like to incorporate Wagner into his own story of the development of a new musical language which culminates in Schoenberg; but he cannot really stomach the leitmotif, which belongs for him in a very different story, namely the emergence of mass culture, kitsch, and movie music.

I want to propose a somewhat different reading of the leitmotif in the spirit of the temporal systems I have just been describing. From that perspective, clearly, leitmotif is the scar left by destiny on the musical present. Musical memory, to be sure: but we must be careful here, since the expansion of musical memory demanded by sonata form is something very different from these apparently crude recalls, and the partisans of Beethoven's musical temporality would clearly not want to identify this vulgar Wagnerian time with the complexity of the older kind. Still, the leitmotif is what destiny gives the new musical language of affect to absorb, to draw into itself, to assimilate into its wondrous new fabric; and in that sense what we now identify as the *Ring*'s basic leitmotifs are little more than the indigestible bones and gristle an affective music has to spit out.

Meanwhile, destiny leaves its mark on the larger forms as well. Not only is destiny the very subject of the *Ring* as a whole, the conceptual material out of which it wishes to fashion some new philosophical meaning. It is also the formal shaping power which deposits the smaller forms of so many interpolated and often long-winded stories or tales, recapitulations of previous action, narratives of offstage or foundational events—what we may call Gurnemanz-moments—along the way. One can only wonder what went through the minds of older audiences during these tedious and seemingly

---

[10] See Theodor W. Adorno, *Versuch über Wagner* (Berlin/Frankfurt: Suhrkamp, 1952).

static accounts which do not even offer the pleasures of the aria: but now that we have subtitles or supertitles, it is up to us to invent new ways of appreciating them, in a culture which has been able to imagine new relationships to repetition generally. At any rate, they are the *part du récit*, the very force of gravity of the older tale-telling pole of such works. Far from being unfortunate traces of the accident of Wagner's composition backwards in time, from *Götterdämmerung* to *Rheingold*, they are substantive moments in their own right, where characters confront the weight of destiny as it drags on their life in the present of time.[11]

Here, too, we may reckon in the very shape of these dramas, which—far from any epic tradition, let alone the *Nibelungenlied* itself, with which they have so little to do—reminds one of nothing quite so much as the old family novel dear to nineteenth-century realism (and culminating with the Wagnerian first novel of that perfect Wagnerite who was Thomas Mann). Nietzsche made merry over the other nineteenth-century resonances: "What surprises one encounters in the process [of retelling Wagner in more youthful proportions]! Would you believe it? All of Wagner's heroines, without exception, as soon as they are stripped of their heroic skin, become almost indistinguishable from Madame Bovary! And conversely one understands that Flaubert could have translated his heroine into Scandinavian or Carthaginian terms and then offered her, mythologised, to Wagner as a libretto."[12] Nietzsche here offers us a valuable lesson in the modes of ideological analysis or unmasking, as he introduces one more piece of damning evidence into the dossier of a decadent and neurotic Wagner, of Wagner as a fundamental cultural sickness. The procedure is powerful and still has its relevance (Adorno will simply translate it into the terms of fascism and the authoritarian personality). Yet it remains to be seen whether such

---

[11] It is well known that Wagner first wrote *Siegfried's Tod* (the script that occupies the place of *Götterdämmerung*), and then felt obliged to situate it in an earlier history, which turned out to be the scenarios of *Siegfried*, *Die Walküre*, and *Das Rheingold*, in that order. He then began to compose the music, as it were, backwards, beginning with the last-written (*Das Rheingold*) and then advancing as far as *Siegfried*, Act II, upon which he stopped, and in the twelve-year hiatus composed *Die Meistersinger von Nürnberg* and *Tristan und Isolde*. At length, in 1864, and under pressure from the king, he began again and wrote the last act of *Siegfried*, and finally *Götterdämmerung* itself.

[12] Friedrich Nietzsche, "The Case of Wagner" (1888), in *Basic Writings*, trans. Walter Kaufmann (New York: Random House, 1995), pp. 601–54, at p. 632.

culture critique is still appropriate, still carries conviction, in our own postmodernity today. If not, why not? Why is the once powerful idea of decadence no longer meaningful for us?

The family novel may also no longer be so relevant either, in the age of the nuclear or even post-nuclear family. Yet all these generations are in the *Ring*, entangled in their endogamy—Brünnhilde is after all Siegfried's aunt (shades of *The Charterhouse of Parma*)! The transgressive theme of incest has perhaps lost its edge in the contemporary world, overtaken by a host of other once even more shocking "perversions." Yet there is a sense in which this seemingly conventional romantic motif in Wagner can be re-read in an astonishingly post-contemporary way. Indeed, to Fricka's outrage at the incestuous coupling of the Walsung brother and sister ("When came it to pass/that brother and sister were lovers?") in *Die Walküre*, Wotan has a prophetic reply:

Heut'—hast du's erlebt:	Today you have witnessed it happen:
erfahre so,	learn thus that a thing
was von selbst sich fügt,	might befall of itself
sei zuvor auch noch nie	though it never happened
es gescheh'n.	before.[13]

All of which can colloquially be translated as "You have no idea!" in which sense Wagner's conventionally scandalous practice of love and adultery opens up into the far more revolutionary and utopian "overturning of values" of the 1960s—in Norman O. Brown's celebration of the polymorphous-perverse—and, in a later avatar, in "queer theory," in which the category of gender is itself dismantled. But that such an implicitly progressive perspective has another face is then re-emphasized by Lévi-Strauss's kinship analysis of the *Ring*, where the return to endogamy suggests an imprisonment in ever narrowing circles of consanguinity.[14]

As for the socioeconomic context, the struggles of the two great families—Wotan's and Alberich's (the Fafners are, after the Freia episode, confirmed bachelors)—do recall the titanic rivalries of the old robber barons. The saga of the Wagner clan (as Jonathan Carr so

---

[13]   Richard Wagner, *Wagner's Ring of the Nibelung: A Companion*, ed. Stewart Spencer and Barry Millington (London: Thames & Hudson, 1993), p. 142. Hereafter followed by opera act and/or scene, and page number: here, *Walküre*, II, i, 142.

[14]   Claude Lévi-Strauss, "De Chrétien de Troyes à Richard Wagner," in *Le regard éloigné* (Paris: Plon, 1983), pp. 301–24.

captivatingly tells it) reminds us that there too the good or bad luck of some primal destiny gets passed on down through the generations.[15] And all of this can also be assimilated to the classical Shavian account of Wagner's Marxism: the *Ring* is primitive accumulation; the giants stupidly hoard the gold without turning it into capital (that is, into money that begets itself, profit that "productively" generates an even more productive profit). The action then corresponds to the era of the robber barons, as recounted in Gustavus Myer's famous book, *The History of the Great American Fortunes* (1907), which was one of Brecht's favorites.

As for the ending—and whether it merely designates the end of the gods and of religion, or the end of the world itself as a whole—this is one of the two great unsolved problems of the *Ring*, along with the character of Siegfried. We cannot solve it here, or anywhere, because it is as they say undecidable. We will see that Nietzsche perspicaciously places us between the two alternatives: Feuerbach or Schopenhauer. Yet Wagner has boxed himself in, by virtue of the chronology of his composition, and even the three variants on Brünnhilde's final monologue do not leave much room for interpretive variety (although the literature on the matter is enormous). We may assume that it is as a survivor of the ancien régime (even though she is now human and not even a demigod any more) that Brünnhilde must be condemned to sati: all traces of the former gods and their superstitions must be swept away; the slate must be wiped clean in revolutionary fashion. Yet Chéreau found a different way to implement the Feuerbachian solution: in his great centennial production in Bayreuth in 1876, he followed Wagner's stage directions to the letter—the mass of curious human onlookers slowly turn and face the audience after Valhalla has gone up in flames. It is not yet Utopia, but only the beginning of the human age, something like the surviving population in the rubble of Germany Year Zero (1945). Meanwhile Kasper Bech Holten's magnificent Copenhagen *Ring* (2006) cuts the knot brutally, discards Wagner's ending, and has Brünnhilde survive to bear the child of the superman, à la Shaw. Wagner's ending, indeed, is paradigmatic of all great art in the way in which it foregrounds not this or that solution (bound in any case to be ideological), but rather the contradiction itself.

---

15 See Jonathan Carr, *The Wagner Clan: The Saga of Germany's Most Illustrious and Infamous Family* (New York: Atlantic Monthly Press, 2007).

But on the character of Siegfried there is much more to say, and we will approach it from the standpoint of the hypothesis of the two temporalities—récit versus scene, Beethoven and the end of the sonata form. The leitmotif thus assures the temporality of the past-present-future, of the before-and-after: along with the long-winded récits within the music drama itself, it secures something like that "telling" or foreshortened plot summary which Henry James so deplored in the "endless melody" of the novel, but whose local necessity he grudgingly admitted.[16]

But of course the leitmotif also occupies and consummates a different kind of temporality, which, adapting Hegel, we may call "the immense privilege of the musical present." Here it interacts with a variety of other motifs, and is scored and orchestrated in a sonorous density of a unique properly Wagnerian type, becoming the space of a new kind of hearing and listening attention. Such a space of attention is radically different from the old commodified hearing denounced by anti-Wagnerians from the hostile contemporaries all the way to Adorno, and replaced by the subtle commentaries and analyses of the best contemporary musicology. And if it should be objected that it is scarcely possible to conceive of some pure present in a temporal art like music, I would respond by describing it in terms of that attention to the timbre and color of the musical event, to the body of its instrumentation and the peculiarity of the sound combinations which is bound to shift the experience of sound away from its movement in time, and far more decisively to the approach of some paradoxical new musical atemporality.

The two temporalities thereby become something like a musical diachrony and a musical synchrony, and this is the spirit in which I now wish to turn from music to drama and to approach the problem of Siegfried, which is to say, ultimately, that of the magic potion that deprives him of his memory of Brünnhilde in the first act of *Götterdämmerung*. What do we do with this character, about whom the great East German director Joachim Herz has observed that from the perspective of the liberation of humanity Siegfried is little more than a casting error? Chéreau has meanwhile described his own perplexity:

---

[16] As James put it: "the odd inveteracy with which picture, at almost any turn, is jealous of drama, and drama (though on the whole with greater patience, I think) of picture." See Henry James, *The Art of the Novel: Critical Prefaces*, introduction by Richard P. Blackmur (New York: Scribner, 1962), p. 298.

Faced with Siegfried, I did lose my cool; but I'm waiting to hear any director tell us he has no problems with Siegfried. The director doesn't need to know anything about Wagner, his compositional problems, or about Cosima and what happened in their lives. He only knows the characters on stage, and those are the characters he has to bring alive. How to bring Siegfried alive? The only possible guideline for the rehearsals seemed to me to be that every so often, furtively, he has the suspicion that something is expected from him that he cannot quite face, something too heavy to carry. But if he really is "somebody who doesn't know fear," how can one reconcile that kind of naïve stupidity with the malaise I just mentioned? So I suggested that the actor every so often and very briefly show himself on the point of a kind of realization, and that he express his fear through anxiety, through despair, or more generally through doubt; that he show a feeling of missing something, a kind of doubt about himself, and have moments of distraction when he tries to think (going back into his inner room, as Carson McCullers might say, and finding nothing he can use). All that is obviously fairly literary: the role is poorly written, that's all one can conclude.[17]

It is a serious reproach, and there is a sense in which the director has the last word here, for if the director cannot achieve dramatic intelligibility in performance, then—however ingeniously the role is interpreted by theorists—the verdict is final. It is thus truly disheartening to find a director of Chéreau's extraordinary intelligence and imagination, his inventiveness and his virtuosity in stage-craft, throwing up his hands in desperation in the face of Wagner's dramatic demands.

Now it is true that we need not simply opt out with the summary judgement of bad writing. We may, on the contrary, have recourse to T. S. Eliot's old idea of the "objective correlative," in the name of which he condemned *Hamlet* on the strength of the incommunicability of Hamlet's subjective disgust with the mother and her adultery, accusing Shakespeare with not having found an objective (and dramatic) form in which to render this strange complex of emotions (or, if I dare say so, of affects).[18] It is a reproach we may also level against Wagner at several points in his work, it being understood that for the music drama an "objective correlative" will include music along with words and action. So it is that I have often

---

17   Pierre Boulez, Patrice Chéreau, Richard Peduzzi, and Jacques Schmidt, *Histoire d'un "Ring": Bayreuth, 1976–1980* (Paris: Lafont, 1980), pp. 76–7. My translation.

18   T. S. Eliot, "Hamlet and His Problems," in *The Sacred Wood*, 2nd ed. (London: Faber & Faber, 1997 [1928]), pp. 81–7.

felt the climactic moment of *Das Rheingold* to be deficient in just this respect. You will remember that this *Vorabend*, the opening of the *Ring*, begins with the conclusion of the great project. "Vollendet das ewige Werk!" (*WR* i, 70), cries Wotan: the eternal work, the great project (Valhalla), has been brought triumphantly to completion! The project has been fulfilled, time to think of new ones—and into this curious beginning at the end we may read all the philosophical analyses of labor and the project from Hegel and Marx to Heidegger and Sartre: when the project is completed, it is externalized, it is alienated in the neutral sense of the word and ceases to belong to us, and so on and so forth. We even have here a remarkable proto-philosophical critique of the notion of *Entaüsserung* (externalization and objectification all together) in Wotan's discovery in *Die Walküre* that he can never really produce anything but himself, that true otherness is not susceptible of human production:

Zum Ekel find' ich	To my loathing I find
ewig nur mich	only ever myself
in Allem, was ich erwirke!	in all that I encompass!
	(*WR, Walküre*, II: ii, 152)

In any case, as we all know, there remains the matter of the bill, and thereby begins a long and unforeseeable journey (remember that in the beginning here, the gods know nothing about the gold, and neither do the other suprahuman species, the giants and the dwarfs—at least until Alberich's discovery). So at the end of this first pre-evening of the cycle, Wotan is obliged to invent a new project, whose execution will—success and failure alike—occupy the next three evenings and the rest of the work itself.

But how is this new project conveyed to us, and what could be its "objective correlative"? All we have are the words in Wagner's stage directions in *Das Rheingold*: "wie von einem grossen Gedanken ergriffen, sehr entschlossen"—"very resolutely, as though seized by a grandiose idea," a characterization that presumably merely designates the subsequent words, "Thus I salute the stronghold, /safe from dread and dismay" (*WR* iv, 116). But this is a gesture and an action that in no way conveys the spirit of the "mighty thought," which is indeed not revealed to us until the lengthy explanations and narratives of the next drama, *Die Walküre*, as the creation of the superman. This is then truly a form-problem in Wagner, or if you prefer a formal contradiction. How to solve this dilemma of the unrepresentability of his fundamental theme—the forming of a project whose realization will open destiny to the vagaries of objectification and alienation, and to the impossible freedoms of human beings?

To be sure, returning to Chéreau's judgment on the role of Siegfried, we can always return to the encouragement of the Master himself: *Kinder, macht Neues!* Children, invent, think of something new, make it new! And we can remember the unrealizable stage directions and set requirements, impossible in Wagner's own time but now triumphantly fulfilled by modern systems of special effects. With the utmost thanks and admiration, taking leave of the by-now thirty-year-old Chéreau realization, we today look forward to the unpredictable genius of the directors of the present and future "Rings." Yet I must continue to feel that the two great representational dilemmas—Wotan's "mighty thought" and the character of Siegfried—must for us remain the object of theoretical perplexity.

There are indeed a number of theoretical frames in which to place, and thereby reevaluate, the role of Siegfried. From a certain historical perspective—for example, that of modes of production and social systems—we can substitute the evolution of the clan system for that of the primitive accumulation of capital and emergent individualism. We can also read the rivalry of the dual heroes—Siegfried and Hagen—as a rivalry between the stages of evolution of two hostile clans, either of which might well be taken as the positive figure (it is worth recalling that in the *Nibelungenlied* Hagen is the heroic central protagonist, Siegfried being reduced to an episodic role which comes to an end early in the poem). If so, then the existence of the clan may be projected backwards in time onto totemic figures, and we thereby glimpse the gods—with their leader "LichtAlberich" (Wotan), and the dwarves, with theirs in so-called "Schwarz-Alberich"—in a new perspective. Meanwhile, the travails and anxieties of both these totemic leaders suggest the instability of the position of the "big man" or clan chieftain in this essentially decentralized social system, which has its analogy later on in feudalism. (As far as capitalism is concerned, we may also recall Thorstein Veblen's idea of an essentially feudal capitalism at the turn of the twentieth century, and also, transforming the clan into the criminal mob, Horkheimer's notion of history as a succession of "rackets" and racketeers.)[19] The archaic elements of Wagner then take on the

---

[19]   Max Horkheimer, *Dämmerung* (Zurich: Oprecht u. Helbing, 1934).

sense of a critical diagnosis rather than a regressive or reactionary nationalist celebration.

But we must now confront the character of Siegfried directly, inasmuch as he is positioned to bear the meaning of hope for the future and for the resolution of the baleful effects of the ring and its curse. Three features would seem to set this "hero" off from the other characters, even from his altogether more attractive and tragic father Siegmund. First, he is the boy who, like the eponymous Grimm character, fails to learn fear. Then, and perhaps as a result of this youthful innocence, he embodies a more general ignorance about the world and about his own genealogy, something that could also be taken to signify his nascent individualism (as a bourgeois subject, for instance). And finally, and more enigmatically, and perhaps as a consequence of all the aforegoing combined, he seems to stand for "freedom," a philosophical concept not generally associated with Wagner unless we hearken back to the barricades in Dresden in 1849, to Bakunin, and to Wagner's alleged revolutionary anarchism. (Indeed, Siegfried has occasionally been identified with Bakunin himself, something more plausible for the older, traditional, more shaggy productions of the opera than with any of the recent ones: Hagen we can imagine with a Viking-like beard, but the young Siegfried less easily.)

And to all these ingredients we add the mystery of the forgetfulness potion—or is it a love potion? (Wagner is never very clear on this)—together with the aesthetic judgment it always seems to call for. Mann thought Wagner could have left the magic potions out; others see it as a piece of melodramatic claptrap not unrelated to the conventional grand-opera machinery still surviving in the final music drama, which was of course the first playbook whose fledgling text was written out.[20] Furthermore, we have the philosophical issue raised by the ungrateful son Nietzsche. Is Siegfried the superman (Übermensch)? If not, why not? Nietzsche would have been very familiar with the *Ring* and in particular with Siegfried long before the premiere of the entire *Ring* (and of Bayreuth itself) in 1876, the year in which Nietzsche most decisively moves to distance himself from the Master: particularly inasmuch as Wagner incessantly played and sang his music dramas to his inner circle and had

---

[20]   See Thomas Mann, "Sufferings and Greatness of Richard Wagner," in *Essays of Three Decades* (New York: Knopf, 1947), pp. 307–52.

already published both libretti and scores which the disciple, himself a gifted musician, would have been able to play on his own piano. To be sure, the object of Nietzsche's most fundamental disgust and disillusionment was the heavily pseudo-religious *Parsifal*. Siegfried does not seem to bear out that fundamental diagnosis of decadence Nietzsche passed on Wagner generally; and indeed, the philosopher is probably the first (in *Der Fall Wagner*) to have staged Wagnerian interpretation in terms of the opposition between Feuerbach and Schopenhauer:

> "How can one abolish the old society?" Only by declaring war against "contracts" (tradition, morality). *That is what Siegfried does* … [T]he rise of the golden age; the twilight of the gods for the old morality—*all ill has been abolished.*
>
> For a long time, Wagner's ship followed this course gaily [the Feuerbach-Bakunin revolutionary course]. There is no doubt that this was where Wagner sought his highest goal—What happened? A misfortune. The ship struck a reef; Wagner was stuck. The reef was Schopenhauer's philosophy; Wagner was stranded in a *contrary* world view.[21]

It should be noted that not only is the Siegfried who emerges from this sketch a truly revolutionary one (and far from the comic figure he inevitably cuts for a modern audience); the ideals for which he stands—destruction of religion, end of the law and of morality—are very precisely those which Nietzsche himself championed with single-minded passion until the end of his conscious life. In that sense, Nietzsche was the fulfillment of Feuerbach (who retired from the intellectual and political scene rather early in life), and his idolization of the father-figure Wagner must surely have been at least partly inspired by the traces of the Feuerbachian revolutionary now dwelling in Tribchen's domesticity.

We must go further than this, however. Even after the break Nietzsche is suspiciously silent on the figure of Siegfried with all its ambiguities; the concept of the Übermensch however—call it superman or overman as you like—does not really swim into being until the work on *Zarathustra* in the early 1880s. Is it not permitted to conjecture that it is precisely this problematic ambiguity about Wagner's dramatic representation of the hero of the future that

---

21 Nietzsche, "The Case of Wagner," pp. 629–30.

impels Nietzsche to some new attempt at theorization, one which will result, not in any representation of the new figure, but rather simply in Zarathustra's call for him: "I teach you the superman. Man is something that should be overcome."[22] Nor is Zarathustra himself in any way to be taken for the superman (and certainly not the sickly and neurotic Nietzsche whose entire work is an attempt to overcome *himself*). This prophetic *ajournement* into the future, this deliberate omission of any positive detail, any desirable features, let alone any fuller concrete description (as in the Leninist non-account of a future communism), is a signal revision of the Wagnerian experiment, which nonetheless shares with Wagner a profoundly annunciatory future and, we may even say, following Bloch, utopian orientation—what the later Nietzsche might acerbically have called an "intimation" (*Ahnung*).

In this sense, it may therefore further be conjectured that Nietzsche sensed enough of what is unrepresentable (or even comical) in Wagner's Siegfried to take precautions with his own tentative conceptual efforts in this direction. Still, along with the "transvaluation of all values" he endorses in Wagner (away with the old morality, with custom and Law), there is another feature of the Zarathustrian prophecy which may have some interesting lessons for us. It is not the famous "will to power," which is calculated to undermine the classic Wagnerian opposition between power and love, on the grounds that for Nietzsche—here the far more subtle and unflinching "psychologist" (as he called himself)—love is itself, like everything else, a manifestation of the will to power. No, that feature of Nietzschean doctrine which will be of greater interest to us here is rather the doctrine of the eternal return.

I suppose that there are as many ways of interpreting the eternal return as there are of expounding the Freudian death-wish; and indeed any self-respecting intellectual and theorist will surely want to try his or her hand at devising a new one. At any rate, I here propose to read the eternal return as a commitment to an eternal present of consciousness whose rapidly shifting contents and configurations are always to be affirmed no matter what their conse-quences for future (or past). You may, if you like, see dawning in this interpretation the outlines of the theory of the two temporalities I

---

22   Friedrich Nietzsche, *Thus Spoke Zarathustra* (1883–85), ed. and trans. R. J. Hollingdale (London: Penguin, 1969), p. 23.

outlined above. There is a war between chronology and the eternal present of consciousness. The eternal return of the same means that consciousness—as impersonal as you like, and as unrelated to any idealism or any materialism either—is always "the same."

Will it prove arbitrary to seek to apply such a strange yet thoroughly philosophical concept to Wagner? But he invents it himself, and very precisely along the lines theorized by Blanchot, Klossowski, and Deleuze, as we discover in the stages of Wotan's struggle with his own defeat. On a general level, the philosophical problem (if it may be called that) emerges in the seeming inconsistency—which is to say the gap—between the presumed immortality of the gods and the passage of time in a Heraclitean universe in which even their timelessness is not immune to moira or fate (the Anaximander fragment, dear to Heidegger: *they must pay back their debt to time*).[23] The contradiction is, to be sure, a representational one. It does not exist in Christianity, where the temporalities are divided up and God (unrepresented and unrepresentable) remains timeless, while Christ (in his human representation) submits to the passage of time and fate. But if the gods are to be given anthropomorphic figuration, then the latter must be somehow challenged, either by monotheism as such or by more primal myths which constitute, as it were, their backstory. Thus, Zeus dethroned Chronos, the gods are born, marry, and the like, until finally, under Christian auspices, they are transformed by the coming of Christ into so many devils and demons (see Jean Seznec's encyclopedic account), or else, as wondrously in Flaubert, they die out.[24]

It will be seen that this is exactly the process *Das Rheingold* dramatizes for us, when the gods are deprived of Freia's "golden apples" (leaving only the latter's music behind). But it is this very vulnerability of the immortals which prepares the possibility of their final destruction. It should be noted that this paradox holds for all modern representations of the gods all the way to Sartre's *Les Mouches* (1943);

---

[23]   Anaximander: "And the source of 'coming to be for existing things is that into which destruction, too, happens,' according to necessity: for they pay penalty and retribution to each other according to the assessment of Time." And see Martin Heidegger, "The Anaximander Fragment," in his *Early Greek Thinking: The Dawn of Western Philosophy* (New York: Harper, 1975), pp. 13–58.

[24]   Jean Seznec, *La Survivance des dieux antiques* (London: Warburg Institute, 1940); and see of course Gustave Flaubert, *La Tentation de St Antoine* (Paris: Charpentier et Cie, 1874).

and that it is a representational dilemma which in a way returns us from Feuerbach to Hegel again: for the very existence of the gods as representation, as dramatic figures (and not mere idols or images), means that they are a little more than mere fantasies and projections of the human mind. In a Hegelian sense, then, their appearance has a reality, an objectivity of its own, even if their reality is nonexistent. I sense here then an autoreferential dimension of such texts in which, without intending to, their own externalization as objective appearance becomes the deeper subject of the work, where now, whatever it overtly claims to assert about the gods—they exist, they don't exist—in reality primarily foregrounds the problematic necessity of representing them as though they existed in the first place.

However this may be, the eventual "defeat" and destruction of Wotan himself will also have an autoreferential overtone. More immediately, however, the text, here following the great final battles of the Scandinavian epics, presupposes the possibility that even the leader of the gods himself can ultimately be annihilated together with all his "race." We have already learned that, like Zeus, Wotan also is subject to the higher power of fate, in the runes of the world-ash-tree. Yet this constraint he freely chooses (hacking the wood for his spear from the immortal tree of the world, which then itself begins at once slowly to perish, in a kind of causal overdetermination of the final catastrophe).

What is however post-contemporary about Wotan's end in *Die Walküre* is that the failure of his plan—the law and the runes force him to kill his chosen agent Siegmund—generates despair only at the outset:

O heilige Schmach!	O righteous disgrace!
O schmählicher Harm!	O shameful sorrow!
Götternoth!	Gods' direst need!
Götternoth!	Gods' direst distress!
Endloser Grimm!	Infinite fury!
Ewiger Gram!	Grief neverending!
Der Traurigste bin ich von Allen!	The saddest am I of all living things!

(*WR, Walküre*, II: ii, 148)

There then follows a suicidal impulse:

Auf geb' ich mein Werk;	My work I abandon;
nur Eines will ich noch:	one thing alone do I want:
das Ende—	the end—
das Ende!—	the end!—

(WR, Walküre, II: ii, 153)

I hope it is not to abuse the notion of autoreferentiality to suggest that when Wotan calls for "das Ende!" the drama is also calling for a way to end itself and wrap things up. In this sense the final conflagration not only fulfils Adorno's Bakunin anecdote (if this is water, the great anarchist is supposed to have said of *The Flying Dutchman* [1843], what will it be like when he gets to fire?). It also at once displaces the conventional critical debate about the three endings of Brünnhilde's final monologue. What then becomes significant is not what it means, but to what degree it becomes a kind of archetype of our sense of an absolute ending: it means "das Ende" as such, rather than this or that end of something.

He next seeks counsel with Erda, not simply to learn the course of events and of history, but also as a last resort to find a remedy in extremis:

doch deiner Weisheit	but I'd thank
dankt' ich den Rath wohl,	the store of your wisdom
wie zu hemmen ein rollendes	to be told how to hold back a
Rad?	rolling wheel.

(WR, Siegfried, III: i, 255)

But there is no last resort here, and not the least interesting feature of the historical vision embedded in the *Ring* is the radical shift in the very dynamics of history itself as soon as money (gold, the ring) is introduced. In the early moments of the cycle—as it were the precapitalist landscape—acts as such (whether of gods or humans) set forces in motion and constitute genuine causes: whence the power of Alberich's curse and even of Siegfried's fearlessness, let alone Wotan's conspiratorial plans. In this world there is much interaction of the lines of force, of the causes and effects of praxis, irrespective of defeat or victory: action and events are still on a human—or perhaps better said, an anthropomorphic—scale, and the language of "freedom" is thereby still justified.

But little by little the other face of this web of actions shows itself, and that is a systemic determination beyond all anthropomorphic control. Here even destiny changes its meaning, and from the fate of an individual it becomes the blind force of necessity of a process. Money is here the new element of noise in the communicational system, as Habermas puts it in *The Theory of Communicative Action* (1981): it is the foreign body, the chemical ingredient, which crystallizes another order of things. It sets "the rolling wheel" going, as Wotan perceives, and from the multiple and independent histories of isolated communities a single overarching historical totality emerges which no one can master or inflect; nor is it clear that the return of the ring to the Rhinemaidens themselves can restore anything of that primal state as it were before history in this new and second sense, the sense of system and indeed of capitalism itself.

That this is in fact Wagner's vision, inscribed in the text and not imposed on it in the spirit of some external and unrelated philosophy or theory of history, may be judged by the reactions of Erda and her daughters, the Norns, in *Das Rheingold*. Erda clearly enough represents *Wissen*, the knowledge of all historical events and outcomes:

Wie alles war, weiß ich;	How all things were—I know;
wie alles wird,	how all things are,
wie alles sein wird,	how all things will be,
seh' ich auch …	I see as well …

(WR, Rheingold, iv, 112).

This Wissen is clearly enough that of the destiny of individuals and the interweaving of their chronological wissen of the récit, of the temporality of causality, the before and after, the past-present-future.

It is precisely this system of human acts that the Norns weave in their web, a warp and woof which, it will be remembered, dramatically breaks off in the *Götterdämmerung* "Prologue":

Zu End' ewiges Wissen!	An end to eternal wisdom!
Der Welt melden	Wise women no longer
Weise nichts mehr.	tell the world their tidings.

(WR, Götterdämmerung, 284)

To this climactic break corresponds Erda's confusion in her second scene (in *Siegfried*), when she hears of Brünnhilde's fate:

Wirr wird mir,	I've grown confused
seit ich erwacht:	since I was wakened:
wild und kraus	wild and awry
kreis't die Welt!	The world revolves!
	(*WR*, *Siegfried*, III: I, 256)

It would be wrong to interpret this decisive break in the very nature of Wissen, of the vision of anthropomorphic events past, present, and future, in terms of the impending end of the gods. Rather, it is the advent of a radically new historical temporality, that of money: and what henceforth looks confused in the focus of individual acts, takes on all the clarity of a "rollendes Rad," an impersonal determinism, from the standpoint of the now inhuman, superhuman, henceforth economic system.

Thus what the *Ring* registers here is the radical difference between the historical dynamic and indeed determinism of capitalism and that of earlier modes of production as they stretch back to village culture, isolated huts in the forest, or even the self-contained clans of gods and men, of dwarves and giants.

Returning then to Wotan and his anticipation of the eternal return, the fundamental changing of the valences of his despair and his failure simply involves a passage from passivity to what Nietzsche calls affirmation, or in other words, the eternal return. This is not resignation or stoic acceptance; it is something far more active than that: to welcome this outcome as though you had willed it in the first place, as though you had willed it from all eternity (over and over, again and again, in the language of "recurrence"): this is now Wotan's new choice; at the climax of the second Erda scene (in *Siegfried*) and until the end of the cycle:

Um der Götter Ende	Fear of the end of the gods
grämt mich die Angst nicht,	no longer consumes me
seit mein Wunsch es—will!	now that my wish so wills it!
Was in des Zwiespalts wildem	What I once resolved in
Schmerze	despair,
verzweifelnd einst ich	in the searing smart of inner
beschloß,	turmoil,
froh und freudig	I now perform freely
führe frei ich nun aus …	in gladness and joy …
	(*WR*, *Siegfried*, III: i, 257–8)

But Wotan mistakes this affirmation for his own choice; the choice —the end of the gods—has been made for him; he re-chooses it, *amor fati*: he assumes it in the form of a new choice or rather an affirmation. It is the sense in which Blanchot's Juliette, subjected to exactly the same tortures and indignities as her Sadean sister Justine, masters her destiny by choosing precisely those indignities rather than suffering them.[25] And this is the desperate Nietzschean invention of the eternal return, to affirm the horror as if you had willed it in the first place (note the active persistence of the Schopenhauerian term "will" in both Wagner and the allegedly post- and anti-Schopenhauerian Nietzsche).

I conclude this long excursus with a return to the question of the way in which Siegfried also may be said to incarnate the Nietzschean eternal return, or at least to prefigure it in a significant and revealing way. For the other feature of the eternal present of the eternal return is strong forgetfulness, that is, the willful obliteration of the past (and indeed, presumably also of the future). No episode in the *Ring* has been subjected to as much critical grumbling as the magic potion administered to Siegfried in *Götterdämmerung*, which has the simultaneous effect of obliterating his memory—in particular, his memory of Brünnhilde—and of causing him to fall in love with Gudrun: distinct outcomes no doubt meant to be identified as a single unique experience. The utterly different love potion in *Tristan* then inevitably comes to mind (as I already observed, Thomas Mann thought that Wagner should have left both out), and the overtones of magic also subtly interfere with other kinds of non-natural forces, such as that of Alberich's curse. It is disconcerting, for example, to learn that the now-human Brünnhilde is also a witch, having brought at least some of her more transcendent attributes with her into mortality.

I myself disagree with these judgments. In order for emotion to be transformed into affect (or at least overlaid with it in a new kind of affective surcharge), it seems to be logical for whatever exists as an emotional component of the dramatic intrigue to be doubled with a purely bodily or physiological dimension, that of the suffusion of the body with the fever of the poison, the fateful burning of the blood, and the sudden impact of the intoxicating drug. I take the named emotion here (amnesia, coup de foudre) as a building-block of the chronology and of "telling." The potion's surcharge of the

---

25   Maurice Blanchot, *Lautréamont et Sade* (Paris: Minuit, 1949).

affective dimension on the emotional events is then very much, in that spirit, an allegory of the emergence of the present of scene, and of the tension between the two now coexisting temporal dimensions.

But the defense of the melodramatic mechanism of the potion can also be waged on a less theoretical, a more everyday psychological level. Indeed, inasmuch as Siegfried may be said to retain a childlike mentality, one that is easily distracted, given over to the moment and its immediate enticements, it is not at all out of character for him to succumb to such a charm; or, if you prefer, the charm itself merely dramatizes and exaggerates an already existing condition, a preexisting feature of his personality in which the immature and the impulsive are already combined. Nietzsche will later on recommend "strong forgetfulness" for the Übermensch, but he is not likely to have missed the unattractiveness of this aspect of that future being—yet another reason why he should leave this figure unrepresented in Zarathustra and the object of a prophetic appeal, rather than a lovingly detailed portrayal. Later on, the predatory cruelty of a Cesare Borgia will be added to the Nietzschean evocation of the "strong" in order to dispel all traces of Siegfried's naivety, while that Athenian "rhathymia" celebrated by Pericles—"boldness and wickedness," "mad, absurd, and sudden in its expression, the incalculability, even incredibility of their undertakings"[26]—is as far from Siegfried's Germanic fearlessness as Bizet is from Wagner. To be sure, the twelve-year gap between Siegfried's youth and the third act of the eponymous opera, let alone of *Götterdämmerung*, must also be reckoned into a kind of maturation of his portrayal, if not his character itself; and the death of Siegfried, his reawakening to the memory of the equally reawakening Brünnhilde, can surely be said to mark an evolution of this figure.

Now I want to look at the issue of Siegfried's character and its meaning from a somewhat different angle. The seemingly strident and implacably heroic mode in which Wagner's music has been stereotypically characterized—an impression reinforced by the traditional blare of many orchestras (Boulez is especially mordant on this subject), as well as by innumerable political caricatures of

---

[26]   Nietzsche on Pericles's funeral oration in Thucydides, whom he quotes as praising the Athenians' "boldness … goodness and wickedness." See Friedrich Nietzsche, *On the Genealogy of Morals, and Ecce Homo*, trans. Walter Kaufmann and R. J. Hollingdale, ed. Walter Kaufmann (New York: Vintage, 1969), Part 1, Section 11, p. 41—emphasis in original.

Wagner himself—has tended to obscure moments in which both drama and music achieve other, far more subtle and delicate effects. Bloch is especially good on such effects in the music itself.[27] I want to underscore analogous features of the drama, often drowned out by the sound and by a properly Wagnerian "style" (and for which the composer is sometimes himself responsible).

So it is that the seemingly endless procrastinations of the love duet (in Act III of *Siegfried*) have often, particularly when the sub- or supertitles are lacking, exasperated even the most sympathetic listeners/spectators. What we lose thereby is the most subtle drama of the anxieties and hesitations of two virginities, of an approach and withdrawal of what it would be incorrect to call seduction, a remarkable dramatization of that "fear" Wagner deliberately inscribed in the discovery (by both parties) of sexual differentiation—it is an account worthy of the most acute "psychologists" so admired by Nietzsche in that French tradition which runs from Racine to Paul Bourget. Yet it is true that Wagner's magnificent music tends to distract us from this far more intimate drama in the words and their exchanges, or indeed to cause us to overlook it altogether.

But I want to bring out another, related property of Wagnerian drama which has drawn even less attention, and that is what I will call an allegorical division of labor between the characters in certain scenes. Foremost among these is surely the "deconstruction" of Wotan's "wish" beginning in Act III, Scene ii of *Die Walküre* and culminating in the third scene of its last act. This is no ordinary portrayal of thwarted wishes and ambitions, although it is theatrically useful to have its grand lines acted out as the submission of Wotan to Fricka's Law, and the subsequent disobedience of Brünnhilde not so much to the law as to Wotan's own submission. But it is precisely this distinction which is here at stake and which Wotan expresses at great length. We have already observed the cool disapproval of the lawful spouse for this illegitimate daughter whose official function is to people Valhalla with dead heroes (a use for which this facility was not originally designed) and who otherwise serves as Wotan's right hand in a variety of extracurricular situations. All this is wonderfully effective in thickening the drama and multiplying its internal relations in appropriately "dramatic" ways.

But what Wotan objects to is something far more complex than ordinary disobedience. In *Die Walküre*, at the climax of the great

---

[27] See p. 35, footnote 4, above.

farewell scene, Wotan articulates the meaning of Brünnhilde's insubordination as a virtual theft of jouissance:

So thatest du,	And so you did
was so gern zu thun ich begehrt—	what I longed so dearly to do—
doch was nicht zu thun	but which I was doubly
die Noth zwiefach mich zwang?	forced not to do by need.
So leicht wähntest du	So lightly you thought
Wonne des Herzens erworben,	that heartfelt delight might be won,
wo brennend Weh'	when burning pain
in das Herz mir brach,	broke into my heart
wo gräßliche Noth	and hideous need
den Grimm mir schuf …	aroused my wrath …
	(*WR*, *Walküre*, III: iii, 186)

What is intolerable for Wotan is not so much the collapse of the great project, and the misery of submission, the pain of renunciation, nor even the death of a beloved son. All that is, so to speak, normal pain, normal suffering. What really infuriates him, however, is Brünnhilde's enjoyment of what he has had to renounce: her assumption, in his place, of that immense libidinal satisfaction, including past and future, desire and fulfillment:

Wo gegen mich selber	When I turned on myself
ich sehrend mich wandte,	in consuming torment,
aus Ohnmacht-Schmerzen	starting up, chafing,
schäumend ich aufschoß,	in impotent pain,
wüthender Sehnsucht	furious longing's
sengender Wunsch	fervent desire
den schrecklichen Willen mir schuf,	inspired the terrible wish
in den Trümmern der eig'nen Welt	to end my eternal grief
meine ew'ge Trauer zu enden—	in the ruins of my own world—
da labte süß	then blissful abandon
dich selige Lust;	solaced you sweetly;
wonniger Rührung	rapt emotion's
üppigen Rausch	heady delights
enttrank'st du lachend	you drank from love's cup
der Liebe Trank—	with lips parted in laughter—
als mir göttlicher Noth	while *my* drink was mixed
nagende Galle gemischt?	with the griping gall of
	godly distress?
	(*WR*, *Walküre*, III: iii, 186)

No doubt this is taking place against the background of increasing individuation. In the earlier scene, Brünnhilde affirmed herself as his wish, as identical with the father in much the same way that Tristan identified himself as Isolde and Isolde as Tristan. You will not be telling another person, another subject, when you tell me your innermost thoughts, she assures him; and in Chéreau's production Wotan's "self-expression" takes place before a mirror, and with his eye-patch removed to show his true face—a situation with three subject positions rather than two. But in the later moment, clearly, Brünnhilde has separated herself off as a subject in her own right.

Nor is this interesting moment to be understood as simple envy; but perhaps we may here open a parenthesis on the Wagnerian psychological system and its peculiarities. It is wrong to imagine that this system is organized around any conventional opposition between good and evil, despite the melodramatic appearances and even allowing for the Nietzschean interpretation of good as the affirmation of a central subject's desire. For what takes the place of evil in the *Ring* is rather *Neid*: an intense mixture of jealousy and envy which permeates the whole range of Wagnerian emotions and motives. Thus it becomes conventional here to praise the great sword Nothung as a "neidliches Schwert"—"enviable sword"—which Porter mistranslates as "sword of my need" (no doubt the precise meaning of the sword's name but not of the celebratory adjective). The glory of the sword is rather that it awakens envy in others: it is a properly feudal conception of fame and of heroic honor—to be great is to be envied, and fealty becomes something included in that primal envy of the great—as when Gunther politely offers to become Siegfried's vassal (*mi casa es su casa*), to which Siegfried significantly replies that he has no house or vassals to offer in return, only his own body.

Neid is here the primordial driving force of this feudal world; and what might in some later moral system be identified as evil is here subordinate to it. Wotan's supremacy as a god is that he need not envy anyone (not even Alberich as possessor of the ring). Meanwhile, we may venture a biographical speculation that Wagner's own paranoia (and his anti-Semitism) are the expression of the feeling, not only that the world owes him an income, but that everyone else, and very especially the other composers, all envy him. Whence his relief (generally only temporary) at finding other beings, disciples, lovers, Cosima above all, and the King, who have transformed their putative envy into adulation.

Were one then to construct a system of the Wagnerian emotions, it would no doubt be organized around a fundamental opposition between Neid and "fearlessness," with the ill-defined notions of freedom, love, and the Law semiotically clustered around this primary tension. This is not the place to work out such a system; yet it remains to observe the way in which it becomes modified in Wagner's greatest disciple, Nietzsche. For the Wagnerian system was still individual in nature. The originality of Nietzsche—to be sure, himself a far more unassuming and modest social being than the outrageous Wagner—was to have transformed the concept of Neid into a collective category, namely that of ressentiment, assuredly one of Nietzsche's most influential philosophical achievements. The opposite of ressentiment then in Nietzsche's hands becomes a different kind of freedom (and even, if one likes, of fearlessness), namely solitude; and the new system then pursues its own independent fortunes in a later political and ideological universe.

But we must now, after this lengthy excursus, return to what we have called "psychic allegory" in Wagner's drama. No doubt, it is not particularly unusual for individual characters to bear the meaning of this or that psychic drive (indeed, for Neid we already have the inescapable figure of Iago). What gives the music drama its unusual purchase over such a structure is the way in which all the characters and their dialogue with one another are subsumed by the musical element in such a way as greatly to reduce the conventional distance established by allegorical personification. The music takes on the function of a psyche in which the various impulses emerge, differentiate, and recombine, and which thereby, in the terminology I have been seeking to establish here, serves as the medium wherein the distinct diegetical elements—the various named emotions and motivations—become identified and transformed into a stream of affect.

This is indeed what we find in the second allegorical sequence I wished to gloss, namely (once again) the love duet at the end of Siegfried. What is it that the older woman offers the younger man, as it were the neophyte and indeed the pupil? Strangely enough, or on the other hand perhaps unsurprisingly, it is her Wissen (knowledge). It is something that seems to range from the magical powers touched on earlier (she will make his body invulnerable, except, as we well know by now, from the back) all the way to a knowledge of the web of fate or destiny, a knowledge in which she is herself deficient (the

Copenhagen *Ring* indeed has her researching the earlier episodes in a kind of library). In fact, no character in the *Ring* has any kind of genuine omniscience. We have seen that even Erda herself loses her foreknowledge in the aftermath of the forging of the ring. And any number of riddles and questioning scenes (*weisst du wie das wird?*) elevate this mode into a virtual "simple form" in Jolles's sense, if not a genre in its own right (Wotan is the supreme practitioner of this riddling form, first with Mime, then with Siegfried himself).[28] We have already commented on the well-nigh medieval ignorance on the part of the inhabitants of the various and separate primeval worlds in the beginning of the music drama. I have then argued above that omniscience (wisdom) of Erda's type, and later on of the Norns, is really only possible against the background of that well-nigh geographical ignorance of the early clans and species. The loss of such a possibility is the sign of the beginning of a newly unifying, totalizing historical dynamic—that of money or even industrial capitalism.

Yet Brünnhilde's "Wissen" is still of that earlier variety: she knows the destinies, which is to say the récits, the legends, of the various characters and forces, and foresees (in *Siegfried*) the fates that wait in store for them:

Was du nicht weißt,	What *you* don't know
weiß ich für dich:	I know for you:
doch wissend bin ich	and yet I am knowing
nur—weil ich dich liebe!—	only because I love you!—
	(*WR, Siegfried*, III: iii, 268)

But it is precisely this Wissen, this "wisdom" of the temporality of the before-and-after, the past-present-future, which Siegfried is unable to grasp—indeed, whose incomprehension defines what we might otherwise call his naivety or his immaturity:

Wie Wunder tönt	Wondrous it sounds
was wonnig du sing'st;	what you blissfully sing;
doch dunkel dünkt mich	yet its meaning seems obscure
der Sinn.	to me.
	(*WR, Siegfried*, III: iii, 269)

---

[28] See André Jolles, *Einfache Formen* (Tubingen: Niemeyer, 1930).

This incomprehension is not to be assimilated too completely to rapt and sensual contemplation, to desire and its senses, even though that is the pretext for expressing it:

Nicht kann ich das Ferne	With my senses I cannot
sinnig erfassen,	grasp far-away things,
wenn alle Sinne	since all these senses
dich nur sehen und	can see and feel only
fühlen.	you.

(*WR*, *Siegfried*, III: iii, 269)

The exchange confirms the notion of the two distinct temporalities that here confront each other—Wissen versus *Sinnen*, Brünnhilde the tale, Siegfried the scenic present—and illustrates the twofold way in which the standard mechanical separation of allegorical tenor and vehicle is in Wagner attenuated and transformed into an event rather than a static structure by the love union on the one hand, and the musical texture on the other. Wagner thus idiosyncratically solves the great form problem of the theater between the collapse of the genre system with the ancien régime and the emergence of naturalism in full industrial capitalism: the separation of particular and universal, or of individual experience and some more generalizable meaning. Siegfried himself meanwhile stands as the survival of that older ignorance of heterogeneous world geography by the isolated clans up into the new social world of dynasties and alliances (from consanguinity to affiliation, Deleuze calls it, following Lévi-Strauss).[29] This ignorance is his isolation as an individual separate both from clan and alliance alike, and if anything can, it serves as the only meaning "freedom" can have in the *Ring*.

For Wotan faces a political dilemma characteristic of all lawgivers and their theorizations from Lycurgus on, namely how to avoid imposing a law that must be freely chosen.[30] This is a theoretical dilemma far more complicated than the conventional opposition of law and power which has so often been designated as the crux of the *Ring*, and most often associated with dictators or usurpers. Here, however, even Wotan's power must in this new human world

[29] Gilles Deleuze and Félix Guattari, *L'Anti-Oedipe* (Paris: Minuit, 1972), p. 170 (Chapter 3, Part 2).

[30] See Fredric Jameson, "Rousseau and Contradiction," in *Valences of the Dialectic* (London: Verso, 2009), pp. 303–15.

be somehow endorsed and affirmed by his subjects. It is the problem of the adoption of constitutions rather than the organization of armed forces, and corresponds to that peculiar suspension Negri has so subtly analyzed in terms of the passage from constituent power to constituted power.[31] To take a contemporary reference, we may recall the paradoxical dynamic of the Chinese Cultural Revolution: Mao Zedong wishes to destroy the old power and institutions of a bureaucratic communist party state. "Bombard the headquarters!" is however a classic example of the double bind, insofar as, emanating from authority (and from a new "headquarters"), it asks the population freely to follow new orders and to repudiate the old ones. It thereby commands its citizenry to be free—not necessarily the best formula for genuine freedom.

But Wotan is precisely in this same situation. He must create free human individuals who execute his pre-established plan, who somehow freely reinvent it in their own right without any reference to him. Siegmund, who has lived with the Wanderer his whole adult life, and to whom an invincible sword has been furnished in advance, is not in a position to execute this project. Siegfried, however, is; but only on the condition that he understand nothing and have no idea of what Wotan aimed for in the first place. In practical terms, this independence means that Wotan must relinquish his own power (and even his divinity). Siegfried thus shatters the spear (but significantly, in the Copenhagen *Ring*, it is Wotan himself who breaks it in two). Wotan, therefore, like Lycurgus before him, in effect commits suicide.

Siegfried, however, as soon as he has accumulated enough deeds to have a destiny—and to remember it!—passes from the temporality of the pure present to that of chronology and is consequently killed. Brünnhilde herself still belongs to that temporality of destiny associated with the old world and the gods, and she chooses also to perish with it, as though this new mortal world had no place even for the memory of immortality. It has no place for heroes either. Far from dramatizing the advent of Nietzsche's "last men" it is rather as though the superman were here defined not only as the overcoming of "man," but also of human heroes as such.

---

31 Antonio Negri, "Constituent Republic," in Michael Hardt and Paolo Virno eds, *Radical Thought in Italy: A Potential Politics* (Minneapolis: Minnesota University Press, 1996), pp. 213–21.

Chapter 3

Transcendence and Movie Music in Mahler

for Ramón del Castillo

This (1927) was the year of the high and miraculous harvest of chamber music: first the ensemble for three strings, three wood-wind instruments, and piano, a discursive piece, I might say, with very long themes, in the character of an improvisation, worked out in many ways without ever recurring undisguised. How I love the yearning, the urgent longing, which characterizes it; the romantic note—since after all is treated with the strictest of modern devices—thematic, indeed, but with such considerable variation that actually there are no "reprises." The first movement is expressively called "fantasia," the second is an adagio surging up in a powerful crescendo, the third the finale, which begins light enough, almost playfully, becomes increasingly contrapuntal and at the same time takes on more and more a character of tragic gravity, until it ends in sombre epilogue like a funeral march. The piano is never used for harmonic fillings, its part is soloistic as in a piano concerto—probably a survival from the violin concerto. What I perhaps most profoundly admire is the mastery with which the problem of sound-combination is solved. Nowhere do the wind instruments cover up the strings, but always allow them to have their own say and alternate with them; only in a very few places are strings and wind instruments combined in a tutti. If I am to sum up the whole impression: it is as though one were lured from a firm and familiar setting-out into ever remoter regions—everything comes contrary to expectation. "I have," Adrian said to me, "not wanted to write a sonata but a novel."

Thomas Mann, *Doctor Faustus*[1]

I.

To identify the formal contradiction at the heart of a work is not to criticize it but to locate the sources of its production: it is in other

---

[1]   Thomas Mann, *Doctor Faustus*, trans. H. Lowe-Porter (New York: Knopf, 1948). pp. 455–6.

words, following Lukács's useful formula, to articulate the form-problem the work attempts to solve. Without confronting such a form-problem, without in other words grappling with a genuine contradiction, it is hard to see how a work could have any distinction or win any value. The form-problem (and not necessarily its solution, for contradictions are never resolved and problems are "solved" only by being articulated) secures the work's position in history: in the history of form, first of all, and by way of that, in the various levels of social history, of subjectivity, and of the mode of production.

Mahler's commentators often begin with his songs, which are wondrous and truly unique and which can also be documented as the sources for important stretches of the orchestral music. Inasmuch as they are poems, consisting of verbal language, however, they also tend to steer the commentaries in the direction of meanings, biographical or existential, and dangerously approach that quagmire of interpretation which any resolutely formal analysis will want to try to avoid.

(It is worth adding, not only that these reflections omit the songs—that extraordinary body of lyric work that must from any point of view represent the climax of the German Lied as a form—but that the songs are so distinct from the symphonic work that they might be considered the practice of a different art or medium altogether, like a great painter who writes lyrics, or a great playwright who indulges in a sonnet sequence, a novelist who also paints, a poet who makes a film—or even a painter who tells stories! The songs transform the raw material of the symphonic work into melodies, thereby reifying a sonorous matter in flux into unforgettably lyric moments of expression. The *Lied von der Erde* is a farewell to life, in which the intensities of living are not mourned but lifted into extraordinarily memorable affirmations—"bittersweet," as the cultural journalists might put it. This is indeed the place to speak of old-fashioned kinds of interpretative meaning—optimism and pessimism—and to evoke emotion rather than affect, as I will in describing the symphonic work; but it is a radically different language or medium than what the voice stands for when, in Nietzsche's great lyric, it is embedded in the Third Symphony, or even, when in certain passages of the *Song of the Earth*, the symphonic comes perilously close to overwhelming the Chinese verse and the singer who is momentarily at one with it. The songs are uniquely precious moments, for special occasions: the symphonic elaborations are an endless, ongoing work into which one may plunge at any time, asking new questions, finding new answers.)

For even before he was a composer, Mahler was first and foremost an orchestra conductor. ("Any fool," Adorno warns me, "can detect in his music traces of conductor's music";[2] and perhaps the intemperate remark entitles me to some of the criticisms I will aim at Adorno in the following pages.) Surely it is just as legitimate to begin from the more formal consideration of the voice as one more musical instrument among others, whose unexpected introduction at the very moment in which all the other instruments have had their say and exhausted their possibilities (in the fourth movement of the Third Symphony, for example), is an even greater shock than the jangling of distant cowbells.

Meanwhile, the choral interventions traditionally designate that transcendence of which our title promises to speak, while the fact of the song or Lied itself, is to be formally registered as a kind of closure unavailable to orchestral developments (to which its relationship is distantly comparable to that of the short story to the novel) and serves to avoid the problem of endings (of which we will also speak later on) by providing a more traditional full stop (to the Fourth Symphony, for example): it is a solution which has nothing to do with that symphony's notorious cheerfulness or pastorality, but which is a purely formal one.

So we must begin with the orchestra itself, greatly expanded in post-Wagnerian times, and a suitably central social institution in the nineteenth-century city, with its budget, its relationship to government, and its bureaucratic or administrative positions, of which the relatively new status of the conductor is paramount. Adorno compares it to the emergent role of that new kind of political leader (or even dictator) exemplified by Napoleon III or Bismarck, something which might encourage us to speculate about power and its satisfaction, but which should also more materialistically draw our attention to logistics and the ways in which managing a great orchestra is more comparable to the running of an army than to the writing of a novel (even though a Zola was capable of turning his composition into elaborate projects, involving research, files, inspection trips, and planning of all kinds).

---

2   T. W. Adorno, *Mahler: A Musical Physiognomy* (Chicago: University of Chicago Pres, 1992), p. 30. All future page references in the text are to this edition.

Meanwhile, we must also recall the fundamental analogy under-scored by Darko Suvin for that other comparable artistic institution of the time which was the theater, itself also the microcosm of a complex industrial society in its own right, with its materialities and hierarchies, its divisions of labor and associated métiers, skilled and unskilled, its ancillary copyists and bureaucratic satellites and subor-dinates, not to speak of a kind of electoral public seated in judgment in front of it. Like the theater, then, the symphony orchestra stands as a figure of the social totality itself, a social world in which the state and its functions also figure symbolically, and whose debates (of which, for the theater, we have a rich variety from those of the Paris Commune documented by Suvin[3] to the manifestos of Artaud and Brecht, the concept of the happenings, and to the practices of performance in our own time) are then, in musical and orchestral theory as well, in and of themselves political: they replay the various political philosophies and ideologies, the strategies, the constitu-tional and revolutionary crises, familiar in the extra-aesthetic life of the real world, of which they can so often be allegorical.

Meanwhile, this emphasis also places the question of style in a new light. No doubt the deployment of ever larger orchestras opens up new stylistic possibilities, at the same time that it acts as a con-straint, excluding older simplicities and the melodic forms they were able to vehiculate and demanding the invention of new and more complex expressive phrasing.

Styles are, to be sure, the implicit articulation of ideologies and what used to be called Weltanschauungen, as Spitzer and Sartre showed us; but they also function as historical limits on what a work can say and how it can be historically received. Both Beethoven and Mahler have distinctive styles, but in a sense their formal achieve-ments stand in tension with those more persistent and personal forms of expression, in which period styles and a certain kind of history of style (or fashion) is also inscribed.

Nor should we forget something like an "institutional style." Perhaps we may reinfuse the neutral and descriptive adjective, the *symphonic*, with something of that pejorative malice Barthes managed to attach to the word "romanesque" or "novelistic" when used about individual sentences: the connotative evocation of a

---

3   Darko Suvin, *To Brecht and Beyond* (Brighton: Harvester, 1984), Chapter 3: "Politics, Performance and the Organisational Mediation: The Paris Commune Theatre Law."

whole institutional form over the seeming innocence of the execution of a part or a detail, a sentence which was to have been a mere step in the construction of the whole. For he meant that just as a florid utterance can at once be detected as "oratorical," so also the intent to narrate—and to narrative novelistically—can often be felt in the "delivery" of a sentence in passing, a telltale sign of novelism detected not in the great and necessary components of the project (such as beginnings and endings, coups de theatre, etc.) but rather in the most insignificant and dispensable passing observations, which are however there precisely to produce that *effet de réel* so ideologically essential to the novel as an operation.[4]

So perhaps here, less in the composition than in the performance, a great orchestra defeats itself by investing its phrasing and its attack with a pomp and a richness which precisely denotes the "symphonic" as its meaning, and betrays the institution in which orchestra, audience, composer are all complicitous, thereby baring the deeper constitutive relationship of this form to the bourgeoisie itself which brought it forth and nourishes its performances. This is kind of a self-consciousness of the occasion, a satisfaction of its talented and well-paid prestigious performers, the construction of the hall by the city and the price of season tickets: a glimpse even deeper than Bourdieusian "distinction," one which ever so briefly betrays the guilt of culture and its complicity with the system in a way in which a provincial orchestra never could, or a somewhat less supremely perfect "attack," a somewhat less comfortable and self-confident command of the piece (in all its difficulties), might not do. To be sure, the less canonical the music, as Mahler was in his own immediate period, the less useful the occasion for such a telling revelation; the more familiar as well, inasmuch as the great warhorses of the repertoire, however such they remain vehicles for virtuosity, are less likely to attract such momentary attention (since we know the orchestra's ranking, and the conductor's, in advance and by heart).

For the very notion of style—as it is developed out of "stylus," or handwriting—began as a mode of authentication in the visual arts, and in particular the analysis of the chemical contents of paint and the shape of brushstrokes (analogous to handwriting in forensics). It is only with the development of modernism as an individual

---

4   Roland Barthes, "L'effet de réel," in *Oeuvres complètes* (Paris: Seuil, 1994), Vol. II, pp. 479–84. The text dates from 1968.

resistance to all kinds of fixed conventions that the production of a unique style comes to be valorized as the distinctive sign of "genius" and moves to the center of the modernist telos and the coordinates of radical innovation.

But in the time of Beethoven, for example, innovation was still a matter of formal invention and the expansion of what could be done in the various musical genres. Beethoven certainly had a style, as registered in the shape of his themes, but it was still the raw material of his forms: thus the terribilità of his heroic movements—unlike anything in Haydn and essentially, we are told, inspired by and borrowed from that wholly new and different source which was French revolutionary music[5]—is not reducible to the kinds of themes through which this new energy is expressed.

What characteristics the themes as such then remains a "style" in the more "cultural" sense of a fashion which is profoundly marked historically and socially in a different sense: it does not transmit the unique spirit of this new historical thing which is revolution so much as it bears traces of a social culture which Barthes might have called *viennicité* or viennicity (despite the fact that the Rhinelander Beethoven, like the Moravian-Jewish Mahler after him, was essentially a foreigner in this cosmopolitan capitol). There is a characteristic lyricism about these themes which reminds one of Brecht's astonishing critique of Schoenberg on the grounds that his music was "too sweet" (he was perhaps thinking of the more expressionist-hysterical bittersweetness of early works like *Verklärte Nacht*). It is this separate and specific dimension of a kind of personal-cultural style of which one must also accuse Mahler, and this despite the fact that some of this late viennicity may be thought to be pastiche rather than the expression of this or that personal identity. But the fact is that Mahler's themes are always recognizable (even or especially in the absence of their formal context) and that it is this component or level of his production which can eventually tire the listener and cause a kind of Mahler-fatigue unrelated either to the form of the movements themselves or to the specific orchestration of the moments in question.

---

[5] Scott Burnham, *Beethoven Hero* (Princeton: Princeton University Press, 1995), pp. 123–4.

2.

For the moment, we may think of the functions of the composer as a kind of collaboration between two writers, perhaps endowed with two kinds of skills and certainly charged with two distinct kinds of work. It does not matter that in this case, and perhaps most often, it is a single composer who does both; yet one understands that in the normal run of things, the musical composition takes the form of an initial sketch, with basic themes and melodies blocked out, and a fair idea of their development over time and the direction in which they are to be nudged and headed. (For the composer of the opera, of course, there would be yet a third—or rather first, additional—stage which is the composition of the libretto; but once again the order, beginning, middle, end, scarcely matters, except anecdotally.)

At this point of the linear sketch as we may call it, or perhaps even of the fabula or narrative, a different process necessarily sets in which is the scoring of that movement, and not merely its harmonization (which might often be part of the initial sketch itself) but its distribution among the various instruments, the addition of supplementary instrumental developments, for example, or even countermovements, eddies or gyres as we may call them, and so forth. It is then clear that whereas for earlier composers, this might have been a relatively mechanical activity of filling the score out with a limited orchestra and a limited number of voices, often distributed in a conventional way—with Mahler this process of orchestration will become not only immeasurably more complex but also significantly more important and central, inasmuch as our attention is thereby shifted from continuities to a kind of perpetual present. To be sure, this division of labor suggests a twin exploration of this music in terms of the larger form as well as the moment of hearing. Much of Mahler's alleged difficulty in fact comes from the length of these movements and the difficulty of holding them together productively and creatively in the memory, as good listening must do; and the superiority of the truly great Mahlerian conductors, such as Leonard Bernstein, lies above all in the way in which the forward movement of the music gets projected and marked for retention in an active memory. Bernstein's interpretive excesses, which have seemed to many to betray self-indulgence and willfulness, can also be taken as rhetorical emphasis, as modes of underlining specific moments with a view towards their organization in our listening, our memory, and our anticipation. This can, as we shall see, also be understood as a narrative or storytelling process, and indeed one which too often leads to abusive interpretation or abstract retelling. Yet perspective in this narrative sense can be grasped temporally, as when a recapitulation (such as the one central to the "Durchbruch" debate about the ending of the First Symphony)[6] is grasped as a kind of memory of what went before, and the fading of a theme in time fully as much as in space.

And among such self-conscious gestures are surely to be numbered the ostentatious hesitations, suspensions, pauses that dramatize a leap about to be made, a momentous decision, a sudden onrush of the orchestra or else a modulation into something wholly new, generally a change in rhythm and tempo, where the very momentary silence is itself a drawing of breath and an integral component of the momentum itself. Such momentary pauses also have their style; their part of silence is itself a gesture, which can be flamboyant or prosaic: Bernstein or Tilson-Thomas mark these moments well and dramatically, which might otherwise be overlooked: they are as it were features of the operatic Mahler, the self-dramatizing composer-conductor, foregrounding his own effects. But above all, it seems to me that they restore something of the ongoing compositional qualities, I don't want to call them improvised, but rather what used to be called textual production, as though we witnessed speech in its process of elaboration, and not some already recorded score lying there in front of the conductor simply to be recited or repeated. So there is a freshness in such admittedly self-indulgent and rhetorical modes of presentation which awaken us to the very emergence of the music as though it had come into being in Mahler's mind fully orchestrated and coherent, an incomplete *énoncé* in the process of enunciation and developing itself autopoetically as a sentence develops itself virtually without an enunciating speaker who has thoroughly thought through it in advance and "intended" it.

We can imagine this in a different situation, namely of the great virtuoso actor in a repertory company, who assumes all kinds of

---

6   The original idea is to be found in Paul Bekker, *Gustav Mahlers Sinfonien* (Berlin: Schuster & Loeffler, 1921), p. 44. Adorno's appropriation begins at once, on p. 5; and for a thorough analysis of the controversy, see James Buhler's "'Breakthrough' as a Critique of Form: The Finale of Mahler's First Symphony" in *19th-Century Music* 20 (1996), pp. 125–43, as well as his review of Adorno in *Indiana Theory Review* 15 (1994), pp. 139–63.

minor roles or character acting at the same time that he is accorded the great ones, those of the hero or the romantic lead. What kind of play will such an actor imagine for himself? One surely, as Lionel Abel suggested for Hamlet himself, in which a whole range and variety of tones are available to exhibit his virtuosity: pathos, comedy, the wearing of masks, the ridiculous, the touching, the morose and melancholy, all in a single complex role.[7] So also perhaps Mahler's experience as a professional music director may have impacted his sense of what composition can achieve, and stimulated his own technical skills to extraordinary feats of virtuosity and mood change, of the whole gamut of stances and affect, expression and construction alike.

Still, the spatial meaning or musical perspectivism is likely to predominate, as our attention shifts from the role of the composer in framing his plots to that of an orchestrator in which the present of time becomes the place of invention and innovation, indeed of the musical Event as such, in the sense in which the emergence of a new sound behind the others actually happens and is not merely superadded. Indeed at this point the very scoring may well come first and begin to dictate the linear invention; at any rate my interest is not the practical or biographical process as such, as fascinating as either might well be, but rather how this determines our attention to the listening of it, and to the music as a kind of Bazinian depth-shot, in which we perceive not merely a simultaneity of sounds but a wellnigh visual perspective in which layered instruments are discerned, at various distances from each other in the depth of the work: this is of course most obvious when it is the same theme which is repeated at ever greater and more distant, more hushed, spaces behind one another, culminating in the minute sounds of a single solo instrument (the expansion of the technique of the offstage horn call à la Wagner, the evocation of the hunter lost in the great wood, as though in legend or in the mists of time). Here, however, I think it is in the Sixth Symphony, we are likely to follow such receding planes of sound back to the very stillness of jangling barely perceptible cowbells, by which Mahler meant to convey, not the pastoral landscape, but rather the space of another world beyond our own.[8]

---

7   Lionel Abel, *Metatheatre* (New York: Hill & Wang, 1963), p. 47.

8   "The last greeting from earth to penetrate the remote solitude of the mountain peaks": quoted in Michael Steinberg, *The Symphony: A Listener's Guide* (Oxford: Oxford University Press, 1995), p. 317.

3.

With this transition from the work of the writer of plot to the scenic metteur en scène, we confront new possibilities of instrumentation, in which the various sound groups may stand in opposition and in struggle with one another, the woodwinds harassing the string instruments for example, the brass, like *Tyrannosaurus rex*, frightening the other sonorous beings away; a call to order, occasionally, in which one type of sound—no matter whether loud or soft, monumental or chamber-like in its intimacy—rebukes the increasing disorder of the other parts of the orchestra and summons it to combined and disciplined action: or failing that, suddenly releases the pandemonium of sounds of all kinds and descriptions building up and pressing towards the excitement of chaos.

For it is the sound combinations (returning now to the matter of the orchestra as such) which must continue to fascinate and mesmerize the public for which these sonorities correspond to something like an aural *grand spectacle*: a special event like fireworks or the circus[9] in which the listener's jaded palate is given a feast of new and hitherto untested combinations to register; and this is something quite different from the repetitions of Mahler's bodily stylistic mannerisms and that fin-de-siècle history into which he is locked and from which we may ultimately (in our search for new historicist sensations) wish to escape. It is probably because from the perspective of a purely musical history Mahler is on the cusp of the twentieth-century modern and betrays an ambivalence which can be read either as the end of nineteenth-century tonal and symphonic music or as the first powerful impulse towards its overcoming and its replacement by utterly new kinds of sounds—it is probably for this undecidably dual situation-and-response that we are able to find the demands of innovation satisfied in ever newer ways within this music without abandoning traditional form for something else. Pleasure and pain, major and minor combined, the dissonance of instruments rather than notes and tones, "a green so delicious it hurts" (Baudelaire), the sour within the sweet, the raw, the cooked, and the rotten all at once—these are the combinations Mahler was able to demand from his orchestra: "if I want to produce a soft-subdued sound, I don't give

---

[9]   Adorno likens the work of art to fireworks—see T. W. Adorno, *Aesthetic Theory* (Minneapolis: University of Minnesota Press, 1997), p. 81—while Eisenstein's "montage of attractions" refers specifically to the circus.

it to an instrument which produces it easily, but rather to one which gets it only with effort and under pressure—often only by forcing itself and exceeding its natural range," he told Bauer-Lechner.[10] So even the instruments are used against themselves, tormented into ever newer innovations, producing ever newer demands on the senses, ever newer sensations and thrills, until finally (or at least in the traditional narrative) the sensation is exhausted, cries out for rest, for a respite in which all kinds of returns to the traditional can be exploited again, until the sensory restlessness returns, the teleology of consumption and novelty once again demanding its due. And this holds in all the arts, all the dimensions of sensory experience: we want a representation of new feelings and emotions, we want new attention to the oil paint and new color combinations, new sounds, new seasonings and even tactile combinations, we want new spaces as well, we are jaded with the old alternation of monumental public space and Biedermeier overstuffed interior comfort. It is discovered to what degree abstinence, taboos, forced asceticisms of all kinds, can also renew the palate; silences can also heighten the sonorous experience, and not only the massed differences and dissonances of the massed orchestra. The body craves extremes; it is depleted at the same time that it is stimulated: in its moment of emergence the bourgeois body is insatiable and wishes at one and the same time to disappear into its new ecstasies, to be abolished by its own emergent sensations. The world is consumed by a new restlessness:

Suddenly, out of the becalmed mentality of the nineteenth century's last two decades, an invigorating fever rose all over Europe. No one knew exactly what was in the making; nobody could have said whether it was to be a new art, a new humanity, a new morality, or perhaps a reshuffling of society. So everyone said what he pleased about it. But everywhere people were suddenly standing up to struggle against the old order. Everywhere the right man suddenly appeared in the right place and—this is so important!—enterprising men of action joined forces with enterprising men of intellect. Talents of a kind that had previously been stifled or had never taken part in public life suddenly came to the fore. They were as different from each other as could be, and could not have been contradictory in their aims. There were those who loved the overman and those who loved the underman; there were health cults and sun cults and

---

10   Nathalie Bauer-Lechner, *Recollections of Gustav Mahler* (Cambridge Cambridge University Press, 1980), p. 160.

the cults of consumptive maidens; there was enthusiasm for the hero worshipers and for the believers in the Common Man; people were devout and sceptical, naturalistic and mannered, robust and morbid; they dreamed of old tree-lined avenues in palace parks, autumnal gardens, glassy ponds, gems, hashish, disease, and demonism, but also of prairies, immense horizons, forges and rolling mills, naked wrestlers, slave uprisings, early man, and the smashing of society. These were certainly opposing and widely varying battle cries, but uttered in the same breath. An analysis of that epoch might produce some such nonsense as a square circle trying to consist of wooden iron, but in reality it all blended into shimmering sense. This illusion, embodied in the magical date of the turn of the century, was so powerful that it made some people hurl themselves with zeal at the new, still-unused century, while others chose one last quick fling in the old one, as one runs riot in a house one absolutely has to move out of, without anyone feeling much of a difference between these two attitudes.[11]

So if a situational motivation is required to explain the formal description we will eventually offer here—ever greater agitation followed by relative exhaustion and periods of feverish, breathless rest—at least one version can be found here, in the very momentum of the modern as such (it is not the only one).

4.

This is, in fact, what we may call the Standard Narrative of modernism: but it has its specifically musical version, which I take to turn centrally (after the invention of tonality) around the exhaustion of sonata form by Beethoven, after whom a generation of epigones can only repeat the ready-made formal solutions, or, in a following generation, abandon the sonata altogether for tone poems and various forms of descriptive or program music. Thomas Mann's hero Adrian Leverkühn, offers a convincing account of why no further joy is to be found in the sonata:

> I am embarrassed at the insipidness which is the supporting structure, the conditioning solid substance of even the work of genius, at the elements thereof which are training and common property, at use and wont in achieving the beautiful; I blush at all that, weary thereof, get head-ake therefrom, and that

---

[11]   Robert Musil, *The Man without Qualities*, trans. Sophie Wilkins (New York: Knopf, 1995), p. 53.

right early. How stupid, how pretentious it would be to ask: "Do you understand that?" For how should you not? It goes like this, when it is beautiful: the cellos intone by themselves, a pensive, melancholy theme, which questions the folly of the world, the wherefore of all the struggle and striving, pursuing and plaguing—all highly expressive and decorously philosophical. The cellos enlarge upon this riddle awhile, head-shaking, deploring, and at a certain point in their remarks, a well-chosen point, the chorus of wind instruments enters with a deep full breath that makes your shoulders rise and fall, in a choral hymn, movingly solemn, richly harmonized, and produced with all the muted dignity and mildly restrained power of the brass. Thus the sonorous melody presses on up to nearly the height of a climax which, in accordance with the law of economy it avoids at first, gives way, leaves open, sinks away, postpones, most beautifully lingers; then withdraws and gives place to another theme, a songlike simple one, now jesting, now grave, now popular, apparently brisk and robust by nature but sly as you make them, and for someone with some subtle cleverness in the art of thematic analysis and transformation it proves itself amazingly pregnant and capable of utter refinement. For a while this little song is managed and deployed, cleverly and charmingly, it is taken apart, looked at in detail, varied, out of it a delightful figure in the middle register is led up into the most enchanting heights of fiddles and flutes, lulls itself there a little, and when it is at its most artful, then the mild brass has again the word with the previous choral hymn and comes into the foreground. The brass does not start from the beginning as it did the first time, but as though its melody had already been there for a while; and it continues, solemnly, to that climax from which it wisely refrained the first time, in order that the surging feeling, the Ah-h-effect, might be the greater: now it gloriously bestrides its theme, mounting unchecked, with weighty support from the passing notes on the tuba, and then, looking back, as it were, with dignified satisfaction on the finished achievement, sings itself decorously to the end.

Dear friend, why do I have to laugh? Can a man employ the traditional or sanctify the trick with greater genius? Can one with shrewder sense achieve the beautiful? And I, abandoned wretch, I have to laugh, particularly at the grunting supporting notes of the bombardone, Bum, bum, bum, bang![12]

Beethoven's true opposite number was, however, neither his Viennese predecessors nor his German successors; it was, Dahlhaus tells us,[13] Rossini, and the emergence of a distinct yet parallel stream in the

12 Mann, *Doctor Faustus*, pp. 132–3.
13 Carl Dahlhaus, *Nineteenth-Century Music* (Oakland: University of California Press, 1991), p. 8.

Italian opera composers of the nineteenth century. We have already commented on the matter of opera (Mahler conducted all of them); yet to see Mahler as operatic may place him in a new light.

But this splitting of the sources of music into two distinct traditions explains why after Beethoven there could only be a movement of the type of Shklovsky's "knight's gambit," who proposed a history of the various arts in which inheritance proceeded, not from father to son, but rather from the uncle to the nephew, and by way of the activation and exploitation of generic possibilities deployed only secondarily in the previous generation, but which now stand as new channels after the principal ones had been blocked.[14]

It is thus all very well to talk about tone poems and program music, but in the knight's gambit musical history confronts in this period the true inheritor, Wagner, who leaps to the unfulfilled place of German opera and thereby creates an immense orchestral toy for his successors to play with (in the Standard Narrative of musical history they are of course Schoenberg and his followers, whose combination of traditionality and invention is classically and perhaps rather lugubriously narrated by Adorno as a story of closure). But in order to appreciate the ongoing relevance of Shklovsky's "theory of history" here, we must amend Adorno in a somewhat different direction. One remembers that after the disappointment of the first Bayreuth *Ring* in 1876, and after that peculiarly specialized corner into which he painted himself in *Parsifal,* Wagner vowed henceforth only to write symphonies; we may wonder what they would have looked like, without necessarily regretting their loss. Indeed, our consolation may consist in the fantasy that it was just this ensemble of unimaginable Wagnerian symphonic works that Mahler himself wrote, thereby reviving the form whose exhaustion and demise led Wagner to opera in the first place, in a period where others from the late nineteenth century, such as Mahler's friend and rival Richard Strauss, found themselves obliged to substitute the tone poem for the now extinct sonata form.

But what you do, when presented with such an immense gift as the post-Wagnerian orchestra, is not to squander it by turning it to this or that petty personal purpose and obliging its combined practitioners to let some inestimable melody soar or ferociously to blast

---

14 Viktor Shklovsky, *Knight's Move*, trans. Richard Sheldon (Champaign: Dalkey Archive, 2005).

out some deliberately climactic chord, in other words, rhetorically and theatrically to play upon your public's feelings ("do you think I am easier to be played upon than on a pipe?") and to draw them this way and that according to some arbitrary formal or narrative or indeed psychological convention. It is to respect orchestra as a totality: and we may return to Kant for the philosophical concept itself and what it implies (he is defining what he thinks of as a "system" and not the much maligned Hegelian-Lukácsian term):

> the form of a whole—in so far as the concept determines *a priori* not only the scope of its manifold content, but also the positions which the parts occupy relatively to one another … The unity of the end to which all the parts relate and in the idea of which they all stand in relation to one another, makes it possible for us to determine from our knowledge of the other parts whether any part be missing, and to prevent any arbitrary addition … The whole is thus an organised unity (*articulatio*), and not an aggregate (*coacervatio*). It may grow from within (*per intussusceptionem*), but not by external addition (*per appositionem*). It is thus like an animal body.[15]

The Deleuzian repudiation of this here unashamedly avowed organicism is motivated by more than a principled anti-Platonist anti-idealism; but we may leave those other impulses, deeply rooted in our own Zeitgeist, to one side. It is more useful to stress the ambiguity of the organic itself, which certainly affirms a kind of natural unity of the organs that are unified in such an "animal body"; but which can also—see, for example, the various "organs" to which allegedly the chapters of Joyce's *Ulysses* correspond[16]—imply a radical difference between the various organs themselves and their functions; as well as a distance from the organism's ecosystem at the same time that an environmental relationship to the latter is also positively underscored.

The orchestra's various organs, then—its distinct bodies of instruments, made up of different material and emitting radically different sounds and tones—can just as surely lead us in the direction of dissonance and mutual incompatibility as they can to any certainty of consonance and unification. But Kant's account also has the merit

---

[15] Immanuel Kant, *Critique of Pure Reason* (Cambridge: Cambridge University Press, 1997), p. 691.

[16] As outlined, for example, in Stuart Gilbert's *James Joyce's Ulysses: A Study* (New York: Knopf, 1930).

of reminding us of the significance of omission in the organicist framework: "whether any part is missing," and not only "to prevent any arbitrary addition." The latter directs us to the familiar traditional concern with autonomy (which still very much preoccupies Adorno as we will continue to see); the former suggests enlargements of the organism and also deficiencies which declare themselves when not all the organs are given proper use and exercise. This last then encourages a properly Mahlerian ambition to secure the most comprehensive exploitation of all possible instrumental sounds and combinations (whereas the former merely stimulates an obsession with the cowbells and the hammers).

(This is not to deny that a composer might well entertain unique personal relations with various instruments, just as you prefer this or that friend for special occasions. But presumably there will be a kind of self-protection here, whereby such partialities are concealed and other roles distributed to them in order to keep the private symbolism from becoming too obvious. In writers I think this is more likely to fall on syntax and on the predilection for certain kinds of sentences; but in the more limited dimensions of lyric the favorite words can indeed suggest a whole style and tend equally to be avoided for much the same reason, namely to evade reification and recognition).

This view then encourages us to see the orchestral totality as an immense stockpile of all kinds of sonorous possibilities, a Fourieresque collectivity made up of a multiplicity of different instruments, genus and species alike, which are to be used according to the whole range of their materiality as well as to be combined in the most mathematically complex and numerous when not infinite determinable combinations.

"There is much music in this little organ," as, someone once said, and one way of framing this first way of looking at Mahler might be that of seeing him exhaust all the possibilities of this immense toy which it was his historical fate to have been given, of squeezing out of it all the sonorities and sonorous combinations which it was physically capable of producing, of making sounds, in other words, rather than music in the traditional sense, particularly at a moment in which music itself, in this late nineteenth century seemed for a moment to have given all it could, and to have supplied enough "masterpieces" to stock the programs of conductors and orchestras all over Europe for some time to come. Length is obviously one way of refuting such complacency about the need for new production; and it introduces the crucial issue of maximalism versus minimalism which we cannot deal with any further here; except to note that the ambition of exploring the orchestra as a totality certainly implies a tolerance for great length which will be one of Mahler's most absolute demands on us.

But even a layman can imagine all kinds of other possibilities to be explored in the combinations of these various sound groups, as infinite as they may seem, the solo of the one against the massed sonority of the other, the minor clashing with a wondrous dissonance ("a green so delicious it hurts," we have often quoted Baudelaire as saying) which is to be savored as long as possible, like the sourness of a given vegetal substance. This dictates a vertical rather than a horizontal reading or listening: of course the past of the theme is henceforth contained within its present, it includes all the premonitions, all the preparatory variations, its strong and its elusive forms—all that diachrony is now implicit with this vibrant present of the current form. But what we want is its superposition on any number of other themes, the native sounds of the other instruments (with the varying pasts within this particular musical text which they bring with them): and thereby is produced a fullness of the present in which there is for the moment everything, the whole system, except that like the present it is in constant motion and will as such be canceled or corrected by something else—by a variation or a break. New combinations of sonorities will be produced, squeezed out of the orchestra. But this systematic exploitation of the orchestra and its varied resources in instruments and masses must not be thought about simply as a question of the timbre of the various instruments, a concept which presupposes a single sound. We must imagine that each instrument has within itself the virtuality of several distinct themes (or melodies), all very different from one another: so for example—and it is an imaginary, reduced, constructed, artificial example—let's say the woodwinds have in them a joyous theme, a marching theme, a romantic theme, a melancholy air, and so forth. These might indeed reproduce the varieties of affect, or better still of the Indian *rasas* and their eight fundamental affects (love, laughter, anger, compassion, disgust, terror, the heroic, wonderment or amazement); but they are to be generated organically, that is, in such a way that the listener's question about the completeness, about the touching of all the bases, the absence of this or that possibility, is excluded (a better way to talk about the illusion or appearance of completeness). Major and minor are probably only one way of talking about the varying of these (shall we say?) eight melodies or themes: there is also the massed and the solo, the dominant or the subordinate, and so on and so forth.

5.

Such a view has its problems; indeed that is its very interest, to produce further problems, and we will examine them in a moment. But it is also governed by a notion of completeness as a value which demands some initial discussion in its own right. Its first form is, to be sure, that fateful remark of Thomas Mann, which affirms that "only the exhaustive is truly interesting,"[17] thereby suggesting a kind of experimental process in which we try to say everything, like Mann's own masters Wagner and Zola, and in which "saying everything" implies an aesthetic tinged in their historical context with a belief in entropy and an unspoken sense that we will only know we have succeeded in saying everything when we come to the end of everything and reach the point at which we can observe that ending in a more literal sense (*Buddenbrooks, Götterdämmerung*, the end of the Second Empire), in a conclusion which is itself a kind of completion and yet which does not exclude the possibility of some new birth and some new world in the place of the old one.

In these cases too, the drive for completion is also a kind of will to power, which can be imagined as perfectly consistent with the imperious passion of the conductor to exercise his working collectively as a national political leader might form and deploy his prodigious war machine; or the great businessman—we are indeed centrally positioned in the era of the robber barons—his expanding industrial monopoly of the market. But if it is psychology that interests us, we might also take into consideration the possibility that such an "aspiration to totality" might also, for the artist, be a way of getting all this out of his system, or exercising so many impulses and demons, or externalizing the infinite in order to come to peace and to have rest.

None of these motivations, at any rate, will be present when such an aesthetic imperative reappears historically, a moment I take to be

---

[17]   Thomas Mann, *Der Zauberberg* (Stockholm: Fischen, 1950), p. 2.

that of postwar structuralism, and epitomized in the combinatorial aesthetic of Barthes or Greimas, in which the artistic starting point is also a determined set of limits in which a logical permutation scheme is implicit.[18] The work of art is then understood to "exhaust" that permutation scheme in a rather different spirit than that of the late nineteenth century: rather to ring the changes on a very great (but not infinite) number of possibilities—in the relations between the characters, say, or the transformations inherent in a basic situation, the variation on mood or style, the rhythmic dynamics in the instrumental transmission or in the limits of the color schemes—and then to stop. Lévi-Strauss's four-volume *Mythologiques* is something of a monument to this aesthetic and its Pyrrhic victory, reaching a point at which we cannot tell the difference between limits and infinity, and in which the maximal is put to its ultimate test, and "textual production," textualization, celebrates its own funeral in advance. But Mahler's symphonies were not exactly written in the spirit of Morton Feldman's five-hour-long string quartet; and the aesthetic of permutation and/or exhaustion does not ultimately seem to do justice to the temporal satisfactions and fulfillments of either his individual movements or the complete individual works themselves.

What has happened, I think, is that our attention has been diverted into a model in which individual moments are foregrounded, the individual sound combinations, the possibilities grasped as one-time realizations, the production of instants which then seem only able to be added up into Hegel's "bad infinite," and no longer to produce any longer formal units or continuities out of themselves. We must, I think, continue to insist on the "presentism" of Mahler and on the episodic presents from which his work is constructed: thereby implicitly arguing against the temptations of a theme-and-variations approach into which this conception threatens over and over again to fall.

Perhaps indeed the completed musical phrase bears some analogy to Adorno's paradox, that the completed thought is at once identified as Weltanschauung or ideology:[19] bits of it are spun off into

---

18   See for example A. J. Greimas, *On Meaning: Selected Writings in Semiotic Theory* (Minneapolis: University of Minnesota Press, 1987). Of Barthes, however, it must be said that he lived a virtual dialectic between the open and the closed.

19   I take this to be the meaning of his injunction, in the Kant lectures, to avoid any search for the "absolutely first" or the ontological origin: T. W. Adorno, *Kants Kritik der reinen Vernunft* (Frankfurt: Suhrkamp, 1959), pp. 224, 284—a kind of

their own autonomous developments, recombining only for ghostly instants; while what threatens the full restatement (or even the emergence of the phrase in its integrity for the first time) risks, not fulfillment, but the boredom of repetition, or worse yet the sentimentalism of this or that kitsch affirmation (or else the solemn archaism of the chorale). It is presumably this kind of unearned recapitulation that famously caused Stravinsky to "squirm" when he heard it in Schoenberg's First Quartet;[20] the proud gait of achieved identity slipping on a banana peel. It must be said that occasionally it happens to Mahler as well: yet the whole spirit of a fragmentation into innumerable semiautonomies is there as much to ward off such a contretemps as to "develop" what was latent in the motif in the first place.

In fact, in Thomas Mann's fateful program, which we have implicitly compared to the structuralist aesthetic (Barthes comes closest to articulating it openly), namely that a work as a given permutation scheme proceeds by producing as many possible outcomes as its scheme permits and then comes to a close, pronouncing itself "complete"—these two aesthetics are in reality quite different from each other. The structuralist position is that of closure—the work, or its starting point (identified as a permutation scheme, a Greimassian semiotic square) consists of a finite number of possibilities which can in fact be "exhausted"; whereas the Leverkühn quote which serves as a motto for this essay suggests open horizons in which the unknown and the unexplored are always possible, very much in Viktor Zuckerkandl's spirit;[21] in which "development" (if that is still a meaningful term in this context) takes us so far afield we lose sight of our original starting point, thereby shedding all our old habits, our traditional modes of hearing, our old perceptions, our old spatial senses, and approach what is genuinely new and unknown. The structuralist aesthetic then, if we may now call it that, is in effect a renunciation of the modernist Make-It-New, implicitly denying the possibility of novelty or innovation and somehow always returning to its starting point. (It will be objected that it is precisely at this moment that Umberto Eco invents the notion and the ideal of the "open work"; but that may itself be seen

---

methodological inversion of Gödel's law.

[20] Robert Craft, *Conversations with Stravinsky* (London: Faber & Faber, 1958), p. 71.

[21] Viktor Zuckerkandl, *The Sense of Music* (Princeton: Princeton University Press, 1971).

as a dialectical reaction within the structural model itself, and a determinate negation of it.)

Mann thereby keeps the possibility of the New alive; and yet Mahler's practice, and in particular his maximalism and his projection of the musical temporality onto the enormous scale we find in his symphonies, achieves the "New" in practice by annulling memory and making it impossible to return even in thought to our beginnings (except by consulting the experts and their scores): at least a relative infinite, which then does also pose the practical problem of the ending and produces thereby a wholly new dialectical dilemma.

6.

A more productive way of dealing with these paradoxes is perhaps offered by David Green's phenomenological reading of this musical perpetuum mobile, in which he grasped Mahler's musical events in terms of the temporalities they stage: music is indeed by way of being a veritable construction of temporality as such (temporality as a theme then affording a mediation and a bridge to a more explicit reading of subjectivity itself, if that is the thematics we are trying to approach here). In particular, Greene describes a kind of time in which the future is necessarily inscribed and yet "which denies the relevance of any future event," an opposition elsewhere identified as that between melody and mode. "A present may be said to be futureless if no coming event impinges on it—if it does not seem to be generating anything at all."[22] "By changing the relevance of the future, Mahler's movement projects different temporal processes,"[23] "modal chords (that is, chords that do not have tonal functions)."[24] But is this still time in our sense? Better to call it narrative, perhaps, and to try and find some way of conceiving of a narrative which thus "changes the relevance of the future," perpetually absorbing its irrepressible presents into itself, like Saturn eating his children.

Mahler's forms pose the problem of time in two distinct ways, which are not unrelated. This first version is what I have already

---

[22] David B. Greene, *Mahler: Consciousness and Temporality* (New York: Gordon & Breach, 1984), p. 142.

[23] Ibid., p. 143.

[24] Ibid., p. 146.

called the theme-and-variations problem, namely how to prevent the perpetual transformation of this or that theme into an identity which is perceived as simply repeating itself over and over again; in other words how to preserve metamorphosis as an event, rather than a simple reiteration. But if the transformation of a given theme is too definitive and too successful, how to prevent the musical succession (formerly a musical "development") from breaking down into a series of ever new presents of time that have nothing to do with each other?

Meanwhile, I have already observed that the concept of theme and variations as such is not really a solution here, inasmuch as Mahler's practice anticipates that poststructuralist paradox or conundrum of the simulacrum, or the copy without an original; we have variation but no initial theme whose identity we can recognize and reconfirm throughout its multiple transformations. The question is then: Is it all "the same"? Does anything new happen?

It was indeed the great virtue of Rosen's analysis of the emergence of the sonata from eighteenth-century binary and ternary forms to insist on the new form as something like a narrative, in which something new indeed does happen ("the essentially static design, spatially conceived, of ternary form is replaced by a more dramatic structure, in which exposition, contrasts and reexposition function as opposition, intensification, and resolution"):[25] a narratological conception to which I am tempted to add this decisive additional comment: "all the material played in the dominant is consequently [in the sonata-form transformation of ternary form] conceived as dissonant, i.e., requiring resolution by a later transposition to the tonic. The real distinction between the sonata forms and the earlier forms of the Baroque is this new and radically heightened conception of dissonance, raised from the level of the interval and the phrase to that of the whole structure.")[26] The point is that with Mahler we are at the other end of the process, where simple sonata development is no longer adequate to house the multiplicity of musical events he has in store for us. This is then the temporal problem as it presents itself within a given movement: or, the dynamic of identity and difference posed here not as a philosophical but rather a musical dilemma.

---

[25] Charles Rosen, *Sonata Forms* (New York: Norton, 1988), p. 18.
[26] Ibid., p. 26.

7.

A different form of this same phenomenon is to be found on the enormously enlarged scale of the symphony as a whole. Unlike others, Mahler did not abandon this form or seek to invent replacements for it; yet we may also say that unlike many symphonists, each new symphony was for him the occasion for doing something radically different from the last, so that if we can speak of Mahler's style or of his musical strategy in general terms, we cannot really speak of a "Mahler symphony" as though it were a form modified and codified once and for all, as we might with Zola's novels, say (but not with Flaubert's!), or with Cézanne's painting (but not with Picasso's!).

Still, in each of these works so radically innovative and different from the others we do confront a common temporal problem (one which presumably, however, all composers of symphonies have had to face one way or another) and that is how to make the trajectory from one movement to another somehow temporally meaningful inasmuch as in principle each movement is a separate and complete thing. How to create and to build on an anticipation and an overall rhythmic expectation by way of and through the succession of distinct and closed musical statements? Here too the problem is that of unity and multiplicity: are we to encourage a conductor to refrain from any truly satisfying assault on a given first movement, to hold back on the climactic effects, to leave us at least partially unsatisfied with its conclusion and its conclusiveness, in order to spare some attention and appetite for what is to come? It is the composer's problem as well, who surely does not want to deliver an unfinished product, and who must yet mark his first-movement conclusions as merely provisional, until we get to some even more gratifyingly final rounding off and full stop in the last one. To turn the entire symphony into a theme and variations, à la César Franck, is surely the cheapest and most facile of solutions; while at the opposite end of possibilities, only a collection of unrelated pieces awaits us. And what was the phenomenological meaning of the sonata in the first place in this respect? The energetic posing of a problem, a trio, a slow movement, and then whatever winding up seems appropriate: is this some psychological succession of moods, which posits a kind of human nature, a set of quasi-physiological responses as we move from play to rest and back? It seems conceivable that given the gigantic scale on which Mahler is working, these problems will be intensified for him: if each movement is in effect to say everything, and to run the gamut from all possible forms of play to all possible forms of rest, then how is any of that to be left over for some meaningful or satisfying succession of those totalities or musical monads? For Beethoven the succession of distinct moods and rhythms across the four movements was far simpler, and far more sculpturally constructed the listener's subjectivity as a phenomenological consciousness which had to include a few basic experiences, such as joy, mourning, longing, triumph, and the like, in manageable sequences. Mahler's basic ingredients may, on closer examination, also be inventoried in this same fashion; yet it is not their far greater number that is the real problem here, so much as the multiple distractions of a big-city mentality of the type described by Georg Simmel, a bewildering set of demands on our attention at every instant, such that we are unable to settle down into any one mood for long, and, indeed, finally come to crave these constant shifts and take pleasure in their variability, under threat of boredom.[27]

This is, of course, to give forms of temporality meanings that go well beyond mere or neutral phenomenological description; and I must try myself to avoid giving the impression that in this respect Mahler was a forerunner of this or that postmodern "presentism" (or even that his current popularity results from some pre-established harmony between his own formal characteristics and the current Zeitgeist; although that may not be untrue, and Sartre has pointed out to what degree popular success—in his instance, the fortunes of *Madame Bovary*—is often based on collective misunderstanding and misappropriation).[28] That Mahler's maximalism (Nietzsche would have underscored its dialectic of miniaturism, as he did with Wagner) necessarily places a burden on attention to the present, whether in a combination of sounds or an entire episode, seems clear enough; but it might be more appropriate at this point in the consideration of some putative Mahlerian eternal present to see to what degree we can still speak of themes or phrases in his work—smaller temporal units which, even if they are no longer susceptible to sonata-form development, would still serve to organize overall forms and longer temporalities than our insistence on

---

27 See Simmel's classical essay "The Metropolis and Mental Life."
28 Jean-Paul Sartre, *L'Idiot de la famille III* (Paris: Gallimard, 1972), p. 421.

sounds in the present has seemed to make a place for. First theme, second theme, said the sonata; but are these comparable to sentences? Insofar as they are formed, emitted and received, within the tonal system, they share some deeper, pre-given narrative structure which is organized around the keys, dominant, subdominant, tonic, rewritable in major or minor, and promising an inevitable outcome or resolution (a promise which may well of course be broken or never meant to be kept in the first place). The musical "psychology" of a Leonard Meyer, with his expectations and his satisfactions, his retardations and his overshooting the mark, like waving at your ride blindly driving past you without noticing—all these micronarratives of desire and fulfillment are what the tonal system so abundantly offered in its heyday, and what the truly modern ear began to tire of. But within this system one can easily imagine a theme to be a kind of sentence, even a complete one, provided it is not really the last word and stimulates your willingness to wait for that. Does such a sentence even need to be complete? In Joyce, indeed, Mr. Bloom's famous telegraphic thought-sentences are so many abbreviations, which demand continuation far more imperiously than any long rhetorical period of George Eliot or even Proust.

Do we not complete Mr. Bloom's sentences for him, as one is sometimes tempted to do with a hesitant speaker? But what about the multiple outcomes, the ever fresh and creatively innovative or Chomskian new possibilities, which that parsing by tree or diagram (which Gertrude Stein so loved and with which Stanley Fish used to tease the firm believers in the hermeneutic circle) was supposed to hold open for us? Sometimes, indeed, a fragmentary opening musical phrase completely misleads us as to the relatively definitive form the more complete phrase will take later on, only to be reformed and "developed" into something utterly different in its term. This leads us back into the minefield of theme and variations and the relatively more modern situation in which, like copies without originals, we find ourselves confronted with the variations without a theme, and obliged to ask this or that musicologist to identify it, that is to invent one for us arbitrarily in order to assuage what is essentially a temporal discomfort, a *dépaysement* in time itself, whose science-fictional dimensions keeps changing all around us, or whose Greimassian "isotopies" keep shifting underfoot. Here we find ourselves in Mahler territory, in this unique practice of a perpetual or eternal present which seems to be going somewhere, but whose sequential or discursive logic proves quite undecidable, except by our own decision or perhaps by the conductor's. As with film criticism, the theoretical (or semiotic) question about the linguistic status of the "fundamental unit" is central in a certain music criticism as well: is the theme or phrase (the "melody") comparable to a sentence or not? The influential musicologist Viktor Zuckerkandl would seem at first to affirm the analogy: "Every musical phrase has a beginning, runs its course, and reaches a more or less definite conclusion. There are no infinite sentences, whether the language be verbal or tonal ..."[29] The idea finds a curious psychological conformation as well in the well-established aural fact that we recognize a specific melody from only a few initial fragments of its sound, whereas the same cannot be said for visuality or speech. But then Zuckerkandl, turning back (or forward) from tonality to polyphony, seems to retract his judgement: "infinite motion emerging from finite movements: something of the essence of polyphonic music is expressed in his next sentence. There is always something arbitrary about the end of a polyphonic piece: the end has to be imposed from the outside, as it were. Left to themselves, following their own impulses, the tones would move on forever. In this sense polyphonic music is much closer to the flow of *time* than monophonic music."[30]

This is then one form in which the tension we wish to articulate in Mahler can be expressed: that between a complete or intelligible "sentence"—that is, a relatively complete theme which can then undergo development of a traditional kind, familiar from the sonata, for example—and this "infinite motion" in which musical sound perpetuates itself by way of internal "impulses," thereby dialectically producing a new kind of dilemma, namely of reaching some ending at all consistent with that same internal logic.

8.

Perhaps, rather than attempting to assimilate the intelligibility of music to language as such, we might do better to think in terms of those abstract "moments" into which Hegel transformed Kant's

---

[29]   Zuckerkandl, *Sense of Music*, pp. 144–5.
[30]   Ibid., p. 145.

categories: impersonal forms of logical abstraction which convey no messages in and of themselves, nor do they exist on the mode of this or that Absolute, but rather articulate our thinking in specific and limited combinations, on the occasion of specific situations and contexts. This is the sense in which I would like to see the first movement of Mahler's Ninth Symphony with its indeterminable motifs and undecidable fragments: projecting the very category of Indecision which the periodic interventions of the brass are meant to interrupt, proposing "decisions" or better still, the decisiveness and perhaps even "resolution" of a Heideggerian type (*Entschlossenheit*): precisely as the *production* of governing abstractions such as Indecision (and occasionally, in the process, of Decisiveness). These abstract and purely musical categories are not to be transferred elsewhere, or to Mahler's work or style as a whole, but merely as formal designations for a specific play of musical events here, which we are trying to describe in as pure and nonnarrative a manner as possible (but it is never really possible): musical "subjects," as Henry James used that word for the idea or anecdote which triggered the execution of this or that short story or novella.

I have elsewhere characterized this aesthetic, in which a paralysis in the present is combined with a well-nigh infinite succession of those presents in time, problematizing the very concept of an ending or a conclusion other than a mere breaking off, and yet somehow seeming to forfeit the very vocation of the modern composer as one who supremely forms and restructures the temporality of his listeners in a way which transforms subjectivity itself and its habits, at least for a time, drawing into itself what historically alienates them (in the temporality of the modern city or modern capitalism, for example) and alienating that very alienation, using it as the raw material for the bringing into being, however ephemerally, of some radical different state.

The question of the theme or musical phrase then rejoins a whole philosophical debate about identity in the arts: it may first, for example, resemble that around characters in narratives, or better still, about their unity of subjectivity, the centrality of consciousness as it is sometimes called, the persistence of identity throughout their presentation from various angles, as when Proust unexpectedly (or perhaps we should call it his expected unexpectability) reveals an aspect of one of his characters utterly in contradiction with what we had been given at first to understand (that the idiotic Dr. Cottard is, for example, a great diagnostician). But literary narrative works from the inside as well as the outside, and so the problem not only touches on our sense of the other and his identity, but of the narratorial personality itself, and whether there really can be a continuity from the thoughts and feelings with which he (or she) is endowed at the beginning, with later reactions. (And then, of course, there is irony, as when we slowly come to realize that the figure with whom we "identify"—whatever that means—is really ["from the outside"] an intolerable prig or bully or whatever: more on that shortly.) Then there is of course the matter of figuration in painting, which may be somewhat too far afield for our analogy and its productive work.

At any rate, what is certainly at stake here is recognition. Do we recognize ourselves over long periods of temporal continuity and memory? (It is a question I think has often been wrongly posed, owing to the reification of the very idea of memory itself.) Does the unidentified third person[31] prevent our recognition in paradoxical ways (since we will never have known who the character was before this in the first place)? This is perhaps a better place to begin, not least inasmuch it involves beginnings and raises the question of what constitutes a "recognition for the first time" (one of those logico-philosophical paradoxes analogous to repetition for the second time). Is not the concept of identification enough? Why call it recognition? Nonetheless, it is a matter of ranging a particular under a concept, in this case the very concept of character or of musical theme, just as one would have to have some prior idea of the object called a plant in order to attribute a particular green glimpsed in the distance as something organic. But in narratives, the name is often a shorthand way of activating the process of subsumption and the casting around for the general concept to be deployed here.

Meanwhile, the psychologists tell us that recognition has a unique role to play in auditory perception: a glimpse of a color or a shape may well fail to yield sufficient information as to the object in question, just as a few muttered words may well not be enough to convey the whole sentence or message the speaker has in mind. But we are told that two or three notes are enough to identify familiar melodies, so that the process of musical recognition is obviously rather distinctive, and has different dynamics and requirements from that of the other senses (although perhaps a smell does that for many animals.)

---

[31]   See my *Antinomies of Realism* (London: Verso, 2013), Part I, Chapter 8.

But by the same token the process by which a musical unity is achieved is also rather different and more complex: At what point do a few notes fall into a pattern? At what point do they become a whole, and get indentified as a phrase, or motif, a theme or a melody? And how does this vary from century to century, as Western music gradually accumulates its listening habits and the requirements of its new (once new) tonal system? When we come to Mahler, at any rate, it is an acquired culture, a second nature, one perhaps now ripe for playful readjustments and auditory games, if not for deconstruction itself. We have frequently evoked the idea of theme and variations here as a laymen's shorthand for the dynamics of this kind of identity, in which the same can be perceived through difference or even of way of difference, in which perhaps difference itself can be called upon to construct "the same."

9.

This is at any rate what happens when, as in the first movement of the Ninth Symphony, the theme is at first given to us through its variation, comparable in that perhaps to the cataphora in which a pronoun already refers back to a name not yet divulged. So retrospectively a few bars later we understand that the theme itself has appeared, and that it has already been announced by way of subordinate part or anticipated disguise, which are now in retrospect transformed into its preparation, into the preparations, the anamorphic annunciations, teasing premonitory fragments, and so on. But the word fragment—so dear to the German romantics and revived in Deleuzian mechanicity—alerts us to potential yet significant theoretical problems: for the musical Gestalt we have in mind here is so far unlikely to be conveyable in fragments as such; its organic form is not made up of fragments in that sense, even though its parts and pieces are unlikely in themselves to be organs either. Returning to our preliminary focus on recognition, they are more likely to be apprehended as hints, sketches, as the unfinished, as the line to be prolonged or the touch to be filled in. All of which is of course already long since codified in rhetoric, with its retarding devices, and its other named syntactic approaches.

Normally, however, or so we are told, sonata form involves an initial identification of the theme (or themes), their development and variation, and then their reaffirmation—and an accompanying but much fuller recognition—at the end, where recognition now involves familiarity and perhaps even categories less familiar from human social life, such as necessity. Mahler's Ninth Symphony is unique in avoiding this kind of trajectory (which we may or may not want to call a narrative of some kind), and deserves perhaps a different kind of attention than that given to it either by the traditional fetishization of the Platonic idea of a "Ninth Symphony" or by the sentimental and biographical attribution to it of some tragic farewell of Mahler to life, to work, and so forth. It has exquisite moments, but perhaps we could scandalously clear the decks by asserting that it is a relatively minor work, without the stature of the Third, say, or the Seventh, and indeed that it is a peculiar kind of experiment, particularly in its unique first movement.

For here, as we have already suggested, the theme is not identified at all, or rather it only comes to be definitively identified at the very end of the movement; and even this ultimate recognition or "naming" does not really cast a new light back over the minute and episodic developments of the rest of what is a fairly lengthy piece of music. I have no doubt that the musicologists have re-identified all the pieces and shown how practically every segment is a reworking in one way or another of what ultimately becomes the principal theme: but that does not necessarily concern us, the listeners, who are only too willing to admit that everything here comes out of some limited mass of musical material and is thus related to all the rest as cousins might be identified in relationship to other branches of the family.

But that is knowledge rather than experience, if I may put it in so anti-intellectual a fashion; the fact is that experientially we are (not unpleasantly) at sea for most of the movement, searching among what certainly seem to be fragments for some coherence, as one might scan the effusions of a madman for coherent statements of some kind (and I have no doubt that the contemporary reviews, or at least those unwilling to respect Mahler's memory and his tragically curtailed fate, might have viewed it in just that way, as the mental wanderings of a compositionally reduced musician, unable to sustain the more continuous energies of his earlier work, and floundering among complexities he was no longer capable of mastering). Yet it is a delicious confusion, which I have wanted to reinscribe within the work under the heading of "Indecision" as a formal category, whose opposite number we find in those rare moments when the massed brass interventions, followed by drum rolls, try to call all this back to order and assert a "decision" in the midst of this uncertain wandering, which they only interrupt but fail to organize. Better still, I would rather suggest that this music *produces* the categories of decision and indecision, that they are not characterizations we grasp for *après coup*, but rather the very musical "concepts," as Deleuze might say, which the score is itself in the process of thinking.

And that this is deliberate and not simply the result of a loss of energy can be confirmed by the extraordinary force and energy of the variations relentlessly produced at the end of the third movement, whose implacable variety stands at the antithesis of this kind of wandering in the first movement and produces something which is not at all its more conceptual opposite or resolution, but rather a new kind of momentum, which it would be the task of any adequate description to characterize. In fact, however the process of proposing, such characterization turns out to be little more than a play with various models or interpretive narratives, as we shall see.

10.

One of these has to do with the evaluation of the different kinds of phrases, themes or motifs that we are offered in this music, as though, faced with a collection of sentences we sorted them out into categories such as high or low style, popular or learned discourse, dialect, professional jargon, and the like. The dialectic of recognition is necessarily at work here as well, and is indeed presupposed and in a sense extra-musical, extrinsic, extra-aesthetic. The opening phrases, long or short, complete or broken and anticipatory, will not merely set the key of the work and endow a certain group of instruments, most often strings or brass, with the privilege of a kind of de facto dominance, but they will also "strike a chord" in the listener and evoke a certain musical or extra-musical genre: one can enumerate these forms no doubt, the musical ones (allegro, andante, adagio, largo, trio, nocturne, etc., as tempos shade off into the forms themselves) as also the more popular: marches, ländlers, rondos, folk dances, shepherds' pipes, songs, chorales, and so forth. All of these potentially have the status of illusions or even quotations, the classical references fully as much as the popular, reflecting that well-known late-nineteenth-century dilemma of saturation and accumulation of production or overproduction in all the genres, the lament that everything has already been written, self-consciousness of *Epigonentum* and the rebelliousness of a proto-modern on the point of breaking with all that and inventing some scandalous new style. Here we rejoin the malaise of Adorno as well as the smugness of literary categories such as Irony, the latter bearing essentially on what are considered classical borrowings and allusions, the former having to do with the allegedly extra-musical status of the popular, of vulgarity and kitsch.

If we look at Mahler from the standpoint of the antagonism between high art and mass culture, the fabric of the music becomes allegorical, and we see the music of the everyday—vulgar, hurdy-gurdy, marching bands, and even Italian arias and operatic songs—struggling to emerge from the orchestral density of a high-art symphonic orchestral context, a project which embodies the will to artistic autonomy not only in its form but also in its material content as well, institutional, traditionally structured, the concert hall, the orchestra as such, the bourgeois or aristocratic public, with its subscriptions and its loges, etc. All of that is the content of the form of symphonic music at the turn of the twentieth century (Barthes would have named it "connotation"),[32] such that the sonata form deployed in symphonies is itself a signal of social class (or of distinction, as Bourdieu might put it).

To this tension, which is only in part an opposition between the authentic and the inauthentic (inasmuch as the allegedly popular cultural elements are themselves stereotypical, commercial, and in no way genuinely "popular" anymore in the literal sense of that word), we must add what dramatizes it, namely the feeling that a musical language, themes, melodies, and the like, is henceforth only available in mass culture, just as in literature, stories and genuine narratives have sunk into the subgenres, adventure tales, detective stories, horror, romance, and so on. Art itself, as it is incarnated in Mallarmé or Schoenberg's system, or even in nonfigurative painting, is the place of construction, but no longer that of narrative; and we may think of the development of a theme in the classical sonata as a kind of storytelling, even though the musical phrase is finally not linguistic, and the completeness of a melody only analogical to the complete ("felicitous") sentence.

---

[32]   Barthes's central concept in *Mythologies*, later repudiated.

Yet in Mahler symphonic form persists, and along with it the requirement of a kind of musical narration; add to this that other dimension which is one of expression, as in the operatic aria (we must never forget that Mahler's whole professional life was devoted to opera), and we have a situation in which the current home of both these things—a mass culture in which narrative still exists, a commercial music of whatever kind devoted to the expression of the various intense "feelings" of an operatic type—cannot be allowed to vanish into the silences and formal omissions of "modernist" music. That world of the expressive is then something like Mahler's raw material, but he cannot take it on without marking its inauthenticity and acknowledging its distance from "high art": it must therefore struggle against the latter, desperately attempting to rise to the orchestral surface and to master the orchestra in its own right, at one and the same time shouldering aside its competitors, so that the marching bands try to drive out the folksongs and the like. This struggle can be detected, it seems to me, by attention to the completion or not of the musical theme or melody: its complete expression (and here I do think that the concept of a complete sentence is appropriate—we somehow know when a melody has been fully enunciated or is broken off, has not reacted its completeness, etc) signals the triumph of the vulgar-popular and the defeat of art. So it must not be allowed to reach that point, to take over the form.

So with the very beginning of the work we are already confronted with its not-yet existence as genuine art, and it is as though maximalism has the same starting point as minimalism, Mallarmé's blank page, on which one can write nothing, turning out somehow to be dialectically identical with the immense temporalities of all this secondhand music. Adorno invents a little fable to get us going here, one elegantly enough keyed to the very beginning of Mahler's First Symphony, with its mysterious pedal point, holding for bars and bars, under which the music itself, in some middle distance, begins to play. (Here, if anywhere, one would want to remind us of musical perspective itself in Mahler, and the ways in which—as though following Schenkerian concepts, or romantic vistas, distant horn calls in the forest are heard through musical close-ups which otherwise might simply be considered loud, drowning everything out—there exists a deliberate play with layers of sound as in visual perspective, or in the Bazinian "deep shot.")

At any rate, Adorno compares this sustained pedal point to a curtain behind which or through which everything begins to happen; it could equally well be compared to the neutralization of exhibits under glass, or finally to that self-defeating typographical distancing of unacceptable named concepts "under erasure" (which Derrida borrowed from Heidegger), all of these having a certain correspondence with the way in which the function of Irony is conceived, mentioning and discounting at one and the same time, speaking and denying what is being said, affirmation and denial all at once (in the place of outright silence, or negation, or blatant assertion) … What results from this staging is predictable enough; it is the famous "breakthrough" which has become identified with Adorno (even though he borrowed it from the rather different usage of Paul Bekker), and which is supposed to categorize the moment in which Mahler's music—the authentic, the real thing, the genuine article—breaks through its veil of allusion and quotations and touches that reality beyond art, itself presumably as extra-aesthetic as the illicit quotations and kitsch are accused of being.

As for the term "breakthrough" itself (*Durchbruch*), and despite Bekker's prior use (in his 1920 Mahler book), it is Thomas Mann's appropriation of Adorno's appropriation which is the fundamental clue here: for in Mann's *Doktor Faustus* the word designates not only Adrian's doomed attempts to break out of his isolation (*um ihn war Kälte*), at the cost of the destruction of those around him save the humanistic-catholic friend who is his narrator, but also the mortal convulsions of Germany itself, as, caught in its middle-European isolation between West and East, it desperately attempts its breakthroughs, via Hitler's armies, into an outside world and a radical otherness it will never reach.[33] Adorno's borrowing back of the term and the concept cannot be fully cleansed of Mann's late romantic pathos (distantly reflected perhaps in his picture of Schoenberg's "autonomous art" which is the double of his society's "totalitarianism" —yet another elective affinity Mann may have borrowed back from Adorno's manuscript which he read in the course of writing his novel). Nor must we forget that Mann did not personally experience the *Hitlerzeit*, in his richly successful exile in Pacific Palisades, so that *Doktor Faustus* is a little by way of attempting to make restitution to his countrymen who had to live through it.

---

[33]   See Thomas Mann, *Doktor Faustus* (Frankfurt: Fischer, 1947), pp. 219, 266, 363, 365, 450, 459, 482, 723.

II.

I therefore want to conjecture that "breakthrough" is Adorno's own attempt at breaking through: in this case a breaking out of the sealed concept of the absolute autonomy of art to which he was his whole life long committed, and touching for a brief moment that external history and social reality from which by definition the work was isolated. Beethoven's relationship to the French Revolution is thus not an allegorical interpretation, a homology of an art form with a convulsive sociohistorical event;[34] it is thus an instant in which the formal innovations of the *Eroica* not only coincide with its musical content, but also miraculously open into the immense socio-formal innovation of the Revolution itself; reality and form then once again folding back into their distinct realms. The concept is thus, if you prefer, Adorno's own unfulfilled fantasy, locked into his well-nigh religious conviction of the autonomy of (modernist) art, of some deeper relationship between history and form.

But in reality, breakthrough, if we have to go on using this hence-forth freighted and even tainted term, has merely formal and not ontological significance, for it happens as it were from one moment to the next of Mahler's development: each new moment, whether shattering or minutely idyllic, is in reality a breakthrough from the previous one, and a break with it to be broken through in its turn. Here, then, instead of positing even that minimal development which is implicit in the breakthrough, we will experiment with the idea of a series of autonomous moments (of varied lengths, to be sure), a kind of aesthetic or montage of the present, which stages the compositional problem in a different way.

This means that the word development is also here no longer useful, and that a kind of second-degree rhythm—the succession of the moments—is added to the rhythms and temporalities within the moments themselves: so that where the moments may allude to this or that dead or inherited form—a march, say, or an aria, or an allegro, an andante, something *stürmisch bewegt*—their sequence can be none of these and resembles nothing so much as an uncontrollable succession of distinct moods, which like nature abhor the void and flee the boredom of their extension into something utterly

---

34 "One is no more equal to a Beethoven symphony without comprehending its so-called musical course than if one is unable to perceive in it the echo of the French Revolution" (Adorno, *Aesthetic Theory*, p. 349).

distinct and unrelated to what went before. And all this out of the same initial raw material whose perpetual refashioning, however, as has been said, has nothing in common with the old theme and variations.

So in the closing pages of the third movement of the Fourth Symphony, the famous Andante,[35] the *ruhevoll* melodic opening, which promises us a slow movement whose length will depend a little on the conductor's temperament, strange and unexpectedly variable things begin to happen: a kind of scurrying among the smaller animals of the orchestra, hastening the tempo; and then suddenly an extraordinarily languorous lyrical moment which is followed by a truly transcendental outburst of the orchestra at its loudest and its most aspirational reaching upwards for sublimity and height, and followed by those eerie sounds Schoenberg's Hollywood pupils composed for the musical background of horror films or science fiction, the whole then settling back down into the theme with which the movement began, and *basta!* in such a way that we are not really sure of being satisfied by this conventional return, a problem solved for us, as said before (qua! qua! qua!), by the unexpected closure of the song which is the next and last movement. I doubt if even musicologists can name this sequence in any formal way capable of adding some durable technical terminology to their arsenal; that others can construct this or that narrative out of the sequence I have no doubt.

But I want to propose another perspective, which only performances and their comparison can convey let alone validate; and it is a kind of analogy with what Brecht called *gestus*, namely the way in which an actor can draw attention to the actedness of a given act or speech or gesture—an attention designed inevitably to cut that gesture out of the flow and continuity of the action in order to objectify it as a unit; but to do considerably more than that. Some Brechtians, I think of Straub and Huillet, or of the Heiner Müller of the *Hamlet machine*, have seen fit to grasp the famous "estrangement-effect" (*V-effekt*) as a reduction, a neutralization of all conventional feeling in such a way that we grasp the thing itself, the

---

[35]   "In the summer of 1900 Mahler spoke of the third movement of the Fourth Symphony sometimes as an Adagio and other times as an Andante, which irritated Natalie [Bauer-Lechner]. When she asked him about this, he answered that he could just as well call it Moderato, Allegro, or Presto, 'for it includes all of these.'" Constantin Floros, *Gustav Mahler: The Symphonies* (Pompton Plains, NJ: Amadeux, 1997), p. 125.

words, the act, for "what it really is": whence the toneless delivery, by rote, of famous or narrated segments. I believe, on the contrary, that it is by excess that the gestus is to be conveyed, the supplement of theatricality to be added to the more "natural" mimesis, so that we now grasp the latter for what it really is by way of its distance from itself. I have described some of Laurence Olivier's late mannerisms in this spirit,[36] but for Mahler it suffices to listen to the extraordinary languor Bernstein is able to produce in the appropriate moment of the sequence I described above, a truly operatic and theatrical languor that quotes and underscores the musical phrasing in some truly Brechtian exhibit, in contrast to the straightforwardness of the performance of Michael Gielen, say (much the best of contemporary conductors of Mahler and a master of the sound production of his orchestra).

12.

This conception of the Mahlerian will now permit us to draw three uneven conclusions: the first is that of gratitude for Bernstein's most obvious self-indulgence and his inadmissible freedom with some of his material, which may also irritate and prove unacceptable at other moments, but which captures the operatic side of this composer who was, as I have again and again reminded us, a lifelong conductor of the operatic repertoire in all its variety (and who we are told also had a significant hand in all kinds of scenic innovations in the form, innovations we are perhaps only just catching up with today). This is, as it were, Pavarotti's Mahler, and in my opinion, no one who fails to appreciate such theatrical flamboyance can have the truest and fullest delight and indeed jouissance of this composer and even the most somber moments of his art.

One of the more stimulating interpretations of Rosen's classical book is the idea that Haydn's version of sonata form—the fundamental starting point for the very working out of this form in Beethoven and others—was the imitation in music of theatrical comedy, with its *répliques*, its wit, its conversational turns, reversals, and the like.[37] That this interesting analogy might lend to all kinds

36   Fredric Jameson, *Brecht and Method* (London: Verso, 1998), p. 75.
37   Charles Rosen, *The Classical Style* (New York: Norton, 1972), p. 155.

of excessive narrative readings of the music itself, anthropomorphic translations into characters, actions, and so on is a problem we come back to later on in another context.

What such an interpretation might lead to in the case of Mahler, however, is very striking indeed: for it suggests that what has often been taxed as vulgar or excessive (even by Boulez) is itself a kind of mimetic result, and that indeed Mahler's symphonies may well be grasped as a mimesis, not of drama but of opera itself. But we must specify what kind of opera is at stake here: not the Wagnerian, I would suggest, whatever Mahler might have owed to Wagner musically (obviously he could not have composed as he did until after Wagner opened up a certain kind of musical possibility, which is not at all to specify any direct influence or similarity or family relationship). No, the operas in question are the pre-Wagnerian canon, or, since Verdi must supremely be included in this category, rather the parallel development of operatic music alongside symphonic music, the Italian alongside the German, or finally in Dahlhaus's version, the tradition of Rossini alongside that of Beethoven.

This allows us to replace the language of the "vulgar," which is in fact an acknowledgement of the social content of some of Mahler's motifs in Viennese social life, the hurdy-gurdy side of things, the spirit of the waltz, the countryside (already introduced by Beethoven, but without the cowbells), the whole dimension of the tone poem with its Alpine landscapes, but also the cityscape marked as peculiarly Viennese: all this is so to speak the extrinsic and socially connotative dimension so often deplored in Mahler, and it is generally this which is taxed by being vulgar.

But I want to underscore the rhetorical character of this music, its expressive-oratorical dimension, "operatic" excess—precisely the side of things which Wagner, like so many other modernists, wished to eliminate, but which here returns with a vengeance as the music takes on itself the silent-movie-acting vocation of exaggerating every gestus—pain, joy, anxiety, the hectic and the forward-driving or heroic-resistant and so forth. This might be thought to be the reflexive side of Mahler, the music itself becoming conscious of its deeper origins in emotional expression and deliberately foregrounding it (rather than as in modernist minimalism trying to escape it, neutralize it or at least diminish it as much as possible). But I think something else is at stake in this garish overacting of Mahler's music, which is so exciting and yet leaves us feeling soiled, as if guilty of regression into the base feelings and effects of music as they were denounced by the ancients (as well as by the modernist aestheticisms).

The second consequence to be drawn is that the musicologists must stop talking about Irony as though this were some enviable literary-critical discovery calculated to enrich the writing of a fledging musical theory. Irony as James or Thomas Mann indulged it is henceforth exhausted and unacceptable in literary criticism as in genuine literary production today. It was a way of straddling the fence and having it both ways—deeply political in its formal origins and the period style of a transitional moment of bourgeois intellectuals undecided whether to sympathize with both sides or to issue plagues upon both the houses, thereby redoubling their own structural ambivalence which they were fortunately able to name and respectabilize with this newly fashionable all-purpose word (already used in the same way by Friedrich Schlegel). Brecht was not ironic, he was sarcastic; and postmodernity replaces an unfashionable transitionality with pastiche, or affective neutralization. As for Mahler, it is ingenious to theorize his complex solutions in terms of an ironic stance which one can musically situate only somewhere between *Die Meistersinger* and Ravel's *Bolero*; but Mahler's orchestras presumably played all this *leichte Musik* of overtures, Strauss waltzes, and the like, with gusto, and this particular conductor is unlikely to have approached them in a spirit of secret contempt. I think there are better ways of naming the problem (let alone solving it).

13.

In order to do so, however (third consequence), we must really say a thing or two about Adorno and his temperament, which seem to me central in setting the stage here, not only for Irony as an admissible concept but also for the problematization of Mahler generally (he is obviously not be held responsible for the lengthy hiatus in the composer's historical reception, which made Habermas's *nachholende Moderne*[38] as much a duty for him as for so much else stigmatized and stifled as degenerate art during the Nazi period).

---

[38] Jürgen Habermas, *Die Moderne—Ein unvollendetes Projekt* (Stuttgart: Reclam, 1990).

Is it permitted to express the occasional irritation with Adorno's temperamental negativism? Its philosophical and historical grounds are clear enough and defensible: "negative dialectics" consists in an implacable demystification of the innumerable ideologies whose affirmations underpin our social system, without allowing anything of that critical resistance to harden over into an affirmation in its own right, including the very Marxian principles on which it is based in the first place. This position keeps faith with the Frankfurt School's initial analysis of capitalism, a powerful critique which the development of Stalinism deprived of its positive or revolutionary energy: and clearly the historical position of postwar Germany— divided between a restoration staffed by holdovers from the National Socialist regime and a Communist state largely dependent on the USSR and administered by German militants who spent the Nazi period in their Moscow exile—intensified this dilemma in an existential way. Nowhere then is a concrete situation more propitious for the development of ironic stances of all kinds, in which dual sympathies must inevitably result in a kind of Sartrean bad faith. Adorno's intellectual negativity is a desperate attempt to ward off even this kind of profoundly ideological consequence; and the Irony I am concerned to deplore here is not to be attributed to him personally or philosophically.

But what is ironic about his intransigent refusal of "affirmative" solutions[39] is the doubling of this position with a more general aesthetic taste for irreconcilable suffering, if I may put it this way. Adorno's affective "philosophy of history" does allow, if not for happy endings, then at least for the momentary resolution of contradictions: Hegel and Beethoven are the two preeminent historical moments in which this ephemeral "reconciliation" is acknowledged; and their secure positions in the past as an "end" of a history which does not stop and which continues to deteriorate after them (philosophically and musically) deprives us of the right to take any consolation in their achievements. Rose Subotnik has pointed out that Adorno never mentions Haydn, for all his wide-ranging assessments of musical history: which means, as we shall see, that joy does not have the right to exist in his scheme of things. It is this structural absence of a place for the cessation, let alone the absolute negation, of

---

[39] "Affirmative," along with words like "positive" and "emphatic," is a Frankfurt School term for ideology, that is, for the affirmation of this or that metaphysical content.

suffering that occasionally lends his incessant reminders of universal misery their fatuous overtones, something Brecht was quick enough to exploit in his denunciation of the "Tuis," the Left intellectual elite of the capitalist countries.[40] I say all this in order to position his influential Mahler book in its more personal context, and to underscore its profound ambivalence about this composer, who can neither be denounced like Wagner or Stravinsky, nor celebrated for his centrality in the historical development of the musical material, as Adorno will do (not without his own reservations) for the "progressive" practitioners of Schoenberg's innovations. Mahler is therefore a problem for Adorno; his enormous work confronts him with a compositional method which lies athwart the standard narrative of the telos of the modern, but which cannot be assimilated to the nationalisms of a Sibelius or a Bartok, nor to regressions of a Richard Strauss.

Mahler's symphonies are not reactionary attempts to revive the sonata form, nor are they tone poems either. And as for suffering, of which a fair amount can be located in this composer, if you are intent on validating his work with concepts like tragedy or mourning, there are also the other moments, to which this now infamous sentence of Adorno testifies (he is referring to the last moment of the Fifth Symphony, a true crux and dilemma for any Mahlerian): "Mahler was a poor yea-sayer. His voice cracks, like Nietzsche's, when he proclaims values, speaks from mere conviction, when he himself puts into practice the abhorrent notion of overcoming on which the thematic analyses capitalize, and makes music as if joy were already in the world" (p. 137). One does not argue against such remarks, which fulfill that uniquely Adornian aesthetic of the single sentence which says everything, including the definitive success and failure of the insurmountable contradiction. Indeed, Adorno's *Mahler* is by way of being his best book, owing to the supreme effort required to confront that superhuman contradiction which is Mahler's work, and to whose challenge Adorno here rises triumphantly, unerringly denouncing and celebrating him all at once. It is thus an incalculable mass of aphorisms in the present, not only supremely quotable but saying in advance almost everything it is possible to say and

---

[40] Brecht's "Tuis" (short for "Intellectuellen") inhabit a thinly veiled fable about the Frankfurt School, in which a wealthy Mandarin summons his circle of intellectuals about him on his deathbed, charging them to go forth to discover the secret and the source of evil in the world, "not understanding," Brecht adds, "that this was he himself."

think about the composer (and the present essay is no exception). At Adorno's best, as here, the dialectic triumphantly fulfills its promise to be irrefutable.

If Hegel's fundamental motto is the identity of identity and non-identity, then surely Adorno's should be couched in an analogous way as the Impossibility of Possibility and Impossibility. His practice of the dialectical sentence everywhere both affirms this principle and reenacts it: as he puts it in his essay on that most paradoxical of all language experiments, the final scene of *Faust II* (set to music in Mahler's Eighth Symphony) where Faust ascends as it were into a heaven, about which, in this world of degraded reality and debased language, one can say nothing, being thereby reduced to empty and vacuous mysticism at best or some universal nihilism or skepticism.[41] Yet the latter is also, alas, a content and an affirmation, and to express a belief in nonbelief remains an equally self-contradictory belief in and of itself. But by expressing the contradiction Adorno manages to speak at the same time that he denies its possibility: and this is the positive face of the aporia of impossibility: the articulation of non-articulating, taking sides for the impossibility of taking sides, turning Hegel inside out like a glove.

Still, Adorno's revealing wording, in the sentence that indicts the ending of the Fifth Symphony, implicitly and perhaps inadvertently suggests that he himself thereby occupies the position of the naysayer, about which it must also be said that he too is not always convincing. The inveterate "negativity" is sometimes a little glib, in that habitual and well-nigh instinctive appeal to "suffering" to which I have already alluded. I suspect that the affirmative Mahler in question here is not only the final movement of the Fifth Symphony, about which everyone seems willing to express their mixed feelings;[42] but rather the ending of the Second or "Resurrection" Symphony, to question which is a little like Adrian Leverkühn's intention "to revoke the Ninth Symphony" (he means, of Beethoven). But Klopstock's poem is not unqualifiedly "affirmative" either, and I suspect the discussion would be more satisfactorily couched in formal terms rather than those of pessimism or optimism (which are surely closer to moods and ideologies than to philosophies).

---

[41]   "Zur Schlußszene des Faust," in T. W. Adorno, *Gesammelte Schriften II: Noten zur Literatur* (Frankfurt: Suhrkamp, 1997), pp. 129–38.

[42]   Klemperer in particular thought this movement was a failure. See for example Daniel Barenboim's interview of April 27, 2009, available at danielbarenboim.com.

Adorno's Mahler-perplexity—how to admire what ought not to fit the historical scheme of things—is then clarified by the little essay on the ending of *Faust II*, the ascent into heaven, whose artistic and representational qualities turn out to raise the same contradictions "negative dialectics" was invested to resolve (or to avoid) in the realm of pure thought. What ought to be either pure kitsch or outright modernism turns out here to be neither, without the historical excuse of standing so far back in the past (Dante, Sophocles) that it can be said never to have had to face all the modern problems of the degradation of language by the commercial media and the degradation of thought itself (and its representations) by capitalism.

Adorno begins by confessing the double bind of any contemporary consent to speak one's mind, whose naivety at once becomes a Weltanschauung, which is to say an ideology, while the refusal to do so (on precisely those excellent grounds) turns out also to be more ideology, namely what we call skepticism or nihilism. What is perplexing is then Goethe's capacity to express what in English would be the most banal Browning-type maxims ("let your aim exceed your grasp") without falling into the bottomless pit of a sentimental "cultural literacy"; meanwhile a rudimentary nature poetry (waterfalls, lightning, treetops) lacking all Wordsworthian subtlety is able somehow to convey a transcendence devoid of devotional connotations or religious cant (despite the personnel of monks, saints, and the three forms of the Virgin). The issue is all the more relevant for us inasmuch as it is precisely this finale that Mahler set word for word to music in the second movement of his Eighth Symphony, the choral one of "symphony of a thousand" renown. The nature poetry or landscape content is somehow abstract and concrete at one and the same time, conveying another world by way of heights and as it were cinematographic views from above which do not bind it to any specific place (Peter Stein's magnificent production left these organic images to the language itself, conveying the movement of ascension by an immense spiral mounted by the various ages of the Faust-figures and their angelic accompaniment). The style, whose archaisms remove it from the colloquial without "stylization," while avoiding "poetry" by the sheerest simplification, Adorno characterizes as a choice of self-restriction and self-limitation which, holding to the earth in the most minimal way, avoids the empty mysticism of conventional transcendence. "Limitation as a condition of greatness has its social aspect in Goethe as in Hegel: the bourgeois as the mediation of the Absolute."[43] Yet he underscores the logic of the landscape as such, rising to new heights, as it is traversed by plunging waterfalls, "as though the landscape were allegorically expressing its own creation story."[44]

At this point, it will perhaps be helpful to quote Goethe's own account of this scene, in his conversation with Eckermann on June 6, 1831:

> We then talked about the ending [of Faust], and Goethe drew my attention to the following passage:
>
> > This worthy member of the spirit world
> > is rescued from the devil:
> > for him whose striving never ceases
> > we can provide redemption;
> > and if a higher love as well
> > has shown an interest in him,
> > the hosts of heaven come
> > and greet him with a cordial welcome.
>
> "These verses," he said, "contain the key to Faust's salvation: in Faust himself an ever higher and purer activity to the very end, and the eternal love coming to his aid from above. This is wholly consonant with our religious conception according to which we cannot become holy through our own power alone, but through their enhancement by divine grace. But you must admit that this ending, with the redeemed soul rising above, was very hard to do and that I could easily have lost myself in nebulosity with such supersensible scarcely imaginable things, had I not drawn a helpfully circumscribed form and substance from such sharply delineated Christian and ecclesiastical figures and ideas."[45]

Adorno, "Zur Schlußszene des Faust," p. 134.

44 Ibid., p. 133.

45 Wir sprachen sodann über den Schluß, und Goethe machte mich auf die Stelle aufmerksam, wo es heißt:

> Gerettet ist das edle Glied
> Der Geisterwelt vom Bösen:
> Wer immer strebend sich bemüht,
> Den können wir erlösen.
> Und hat an ihm die Liebe gar
> Vom oben teilgenommen,
> Begegnet ihm die selige Schar
> Mit herzlichem Willkommen.

For Adorno, then, what is crucial in these remarks is Goethe's implicit invitation to neutralize the religious content of his material, to grasp the traditional Christian imagery as pure form, traditional narrative which functions, like the myths deployed in an essentially secular Greek institutional theatrical festival, to secure narrative understanding in order to fix the spectator's attention on something else, something we may loosely characterize as metaphysical, or indeed unrepresentable.

As for the famous ethical injunction Adorno has his own extraordinary explanation (which in turn itself serves to neutralize its ideological content):[46] the fundamental recommendation is not one of constant and resolute productivity but rather the healing power of forgetfulness, the Nietzschean call for the obliteration of the past and its guilt. Faust's secret (and he is supposed to be a hundred years old in this final scene) is his capacity to consign his avatars to oblivion and thereby to confront every new present afresh and without the burden of his innumerable sins and crimes, from the abandonment to her death of Gretchen in Part I to the concluding atrocity of the land-grab and the murder of Philemon and Baucis that immediately precedes this finale. Such is then the deeper meaning of the original pact with the devil: do not try to hold onto the instant! That way guilt lies and crippling remorse (Goethe's own life and his various flights and evasions lend biographical support to this unique reading, which Adorno—and the author himself—softens by way of the reappearance of Gretchen and her forgiveness).

The scene itself, however, emphasizes the transformation if not metamorphosis of the soul, rather than its evolution or redemption,

---

"In diesen Versen," sagte er, "ist der Schlüssel zu Fausts Rettung enthalten; in Faust selber eine immer höhere und reinere Tätigkeit bis ans Ende, und von oben die ihm zu Hülfe kommende ewige Liebe. Es steht dieses mit unserer religiösen Vorstelleng durchaus in Harmonie, nach welcher wir nicht bloß durch eigene Kraft selig warden, sondern durch die hinzukommende göttliche Gnade.

Ubrigens werden Sie zugeben, daß der Schluß, wo es mit der geretteten Seele nach oben geht, sehr schwer zu machen war und daß ich, bei so übersinnlichen, kaum zu ahnenden Dingen, mich sehr leicht im Vagen hätte verlieren können, wenn ich nicht meinen poeticschen Intentionen durch die *scharf umrissenen* christlich-kirchlichen Figuren und Vorstellungen eine wohltätig beschränkende Form und Festigkeit gegeben hätte."

Gespräche mit Eckerman, June 6, 1831 (Basel: Birkhäuser, 1945), p. 475. My translation, except the verses here borrowed from A. Atkins, ed. and trans., *Faust I and II* (Frankfurt: Suhrkamp, 1984).

46   Adorno, "Zur Schlußszene des Faust," pp. 137–8.

reminding us of Goethe's dictum that one must not try to be something, but rather to be everything (and indeed the preceding acts
have emphasized the variety of Faust's "engagements" rather than
their successful or single-minded conclusion—all are in fact failures). In fact, as the opening of *Faust II* explicitly testifies, the power
that "saves" Faust is not that of achievement or accomplishment, not
even really that of ambition, but rather that of oblivion.

It is Nietzsche's "strong forgetfulness" that gives him that "flight
forward" out of the guilt of the abandonment of Gretchen all the
way to the destruction of Philemon and Baucis in the last act. This
is the indispensable precondition and as it were the dark side of
that great Goethe-Hegel ethos of *Tätigkeit* or productive activity
which Marx transformed into the collective ethos of production and
productivity itself. This dark side will ultimately emerge in Faust's
final blindness, accompanied by the Heideggerian *Sorge* or worry
which confers on Faust a last mixed blessing, the ability to ignore
Mephistopheles' gravediggers, the lemurs, and mistake their clamor
for the labors of a "free community" reclaiming new land from the
sea. With no little fancifulness, one might spatialize this complex of
motifs thus:

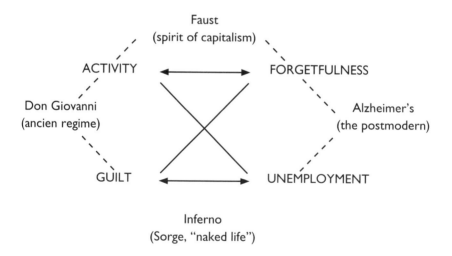

Adorno writes luminously about the language of this final scene,
an instance of his interest in "late style,"[47] and has expressed his
wonderment at the way in which its simple, expressive landscapes

47   The concept is developed in his essay on Beethoven's *Missa Solemnis*, in *Noten zur
Literatur*, but was also important for Edward Said in his own musical writings.

are able to elude the pitfalls of "expressiveness" itself as an ideology along with the stylistic corruption to which the "expressive" necessarily gives rise over time and history: the impersonality of the *Knittelversen* rescues them from personality as well as from the kitsch that lies in wait for "philosophies of life" as well as for "classics." Adorno's essay—or rather his reflections, as they are explicitly conveyed in the form of notes—conveys a chastened wonderment at the ways in which Goethe practices here a kind of literary negative dialectic, not so much by the absolute union and identity of form and content (as in the Hegelian "Ideal") but rather by the participation of both in a neutralization of each other. Religion is here nature in the most literal sense of landscape, yet a landscape which is in fact Spinozan *natura naturata*; while the religious figures (or "characters") are somehow impersonal positions for the drives that speak through them.

Meanwhile, it is just as clear that Mahler did not see it this way, as a remarkable letter testifies:

It is all an allegory to convey something that, no matter what form it is given can never be adequately expressed. Only the transitory can be described: but what we feel and surmise but will never attain (or experience as an actual event), in other words the Intransitory that lies behind all experience, that is indescribable. That which draws us by its mystic force, that which every created thing, perhaps even the very stones, feels with absolute certainty at the very centre of its being, that which Goethe here—again using an image—calls the Eternal Feminine—that is to say, the resting-place, the goal, as opposed to striving and struggling toward the goal (the eternal masculine)—that is the force of love, and you are right to call it by that name. There are countless representations and names for it …. Goethe himself reveals it stage by stage, on and on, in image after image, more and more clearly as he draws nearer the end. In Faust's impassioned search for Helen, in the classical Walpurgis Night, in the still inchoate Homunculus, through the manifold entelechies of lower and higher degree—he presents it with ever greater clarity and certainty, right up to the appearance of the Mater Gloriosa, the personification of the Eternal Feminine. And so … Goethe himself addresses his listeners: "All that is transitory (everything I have presented to you here on these two evenings) is nothing but images, inadequate, of course, in their earthly manifestation; but there, liberated from earthly inadequacies, they will become reality, and then we shall need no paraphrase, no figures, no images. What we seek to describe here in vain—for it is indescribable—is accomplished there. And what is that? Again,

I can only speak in images and say: the Eternal Feminine has drawn us on—we have arrived—we are at rest—we possess what we could only strive and struggle for on earth. Christians call this 'external bliss,' and I cannot do better than employ this beautiful and sufficient mythology—the most complete conception which, at this epoch of humanity, it is possible to attain."[48]

But the Goethean injunction gives support to the development of a Hegelian ethical ideology of what I prefer to call Tätigkeit or activity rather than "striving," itself the forerunner of a Marxian emphasis on living labor and production. The evocation of the "eternal feminine" may also be taken as a premonition of Freud's discovery of the immortality of desire, but the reference more immediately reminds us of Goethe's sense of his daimon and his frequent denial of individuality and originality in human collective life. Mahler, to be sure, had his own daimon, driven as he was by musical production as such; and in the context of late nineteenth-century gender ideology would certainly have associated Alma with Goethe's "eternal feminine."

But it is perhaps in the matter of guilt that we grasp most clearly the distance that lies between the composer and his beloved Goethe. For this final scene in *Faust II* also evokes the infants dead before birth—Margarete's aborted child, the "paths not taken" by Faust himself; and this without any of the searing pathos we hear in Mahler's songs of dead children. For in Goethe the unborn children are the occasion for a unique innocence; the angels have in them the chance to convey the purest experience of the earthly senses and the earth itself they missed: what it was like to see, to hear, to smell the earth's breath and fragrance. This is neither optimistic nor pessimistic: it is truly a nature beyond a fallen human life.

Yet the renewal of the senses was itself a mission of modernism in the arts; and this scene for Mahler offered a supreme formal pretext for the achievement of what we have been calling transcendence, but what perhaps ought now to be identified as the sublime itself.

14.

Yet when we raise once again the question of the sublime, what must be kept in mind is that one rises to it: it is not a sound, or an effect,

---

[48]   Mahler, letter of June 1909, quoted in Steinberg, *The Symphony*, pp. 337–8.

or a level, that one can simply occupy, and in particular that one cannot occupy from the outset. It must be reached and attained, and this is a movement which is always imagined in terms of a rising to a certain height, as with an orator or with music. These are of course two temporal languages in any case, and it might be asked, for example, whether a painting—immobile in its frame and simply approached by a viewer—cannot be sublime.

Is not the finger of God awakening Michelangelo's Adam sublime? But that is already a movement, the intimation in advance of a sublime future moment, the creation of life itself, something on the order visually, of the "Let there be light!" so prevalent in lists of this kind (and it does seem to me significant that while it would be ridiculous to attempt to make a list of beautiful things [the hundred most beautiful things in literature, say, or in painting or in music], for the sublime on the other hand, very much beginning with Longinus followed by Burke, it is common practice to create a chrestomathy of sublime moments, of quotations, whether of the great speeches, or the great verse). This custom thereby ratifies our perception of the sublime as a "moment," and thereby as a moment in time, a moment one reaches. This is, it seems to me, what justifies thinking of the sublime (O Altitudo!) in terms of a rising rather than a falling, of (sub-limis) a "coming up from below the threshold, rising in the air, hence lofty," as the lexicographer tells us,[49] or alternatively, "that which rises obliquely, that which climbs a steep slope, hence lofty."[50]

Each alternative is precious: the first suggesting an eruption from the depths, the second an arduous climbing and movement upward. They do not really convey the Kantian opposition of the mathematical (quantity) to the energetic (power); but insofar as either of those connotations is necessarily the result of movement and of an opposition overcome, then they can also be readily incorporated, and are in most examples. That "altitudo" is sometimes translated "depth" is an interesting twist, in which the low, the opposite, is converted into an elevation in its own right: depth or *profondeur* generally taken in an idealist sense, as depths of spirit. Indeed, the original source (Rom. 11:33) does just that: "O the depth of riches both of the wisdom

---

[49]   Eric Partridge, *Origins: A Short Etymological Dictionary of Modern English* (New York: Macmillan, 1977).

[50]   Ibid., 358. See also the relevant article in Barbara Cassin, *Vocabulaire européan des philosophies* (Paris: Seuil, 2004).

and the knowledge of God! How unsearchable are his judgments and his ways past finding out!"

Besides this, etymology can give us some clues as to the relative weight of the concept in various languages. Thus the German *erhaben* solely expresses the notion of a being lifted up or elevated; it lacks the inner presence of the limen or ceiling that must be broken through. The latter enables the presence of a sense of violence in this emotion or feeling and indeed also a sense of time or narrative process. Here then in the Latinate languages the element of fear finds its place and is retained, whereas the German equivalent can simply pass at once to Winckelmann's classical calm and elevation without it. Kant's tortured conceptuality wrestles with these incompatible elements, attempting to justify the moment of a sublime calm as the recompense for the overcoming of the fear.

As for depth, however, the alternate or antithetical meaning of the Apostle's Altitudo might well be seized as the Nietzschean one, as it emerges in the extraordinary setting of the Third Symphony's fourth movement, the setting of Nietzsche's great poem—the deep midnight, whose depths are not even realized by the day itself—with its radical inversion at the end—"all joy wants eternity," which Mahler is careful to score untriumphalistically, before sweeping it away also with the joyous children's choir which follows it at once in the next movement, and yet which does not itself constitute that "joy" (*Lust*, in German) but rather something else, yet a different affect, namely the delight and merriment of innocence (effacing, à la Faust, the very memory of the preceding moment, not itself melancholy but rather a solemn warning). This reminds us that affect, in such artistic deployments, remains, as Lyotard argued about Kantian political enthusiasm, precisely a purely aesthetic phenomenon: it corresponds neither to depression nor to genuine mania, even though its gamut and scale presumably derive from their realities. As affects, then, melancholy and joy are not opposites, but related moments on a scale on which they define each other by their momentum and their metamorphosis; their true opposites only appear when their transcendences are grasped as movie music, as the orchestration of emotions rather than affects, materials for this or that allegorical narrative which we attribute to the score as its underlying story.

15.

But we must specify distinct forms of transcendence if we do not want to slip into the notion that transcendence is simply to be identified with climax and with some triumphal wrapping up of a simple musical development of the type found in Mahler only in what we have called (following Hegel) the "moments" of a given movement rather than the movement as a whole. Those climaxes exist to be sure, and define more programmatic works like the Second Symphony (even though most often the conclusion of a movement is a false climax in which coda and recapitulation are disguised as a kind of resolution). What we have is rather throughout Mahler a practice of multiple forms of transcendence—relative, situational, or provisional ones—in which a moment (of the kind I have just specified) reaches out and up for an *Aufhebung* strictly bound to this particular complex of motifs in perpetual transformation and is then itself undone (or "transcended") in a movement towards a moment of a quite different kind. So these momentary and altogether relative ecstasies are not so much definitive "statements" (if you like that kind of language) so much as they are distractions from a different kind of attention, the more linear or horizontal kind which would again search for the overall form of the moment as a whole, re-identifying the various local themes with one another and trying desperately to recreate that unique kind of musical memory painfully developed and achieved by a sonata form which is no longer possible (or even desirable). Nonetheless, it remains the case that as with the conventional misunderstanding of St. Paul, transcendence is invariably associated with rising tones and with the higher registers of the orchestra:[51] with the instruments associated with those heights as well, the flute and woodwinds, the violins in their upper reaches, along with the harp and certain trumpet calls. The brass are signals of something else; and it has been observed (by Mahler himself, I believe) that the cowbells were not to evoke anything pastoral, but rather the other-worldly as such (the same would go for the notorious hammer of the Sixth Symphony).

There is thus inscribed here a temptation to associate groups of instruments with certain kinds of meanings or at least with specific

---

[51]   See for example Schopenhauer's speculations: "I recognise in the deepest tones of harmony, in the ground-bass, the lowest grades of the will's objectification, etc." *The World as Will and Representation*, vol. I (New York: Dover, 1969), p. 258.

affects; and I imagine that Mahler's extraordinary orchestration may at least in part be grasped as a constant effort to evade such reifying associations by way of the invention of new combinations and new uses. Only in appearance is there any affinity here with the mystical color schemes and systems of Kandinsky, although the effects of the latter may well be related in a kind of aesthetic "family likeness."

But this is also why the association with narrative genres must be cautiously deployed, when not avoided altogether: so the brass, so insistently utilized in the marches which are an inevitable feature of the musical landscape here, must not I think be too programmatically linked to that "way of the world" Adorno thought he detected in the Mahlerian musical narrative. The phrase, to be sure, is Hegelian (*Weltlauf*) rather than eighteenth-century in its English theatrical sense; the "world" in question is no longer that aristocratic and frivolous prerevolutionary one of a Sheridan but rather the already bustling commercial rhythms of a nascent bourgeois age, from which the "subject" is classically alienated in a romantic if not a Marxian sense. Indeed, it is rather surprising that Adorno should have recourse to this kind of paradigm of society against the individual, unless he simply means to attribute its henceforth conventional narrative to Mahler himself, an attribution against which everything in this music militates. Indeed, the intellectual limits of Adorno's anti-populism, however (I prefer not to call it elitism for fear of awakening a Left anti-intellectualism which results in equally dangerous and damaging political consequences), can be detected when we examine this interpretation more closely, which opposes the "way of the world" to the subject and its resistance: the former "confronts consciousness in advance as something 'hostile and empty' [Hegel]. Mahler is a late link in the tradition of European Weltschmerz" (p. 6). But is this not merely that hoary stereotype of "the conflict between the individual and society," a staple of humanistic and moralizing interpretation, and a most limited instrument indeed for reading the complex interactions in Mahler (nor is it really to be attributed to Hegel either, for whom it was but one "moment," superseded or *aufgehoben* by many other forms). But that embattled consciousness the Frankfurt School so often identified as "the negative" itself and as a critical critique (to use Marx' derisory expression) of a universally commodified society, can easily fall into this stereotypical narrative pattern insofar as it has no social group or historical actor with which (as intellectuals) to identify itself.

But Adorno may in fact here have been expressing his sensitivity to something a little different from mere affirmation, and that is rhetoric. Just as in literary judgments, the awareness of the author's intention may have devastating consequences for the reader's reception (he's trying to make me laugh here, or to inspire sadness in this other passage), so also visible intention is a fundamental feature of musical rhetoric. It is thus less the issue of affirmation than the intent to inspire its mood that can be ruinous for a musical effect as well: the sense of joy is catching and often irresistible, but the intention to express joy and to pass its signal to the listener, to bring about a joyous or uplifting mood, is in contrast a degenerate and sheerly manipulative operation, if not a merely conventional one. When in the midst of the final movement of the Ninth Symphony, an affirmative and officially optimistic note is sounded, we have grounds enough for sharing Adorno's distaste and for viewing this as a predictable and merely conventional mood: there are probably not many such moments in Mahler and there may well have been a formal necessity for this one (the need to shift from one register to another, for example), but as Valéry said, what is necessary in art is what makes for bad art.

At any rate, I would want to separate the matter of rhetoric from that of theatricality (or if you like from the openly rhetorical, which calls attention to itself ostentatiously). Rhetoric and intention in the bad sense fall on the side of named emotion and an aesthetic of expression; I would therefore want to associate the genuinely affirmative movements in Mahler—with affect and the sublime in some more impersonal sense.

Nonetheless, the sentence I have quoted,[52] taken as a symptom, threaten to expose Adorno's deeper embarrassment here, which lies in Mahler's deployment of those mass-cultural materials the Germans call "kitsch," thereby assimilating the sentimental persistence of traditional popular culture to the commercial factory-line productions of the Culture Industry ("jazz" was his most notorious illustration, but America in general and the word "culture" in particular were more general targets of anathemata and loathing). The Berg-Leverkühn use of such materials in their expressionist nightmares was apparently immune to the kind of mixed feelings Adorno had about Mahler, and which return in force on every page of his

---

[52] See above: " … as if joy were already in the world … " (Adorno, *Mahler*, p. 137).

book. What I want to emphasize here is the association Adorno instinctively makes between "affirmation" (ideological yea-saying) and just such degraded mass culture: it is an identification that lies at the heart of all his most powerful social and artistic criticism.

16.

But of course the solution I propose here—"everything is composed within quotation marks" (p. 6)—is also to be found in Adorno: returning to the thing itself I will try to develop it in a somewhat different language. For like Adorno's sentences, Mahler's music also aspires to a perpetual present in which we do not have to wait for "development" to take our satisfaction in the immediate present: not an obvious strategy for a temporal art and one which raises the most insoluble questions about musical memory (and thereby, at one and the same time, about traditional conceptions of musical form). These questions lead one inevitably to the opposition between minimalism and maximalism in modern art, and to Nietzsche's extraordinary observation about the maximalist Wagner that he was a great miniaturist.

But these are still questions about temporality, and perhaps temporality as a philosophical abstraction is the most useful way to avoid psychological expression or narrative mimesis (even though in the long run even philosophical concepts are capable of being unmasked as narratives, or at least such was Greimas's view and his ambition). So the dialectic of the minimal and the maximal is a contradiction between two kinds of time, which have in the modern drifted apart: a unified sequence of events, bound together by causality and having, if not the contingent and arbitrary fact of birth or beginnings, at least the closure of an end and a completion; and then on the other hand a present, the famous "eternal" present, in which we attempt to dwell so instantly and fully that we have even forgotten what memory was (if that is the word for a longer time-sense, something the other side would probably deny: for each position denies the other and rewrites it in its own language, and "memory" is simply a disguised insult with which "presentism," as it now seems to be called, seeks to weaken and discredit the larger time frames so proudly affirmed by the other time-senses).

That debilitated and greatly reduced opponent (also sometimes called historicism) would like to press its case for historical maximalism and feebly to protest that it was not always so, and that the two temporal species were once upon a time far closer to each other than in the current stand-off; that there were periods in which the present was far more comfortable in its chronological niche than is now the case, when it rebels and demands to stand alone all by itself and under its own steam; and when the larger temporal forms—call them periods, narratives, *durées*, historical stories, personal destinies, even "philosophies of history"—shared power with the present, as it were, and participated in what the philosophers call a kind of *Versöhnung* (if not reconciliation) and what the unwary layman might think of as a Hegelian "synthesis" (a "concept" which does not really exist). No, there never was any past like that, cries Lyotard, it was always the same, always like this; while Derrida, more subtly, and enlisting Freudian *Nachträglichkeit* in his defense, explains that this alleged past is little more than a projection of our present, an imaginary wholeness projected back behind us by our own divided present of time.[53]

The history people, then, gamely set forth to locate just such moments, whether in politics, art, subjectivity, or even religion; and we are offered, for the musical history that interests us here, the strange case of Beethoven, who both perfected and destroyed sonata form, leaving his followers in the German tradition the dialectical task of inventing something new in this now devastated and sterile landscape (Wagner, Mahler, Schoenberg are some markers of these efforts), or, as with the French tradition, forgetting about Beethoven and his "traditions" altogether, and with Debussy and Messiaen and the generations of "post-serial" composers turning to non-Western music and exotic sounds and forgetting the dialectic of the modern altogether in the name of something else (which is of course a new kind of musical temporality in which the other side, the eternal present, is endowed with an altogether different status).

Their rediscovery of Mahler, then (I'm thinking of a composer/

---

[53] "Non, décidément, il faut le dire clairement: il n'y a pas du tout de sociétés primitives ou sauvages, nous sommes tous des sauvages, tous les sauvages sont des capitalistes-capitalisés." Jean-François Lyotard, *Économie libidinale* (Paris: Minuit, 1974), p. 155. I will explain in another place how the unique temporality of *Nachträglichkeit* (and with it the dialectic itself) emerges from Marx's conception of a capitalist system or "mode of production" as one that rewrites its own past in the so-called idea of primitive accumulation.

conductor like Boulez), places us squarely back in the temporal antithesis between a Mahler-in-the-present (congenial to American postmodernism fully as much as to French inventor of the concept of *présentisme*—François Hartog[54]—or German followers of Karl Heinz Bohrer's promotion of the ecstatic instant which he called *Plötzlichkeit*)[55] and the more laborious problem of securing a unity for these immense movements and reading them as something more unified and organic than a Hegelian "bad infinite" of one moment after another (and thereby coming close to Henry Ford's definition of History as such).

We have already commented on the danger of a theme-and-variations approach, in which isolated moments or presents of time are then sewn together into an immense process of endless metamorphoses, which we then hastily baptize as a unity. The sonata form, meanwhile, is excluded by so many experts that it is not worth exploring save as that immense formal dilemma opened up by its absence or impossibility. There are, to be sure, many other musical forms to be passed in review, but not by the layman.

Of the technical terminologies that intimidate the lay theorist or amateur philosopher, surely the two most effective and frightening are the musical and the mathematical; and this is no accident, inasmuch as they count among the most abstract languages the human mind is able to handle, and Jacques Attali has indeed on that very basis demonstrated their kinship in his argument, not merely for the kinship of musical innovation with economic structure, but even (in *Noise*) for the ways in which the former has tended historically to anticipate the latter, so that the music of one moment of the mode of production is often prophetic of the infrastructural development to come in the next.[56]

Still, from the insertion of musical examples into the text in visual form, to the reading of scores, the assessment of keys and their intrinsic relationships to each other as tonic, dominant, and the like, the role of the modes (major and minor), all the way through to the foreign words that originally designated this or that tempo and later on became the names for kinds of movement or structure (allegro, andante, etc.), ending up with notations to the conductor,

---

54   See for example his *Régimes d'historicité* (Paris: Points histoire, 2012).
55   Karl Heinz Bohrer, *Plötzlichkeit: Zum Augenblick des ästhetischen Scheins* (Frankfurt: Suhrkamp, 1981).
56   See Jacques Attali, *Bruits* (Paris: PUF, 1977).

such as prestissimo or stürmisch bewegt, we do witness a gradual anthropomorphization of these technical notations, in such a way that proto-narratives seem to emerge, at first visible merely as emotional tonality or mood. "Johann Mattheson talked in 1739 … of how 'an Adagio indicates distress, a Lamento lamentation, a Lento relief, an Andante hope, an Affettuoso love, an Allegro comfort, a Presto eagerness, etc.'"[57] This is then the slippery slope that leads to "interpretation" in the form of what I will call "bad or humanistic allegory," namely the translation of musical sequences into wholesale expressions of optimism or pessimism, triumph or tragedy, titanic struggle, consolation, stoic acceptance or resignation, and the like: the very stuff of so-called "world-views" as these are attributed not only to works of art but to living beings as well, turning the latter into moralizing stories which have the added benefit of legitimizing art in the process as useful adjuncts to life. Narrative is to be sure everywhere, and this is not the place to speculate on the variety of its functions; but this particular one demands constant vigilance and unmasking as a pernicious register of ideology (it is this, I believe, which the Althusserians stigmatized as "humanism"). Not the least vice of ethics as a subfield of philosophy (or of theology) lies in its promotion and perpetuation of such narratives, which certainly serve to distract us from the political, although they clearly do much more than that. It would be tempting, but perhaps also distasteful, to hunt through Mahler criticism for the innumerable variety of such narratives (to which the composer was himself not immune). The polemic purpose of the formalism I have been proposing consists, indeed, of unmasking these "interpretations," which serve to mask the historical nature of the material as well, in ways for which the blanket epithet of "idealism" is insufficient. But it would be a mistake to believe that the return to some objective or technical language of purely musical analysis is any kind of solution to this problem.

For this is our fundamental problem here: how to avoid narrativizing this music, in a situation in which I would equally argument that ultimately everything, even the resolutely nonnarrative or antinarrative, gets narrativized in the long run. Thus, even our description of an eternal present of any given moment of this music

---

[57] Andrew Bowie, *Aesthetics and Subjectivity* (Manchester: Manchester University Press, 2003), p. 35.

in time is easily readapted to a narrative of how we arrived at this point and a narrative situation which poses the various alternative escapes or lines of flight from it.

If music as the temporal art par excellence is one of the fundamental ways in which we construct subjectivity or the individual subject in time, then we have clearly been on the point of suggesting that the Mahlerian present reflects a situation in which human beings are, by virtue of their social and economic constraints, reduced to a kind of diminished life in the present itself (what I have elsewhere called the reduction to the body).[58] This is then a narrative in which a certain kind of relationship of figure to ground is expressed, along with the ambiguous causality of a resistance or a replication: does the Mahlerian present simply reflect this situation or is it a way of answering and redeeming it, lending transcendence to contingency as it were?

17.

But I may venture to propose another narrative model, or at least superimpose a different "image of thought" (Deleuze) on this one, an image, which gives some sense of the irrepressible movement of all this in time, proceeding forward inexorably even in its instants of rest or quiet reflection, a momentum which can somehow never be stilled. But the musical and technical terminology—however carefully revised and amended, however qualified—always suggests familiarity and this or that return: even if this movement is not quite sonata form, we have still mentioned the crucial word; even if variations never bring back the initial theme exactly as it first appeared, we have conveyed a return movement; even if there is recapitulation the persistence of musical memory is affirmed, and the temporality of the sounds reorganized into a kind of subliminal spatiality or diagram of some kind; all of which was to have been avoided in the new description.

I therefore select a new kind of analogy, in which the movements of the Mahlerian theme are compared to ocean currents in their perpetual movement, which cannot be localized nor can it be assigned a

---

[58] See Fredric Jameson, "The End of Temporality," in *The Ideologies of Theory* (London: Verso, 2008).

starting point or a terminus, like any standard human voyage; on the other hand, cyclical conceptualities are not really appropriate either, but simply betray the inability of the human mind to think such natural phenomena, which it is better to mark as unrepresentable or at least as only representable under erasure, to adapt a linguistic experiment to a more visual one. For this is the very problem itself, how to stage time in any of these visual ways, which all tend to reassert the cancellation of our previous mode and to show both up as an impossible opposition. Where that one, static, folds back into points on a line, this one, taking the image of the globe as its surface of inscription (as though this were itself somehow not an image and a mere representation in the first place, even if glimpsed and photographed from outer space), now draws lines in movement ("describes" an ellipse or a circumference, to use the active language of the geometers) and thus underscores a fundamental representational incompatibility between point and line which sends us back once again to the even more familiar unthinkables of space and time, or subject and object, movement and rest, and so forth.

Still, the ocean currents (there are seventeen of them on our world)[59] usefully demand the impossible of us, namely to think a form of matter, the liquid masses, which both are and are not in the same place, and do and do not move onwards. It is not a bad way to approach the mysteries of these sounds, adding to that particular paradox some additional oppositions which complexify it. For the currents can be surface or submarine (one is tempted to have recourse again to perspective and to see some combinations in the foreground, some in the background, some assertive and peremptory, some hushed and approaching the status of the echo). Then too, these same currents can be classified as cold or as warm, and this certainly gives us another, different, perhaps newer sense of their peculiar interaction, which may be momentarily more vivid than the language of major and minor, or of the modes: the cold and the warm currents, particularly in what they germinate or exclude of vegetation, of life, of external climate, suggest something more elemental than the technical language, and perhaps suggest something of the usefulness of the vitalist ideologies which thrived in this period and can be helpful in artistic constructions and the justifica-

---

[59]   The figures are derived from Eric L. Mills, *The Fluid Envelope of Our Planet* (Toronto: University of Toronto Press, 2011).

tion of something that might well have existed without their support in the way of belief (even though from another perspective the two, the music and the ideology, are probably both emanations of the same cause and versions of the same historical and social logic).

As the currents move in what I persist in calling their inexorable movement—for the music also wants to be inexorable and artistically necessary, unavoidable, doomed and fateful, in its momentum (even though as a human construction it can scarcely be any of those things in reality)—as the currents move, they spin off gyres and eddies in their progress, great turning circular movements that surround them as they proceed, a massed but ever-differentiated accompaniment which must accompany the most dense and multitudinous of central sonorities, and as it were the transcendental background of the orchestral sounds themselves in the building and the space within which they reverberate, something which, however measureable, is more like an idea than a tangible aural thing or substance, inasmuch as it surrounds and completes them like the idea of the totality which cannot itself be seen but which is imaginary and real at once (perhaps, in that, like perspective itself for vision).

And then there are those rather different things which are the eddies, as it were the watery episodes spun off the central movement forward in all kinds of new and provisional, ephemeral shapes and form; one is tempted to see in these more minute formal events the very substance of invention itself and of formal play, the digressions which advance nothing and yet without which the musical movement forward lacks all real interest, byways which lead nowhere, picnics in the void, *Lichtung* and *Holzweg*, moments of rest and moments of superhuman intensity, having the family likeness of theme and variations, and yet in all ways lacking any reassuring resemblance with one another or with anything like an original theme, anything like what drives the current forward imperiously and implacably—these are what we have been hitherto describing in the static fashion of the moments of the present as they succeed each other, and yet which also take on a different appearance when they are seen as unintended consequences and as it were collateral damage of the main force and lunge of the moment.

And then there are crests and troughs, the very rhythm of the rhythms themselves, wavelengths of different kinds, each of which is qualitative rather than quantitative; the path or current has its boundaries, where it is forbidden to stray; it has its own internal instabilities, threatening collapse at all times, its average speed, according to which its deviations take on their significance. And the multiple momentums—for each of these currents must be imagined as coexisting with many others, just as this movement coexists with the other four or five (or six), and each collection or symphony co-exists with its neighbors in a kind of synoptic simultaneity—then internally project an as it were extra-musical world outside itself, a world of determinate forces and causes which escape any possibility of registration or expression within the musical material itself but which just as surely shape it, as the Coriolis effect shapes the currents, as the pattern of winds urges this or that development on, and climate and temperature, sunspots, the moon, all ceaselessly play upon this peculiar watery mass with its own peculiar internal structures in movement.

Yet other images, other characterizations, are certainly available, and one might well wish "to compare a stronger, 'modernist' form of such changeability in this music, in which at first we seem to confront a simple opposition between agitation and its soothing, its calming down. But the calming down will itself depend on the variety of forms the agitation can take—noble-heroic, neurotic, anticipatory, anxiety-laden, foreboding, euphoric, rhetorically oper-atic, declamatory, sublime or pathologically sublime, morbid, manic, jolly, frivolous-ceremonial, etc. Each of these must be momentarily subdued according to its dynamic, while the mode of calm—always ephemeral—will itself be dissolved into a new kind of agitation. Temporality is agitation in its very nature; it cannot remain in a state of tranquility for long; the latter always evolves back into a new form of agitation. This is why the whole does not simply resolve itself into a series of variations, why the sonata form does not explain this dynamic, whose fundamental formal question is how this restless alternation from high to low, from somber to ethereal, can possibly be ended, and on what key. (And as for Mahler, it will be remem-bered that Freud's diagnosis of him was based on the composer's childhood memory of turmoil at the parents' violent quarrels, when, shutting himself in the bathroom, at one and the same time he heard the inescapable sound of the hurdy-gurdy in the streets.)"

Yet if more clinical diagnoses are required, we might venture so far as to characterize this agitation only momentarily calmed in terms of the Lacanian version of Freud's death wish (a notoriously polysemic concept). In Lacan, the "death wish" is in fact the force of the drive (or *Trieb* or instinct), which acts through us even when our personal desires and wishes are exhausted, indeed even when our own individual energies are virtually at an end. This impersonal life force, as it were, is unable to find death, resuscitating at even those moments in which we seem on the point of a conclusion— something which would seem to qualify it aptly enough for musical descriptions as well.

Indeed, its most notorious mythological version in music is perhaps that of Bartok's *Miraculous Mandarin*, a fable in which a wealthy mandarin, on his way to the brothel, is attacked by thugs and stabbed repeatedly. Yet the *drive still instinct* within him causes repeated resuscitations, and repeated attacks, the illustrious victim rising up again in his irresistible momentum towards his heart's desire. This is perhaps too somber a parable for the extraordinary varied content of Mahler's musical drive; and yet it may serve to convey a little of that incomparably productive and creative, unquenchable musical energy which more than in any other composer never seems to reach its depletion or its exhaustion, its end point, and in that a figure of what the romantics called the infinite.

"Heavens, what is the public to make of this chaos in which new worlds are being engendered, only to crumble into ruin the next moment? What are they to say to this primeval music, this foaming, roaring, raging sea of sound, to these dancing stars, to these breathtaking, iridescent, and flashing breakers!"[60]

---

[60]   Mahler, letter to Alma, October 14, 1904.

PART TWO

LATE MODERNISM IN FILM

Chapter 4

Angelopoulos and Collective Narrative

for Stathis Kouvelakis

The easier way to explain our failure to grant Theo Angelopoulos the position he deserves in modern cinema[1]—that he is less theoretically experimental than Godard or less politically ostentatious than Pasolini we can grant, but why we fail to love seeing his films more than those of Antonioni or Fellini remains something of a mystery—clearly lies in the character of modern Greek history, which is far less familiar than that of the Western European countries. Greece has gone through a collective experience of which most other modern nations have only known bits and pieces: revolution, fascism, occupation, civil war, foreign intervention, Western imperialism, exile, parliamentary democracy, military dictatorship, and after the sixties, a ringside seat at the horrendous violence of the new Balkan wars, with their flood of refugees recalling Greece's own refugee experience after being driven out of Ionia at the end of World War I[2] (I omit the

---

[1] I am greatly indebted to Andrew Horton, ed., *The Last Modernist: The Films of Theo Angelopoulos* (Trowbridge: Flicks, 1997), pp. 41–2, as to Horton's work on the filmmaker in general; and also to Dan Fainaru's collection *Angelopoulos: Interviews* (Jackson: University Press of Mississippi, 2001). I should add that a first version of the present essay appeared in the Horton collection.

[2] I assume that anyone interested in these films will be as grateful as I was for Dan Georgakas's succinct overview of the history:

The Greek monarchy was restored by a military coup in 1935. One year later, General Metaxas established a dictatorship based on the monarchy. Among the many justifications given for the coup was the need to destabilise the [increasingly influential] Greek Communist Party. Metaxas succeeded in jailing or exiling most Communist leaders. In 1940, Mussolini asked Greece for free passage of his armies travelling to fight in Africa. Popular resistance exploded, and huge signs written in stone were placed in the Greek mountains spelling out "OXI" ("no"). Mussolini attacked Greece only to have his armies thrown back into Albania in the first Fascist defeat of the Second World War. The Germans took up the attack the following spring, and established control in all major cities and most islands. Metaxas died of natural causes, the Greek king went into exile in Britain, and the remnants

current economic disaster only because there was no time left for it to show up on Angelopoulos's registering apparatus).[3] The political passions generated by this unique experience of history were also, no doubt, foreign to a Western public perfectly willing to accommodate the left-wing sympathies of all the other filmmakers I have

---

of the regular army regrouped in the Middle East. Their movements were under the control of the Allies and they did not fight in Greece until the Second World War had ended. In Greece, partisan bands began to form; some were rightist, some centrist, some leftist. The most important of the groups and by far the largest, growing to more than 50,000 armed troops, was the National Liberation Front (EAM-ELAS). This group was headed by a coalition of Republican army officers, hostile to the Metaxas legacy, and Greek Communists. By the end of the war they had liberated most of Greece. The major political issue was the nature of the postwar government. Would Communists be allowed to participate? In 1944, EAM-ELAS attempted to take control of Athens and came within a few streets of success. They were held off by British forces which allied themselves with various forces fearing an EAM-ELAS government. A major aftermath of the struggle was the return of the king and his army. EAM-ELAS agreed to disband under the condition that the pre-war repression would not be resumed. The majority of EAM-ELAS disarmed and disbanded: in the years which followed, those who did not proved to have justifiable fears. Many of the partisans who had stayed in Greece to fight the Nazis were oppressed in an ever-increasing cycle of violence reminiscent of the Metaxas period. Many former partisans went into exile, while others returned to the mountains for what became a civil war. Unlike [during] the resistance period, the new guerrilla leaders were exclusively Communist. For more than forty years, there has been a debate on whether the civil war was forced on them or provoked. During the early years of the war, the Communists operated successfully in small groups throughout the country. Britain soon informed the United States that it could not afford to finance the royalist forces and the United States stepped in with what is known as the Truman Doctrine. The Communist forces regrouped in the north in 1948 to form regular battlefronts. This was largely in response to the Soviet desire to put pressure on Yugoslavia, which had just broken with the Soviet block. The Greek Communists, however, had received considerable strategic aid from Tito. They could not possibly satisfy both Tito and the Soviets, and this break in their foreign support helped contribute to their defeat. During this same period, the United States refurbished the Greek royalist army. This included providing napalm bombs for use in the mountain fighting, the first time such bombs had ever been used in Europe. The Communists were defeated. Although many rebels were killed, most were forced into exile in Soviet nations or were captured. The captured Communists, as well as EAM-ELAS partisans seized earlier as a precautionary measure, were imprisoned on harsh island camps where most remained for three to five years, but a few were still being held as late as the 1960s. Even after [they were] released, these fighters and their families faced difficulties. Their children often could not get college scholarships, government jobs, or even obtain a driver's licence. Throughout the 1950s, anyone who took a dissident position on a political issue risked being identified with the defeated guerrillas. The Communist Party was banned during this period, but a substitute United Democratic Left Party which took part in elections drew the 10 per cent vote which the Communists had typically drawn whenever legal. The junta which seized power in 1967 maintained that the turmoil of 1963–67 was like what Metaxas had had to deal with. Among their first acts was to reopen the camps of the 1950s and re-imprison many aged leftists and their families.

[3]   It would have been central to his unfinished film, *The Other Sea*.

mentioned above, who worked in countries in which class struggle did not reach a state of outright civil war, except during the various wartime occupations in which local reactionary ideologies could be somehow masked by the presences of the Nazis and their armies.

There are, however, other reasons for Angelopoulos's lack of standing in the West and I will come to them shortly. First we need to sort out the periods of his work, and the cycles into which they can be divided (he himself preferred to refer to them as trilogies, an inexact description which seemed useful mainly for publicity). For the first works—I would count the first six in this category—center squarely on the internal Greek situation and in particular, the dictatorship, the occupation and civil war, and the exile of the losers, the communists and the partisans. This period or cycle runs from the Metaxas's dictatorship and the occupation to the end of the civil war (in which we can perhaps include the belated return of the exiles—in *Voyage to Cythera* (1984)—some twenty years later). In the time of their production (rather than that of their content) it corresponds to the radical 1970s (in many countries still part of the 1960s as such) and includes Angelopoulos's most famous film, *The Travelling Players* (1975), which became for a time the most legendary cinematic icon of the Left (until it was replaced, for a non-political age, by his other three-and-a-half-hour work, *Ulysses' Gaze*, twenty years later in 1995).

After that, it is as though the phenomenon of exile were then by some well-nigh Hegelian logic transformed into a mediation on everything dialectical about the border itself: Does something end there? Does it merely divide two distinct spatial and national entities, or does it not slowly under our own obsessive gaze and that of the camera become a phenomenon in its own right, distinct from what it bounds, and a space somehow beyond the world itself even though subject to everything that happens on either side of it? This middle period of the 1980s, oppressive in its melancholy, then culminates in an extraordinary work whose title conveys the peculiarity of this space and this time alike, *The Suspended Step of the Stork* of 1991.

Yet this is also the year in which something happens that shifts the center of historical attention from Greece and even from its frontiers to what lies beyond that border: the Balkan War, the breakup of the "former" Yugoslavia, an immense and bloody internecine conflict which seems virtually to replicate Greece's earlier history on a larger scale. At that point, we might say that Angelopoulos's cinema becomes Balkan, and that history narrows into the question of whether Greece is to be counted as a Balkan country or not (and in the process generates a whole new question and controversy as to what being Balkan might mean in the first place).[4] *Ulysses' Gaze* is the result of this seismic shift, more humanist than historical, I think, and employing international stars to convey metaphysical messages about life and death, time and the past. It is a kind of road movie, a genre which would seem to justify its unabashedly episodic structure, but which will shortly have much to tell us about Angelopoulos's space and time, and also about his conception of narrative and of filmmaking (even though we will deal no further with this film in its own right).

The Weeping Meadow (2004) then returns to Greece in a rather retrospective fashion, reprising many of the earlier themes and episodes as though in a kind of anthology of Angelopoulos's greatest hits or finest moments; while *The Dust of Time* (2008) attempts (unsuccessfully, in my opinion) to break new ground by transferring the paradigm of discontinuous collective temporalities to the drama of individuals, still punctuated by history but more after the fashion of news bulletins and headlines than of qualitatively unique historical situations. It is then one of the earliest of these four periods that we will concentrate here.

After the unfamiliarity of modern Greek history, it has become customary to speak of these films in two other ways: as somehow motivated by a nostalgia for the classicism endemic in this nation-state—something probably more affected by foreigners, from Winckelmann to Lord Byron, from admirers of the polis to those, like Nietzsche, mesmerized by the cruelties of the tragedies; and as an idiosyncratic practice of the long take or "sequence shot," something that immediately classifies him among adepts of a slow cinema from Ozu to Béla Tarr, even though, as David Thomson perceptively remarks, this is a filmmaking which is "not slow so much as preoccupied with duration."[5]

One can no doubt enumerate the classical motifs: the first feature

---

4   See, for example, Maria Todorova, *Imagining the Balkans* (New York/Oxford: Oxford University Press, 1997); and Dušan I. Bjelić and Obrad Savić, eds, *Balkan as Metaphor: Between Globalization and Fragmentation* (Cambridge: MIT Press, 2002).

5   David Thomson, *The New Biographical Dictionary of Film* (New York: Knopf, 2002), p. 22.

film *Αναπαράσταση* (*Reconstruction*, 1970) retells the story of the Oresteia, at the same time that it has a family likeness with Visconti's *Ossessione* (1942), the ancestor of Italian neorealism (and one of the many film versions of James M. Cain's *The Postman Always Rings Twice*). The same classical matricidal drama is enacted (as it were "in real life") by the actors of *The Travelling Players*, whose young hero is in fact named Orestes—"for me the name Orestes is a concept more than a character," says Angelopoulos, "the concept of the revolution so many dream of."[6] As for *Megalexandros* (1980), we are told that the name corresponds not to the classical world-conqueror, but to a historical bandit "who exists in popular, anonymous legends and fables," originating "in 1453 under Turkish domination," and "has nothing to do with the classical Alexander";[7] yet in a sense the classical hero is also inscribed in the film, in its extraordinary beginning, for its Western audiences and for the unhappy philhellenes who are his victims, as we shall see. Yet if the classical means epic and the monumental, the cliché certainly has its relevance here, and also affords a way of converting this cultural stereotype into the technical characterization which so often accompanies it in discussions of these films.

What unites epic and the nostalgia of antiquity is in fact the very concept of the episodic on which we have already touched: for the infamous sequence shot (there are only 80 in the whole of *The Travelling Players*, the experts tell us) is necessarily in and of itself episodic, and so is epic as such. Already, in *The Theory of the Novel*, Lukács had made a place for the survival of what he calls "minor epic forms" on into a modernity which disables the epic as the privileged genre for expressing life: even though he insists on the subjective contingency of these "epic" enclaves (lyric, the short story, humor), in much the same way that we tend to attribute analogous possibilities to something distinctive and contingent about Angelopoulos himself and his "style":

> In the minor epic forms, the subject confronts the object in a more dominant and self-sufficient way. The narrator may (we cannot, nor do we intend to establish even a tentative system of epic forms here) adopt the cool and superior demeanour of the chronicler who observes the strange workings of coincidence

---

6 Fainaru, *Angelopoulos: Interviews*, p. 18.
7 Ibid., p. 28.

as it plays with the destinies of men, meaningless and destructive to them, revealing and instructive to us; or he may see a small corner of the world as an ordered flower-garden in the midst of the boundless, chaotic waste-lands of life, and, moved by his vision, elevate it to the status of the sole reality; or he may be moved and impressed by the strange, profound experiences of an individual and pour them into the mould of an objectivised destiny; but whatever he does, it is his own subjectivity that singles out a fragment from the immeasurable infinity of the events of life, endows it with independent life and allows the whole from which this fragment has been taken to enter the work only as the thoughts and feelings of his hero, only as an involuntary continuation of a fragmentary causal series, only as the mirroring of a reality having its own separate existence.[8]

The notion of enclaves of modern existence which unlike the surrounding contingency of daily life have their own immanent form and meaning is one of the great themes of Georg Simmel, who was a fundamental influence on the work of the young Lukács just as he was on Walter Benjamin. What characterizes such enclave forms is their contradictory combination of completeness and fragmentariness, their only sporadic emergence as a unity of subject and object, or as Lukács puts it, of essence and life. The fragment as a kind of whole was, to be sure, one of the crucial discoveries of the romantics themselves, who paired it with their signature notion of Irony; but it was their archenemy Hegel who, leaving irony aside, detected this tendency to episodic form within classical epic itself and as such:

> The epic work has to proceed in a way quite different from lyric and dramatic poetry. The first thing to notice here is the breadth of separated incidents in which the epic is told. This breadth is grounded in both the content and form of the epic. We have already seen what a variety of topics there is in the completely developed epic world, whether these are connected with the inner powers, impulses, and desires of the spirit or with the external situation and environment. Since all these aspects assume the form of objectivity and a real appearance each of them develops an independent shape, whether inner or outer, within which the poet may linger in description or portrayal, and the external development of which he may allow; depths of feeling or assembled and evaporated in the universals of reflection. Along with objectivity separation is immediately given, as well as a varied wealth of diverse traits. Even in this

---

[8]   Georg Lukács, *Theory of the Novel* (Cambridge, MA: MIT Press, 1971), p. 50.

respect in no other kind of poetry but epic is an outside given so much right to freedom almost up to the point of a seemingly unfettered independence.[9]

We are, however, perhaps more familiar with Auerbach's version of the idea in the famous account of *The Odyssey* that opens *Mimesis*: "Homer ... knows no background. What he narrates is for the time being the only present and fills the stage and the reader's mind completely ... Homer's goal is 'already present in every point of his progress' ... the Homeric style knows only a foreground, only a uniformly illuminated, uniformly objective present."[10] Auerbach here seeks to convey in temporal terms the fundamental syntactic opposition—the paratactic versus the hypotactic—which informs the very structure of *Mimesis*: yet this is a time which has become space as such, a present which has the fullness and completeness of the spatial. It is not a bad way to pass from literature to film.

For it is precisely in these terms that we can describe what is episodic in Angelopoulos: the temporal continuity of the long take (or the travelling shot or the sequence shot, depending on your terminological preference)[11] which however envelops, includes, and exhausts a completed action or episode. Yet this "technique" does not standardize or render homogenous its variety of contents (as Hegel had already suggested with his observation about "the variety of topics ... in the completely developed epic world") (Hegel 1975: 1081). And this is why we can also sort these out into a variety of as it were synoptic categories, and think of them as themes or even obsessions: recurrent types of events and forms which might even be catalogued as such.

Most obvious among these set pieces are the dancing and music-making in cafes, almost always interrupted by armed authoritarian figures; the movement back and forth in the narrow streets leading to the central squares or plazas demonstrators: sometimes organized, sometimes simply massed, at others in desperate flight from gunfire or police assault, and occasionally intersecting in clash or confrontation (and stylized in one of the most famous episodes

---

9   G. W. F. Hegel, *Aesthetics* (Oxford: Oxford University Press, 1975), p. 1,081.

10   Erich Auerbach, *Mimesis* (Princeton: Princeton University Press, 1953), pp. 4–5, 7.

11   For a thorough technical discussion of Angelopoulos's work, see David Bordwell's essay in Horton, *Last Modernist*. For a later version of this essay, see Chapter 4 in David Bordwell, *Figures Traced in Light: On Cinematic Staging* (Berkley/Los Angeles/London: University of California Press, 2005).

of *The Travelling Players*, in which fascist and communist groups exchange songs with each other in a kind of "signifying" duet which is also a duel). Innumerable variations on water—the beaches as some ultimate limit which is not exactly a border (but becomes one when we have to do with a river instead of the sea); flotillas, fishing boats and large ocean-faring vessels most often redolent of the Black Sea, but also the raft on which the lonely couple of exiles is expelled into the mist (as aged Eskimo parents are said to be retired from life)—the maritime and the riverine here echo distant mountains and rocky pastoral meadows, with villages something like natural outgrowths of both and the more urban streets and squares a wholly distinct kind of space: these construct a materiality too close up for any names or geographical identifications except that of Greece itself, and, to play on Auerbach's language, are far too intertwined with the very quality of the events to be called the mere background.

This is the moment, then, to open a parenthesis and to underscore the materialism of Angelopoulos, the passion for the resistance of matter, for the weight and solidity of the village houses and streets, and above all the texture of the walls. Its very emblem might be that from the opening of the *Reconstruction*, in which a bus, whose lumbering movement over the unpatched roads already serves to explore matter itself and to register its unevenness, is found during a stop to have ground to a halt in mud: the efforts to release its tires are themselves a kind of reverse allegory of the spectators' longing, faced with these mere filmic images, to experience matter more deeply, to be mired in it as in a Bazinian or Kracauerian transcendental reality itself. The most significant element in this materiality is the camera, which, an agent of absolute desubjectification, is a passive recipient of the contradictions and the energies of subject and object in turn: here its material autonomy becomes a positive rather than a negative or privative feature, and what we are struck by is its intelligence, as it tactfully pans around a scene, with decent interest returning on its steps, looking again, searching, recording. Nor is this some putative personality trait or subjectivity of Angelopoulos himself: rather, the camera does this on its own—it wishes to delve, to know more; it can also be patient and wait; it knows a temporality which is neither that of author nor characters, a kind of third temporality of its own, capable of sitting out the time of the world until at length events germinate, unexpectedly, slowly, things begin to happen—the time of the ancient φύσις (*physis*) perhaps, so centrally meditated by

Heidegger, a time in which things come into being and go out of being according to their own internal rhythms ("according to the assessments of time").

So now this camera patiently lies in wait for a group of people walking down the narrow streets of a small stone town: it knows these streets, these buildings, so tirelessly and well, but is somehow never bored by them. We are told that Angelopoulos spent months travelling around Greece in order to collect the walls and the buildings he would materially house within the images of *The Travelling Players*. The traveling camera, to be sure, sets this materiality in motion, but within this motion there moves that other fundamental movement which is the frontal approach of the collective characters themselves: most emblematically in *The Travelling Players* with their phalanx of the cast in its perpetual motion towards us, a procession of traditional women's black dresses and the men's suits and hats, in various sizes but always with the suitcases in hand and often umbrellas—this is already what I hesitate to call an archetype owing to unwanted psycho-mythical or Jungian overtones—but it is not yet even the event, which marks its absent presence by the sudden awakening of these faces to something beyond the camera and the audience, something unaccommodated by the shot itself. It is subjective and objective all at once: we witness the slow transformation of the collective gaze into a stare as it grows ever more fixed in rapt attention and horror: it is itself the symptom of the approaching yet nameless object: an advancing police patrol, perhaps, or the hanged bodies that greet them on the steep approach to a mountain village in wartime. It is the adaption of reality and of the human gaze to this peculiar ontological focus which is the contemplative dimension of epic (rather than the static or scientific "objectivity" of a later science and its measuremental observations of staged experiments). Nor is this gaze in any way theatrical, although we will have to come to terms with the theatrical and the dramatic in Angelopoulos in a moment.

Here, however, it is preferable to show how variable these bravura segments can be, sublimated into allusion or drawn down in the crudest violence of the shot that rings out and the body that sinks to the ground. This is the gamut of latency or virtuality, rather than the effects of stylization; and I take as the very emblem of that variability the swift concentration of group or crowd on some central object, multiplicity rapidly uniting into the one, as when, on the comic level the famished players suddenly converge on a stray chicken in the midst of the snowy waste, or on the tragic one, when the disgruntled followers of Megalexandros surround him and blot him out, as though tearing him to pieces like the Bacchae and leaving behind, not bloody limbs, but rather the marble fragments of a classic statue as they once again disperse, like something out of de Chirico.

So it is that the pure form runs its gamut of possibilities: the border with all its philosophical paradoxicality suddenly swelling into the river across which the archetypal Angelopoulos exilic wedding is staged in *The Step of the Stork* (reprised later on in *The Weeping Meadow* as in a kind of *florilegio* of the greatest moments). But what I want to stress here is not only the way in which each of these episodes or moments the old Hegelian/Lukácsian unity of form and content is achieved (or better still: rediscovered!); but also the way in which, uniquely on the occasion of these films, a kind of unity of critical and theoretical discourse is also achieved. Indeed, film offers a privileged space in which to observe this dilemma of the alternation of the discourse of interpretation or meaning and that of technique or construction: the choice between a reading of the content and an analysis of medium or method. The first ultimately leads us back to history and is convulsions, individual and collective; the second on towards the camera apparatus, to the equipment and above all its mobility, and the distinctive nature of the sequence shots that follow the action unfolding within them and include everything; in *The Hunters* (1977), "we had some sequence shots of seven to eleven minutes each; consequently there was no room for errors or improvisations. The slightest mistake meant that we had to start the shot all over again."[12] Angelopoulos's "method" is thereby the polar opposite of Eisensteinian montage and of Hollywood editing, cutting the images up and recombining them into a specific narrative sequence. It is far closer to the Bazinian deep shot (exemplified in Welles), save that it is a deep shot in motion and results in a single narrative block to be aligned alongside the others; thus, as has already been observed, there are only eighty such sequence shots which make up that immense three-and-a-half-hour film called *The Travelling Players*.[13] This technical approach to cinema—as paradigmatically described by David Bordwell (Bordwell 1997: 32–4)—then has the added advantage of marginalizing the interpretive one and

---

[12] Fainaru, *Angelopoulos: Interviews*, p. 23.

[13] Horton, *Last Modernist*, pp. 32–4.

expelling it from film studies into a kind of humanistic and literary no-man's land, in which endless scholastic discussions among dilettantes about meanings are pursued which have no relevance either to producers and their distribution (yet another technical but more sociological "objective" area) or to the filmmakers themselves (just as critics are so often irrelevant for writers).

But this is a rift that is not limited to film studies: it dramatizes the subject/object split which has obsessed philosophy at least since Descartes, and which leaves its mark on the materialist/idealist debate in political ideology and is indeed even more deeply inscribed in the daily life of modernity and postmodernity in "the question of technology" and the relationship of capitalism to the individual subject and of determinism to freedom. The subject/object opposition is thereby central to aesthetics and the debate over the autonomy of art and its possible relationship (ideological, subversive, etc.) to the multiple externalities in which it is embedded. What is important about Angelopoulos—and the point of reviving an ancient Hegelian notion of epic to examine him—is that here, for one long moment, this opposition is lifted, and to talk about technique is also here to talk about meaning: the temporality of the sequence shot is at one with the question of history, or better still, with the uniqueness of Greek history, which is not modern in the Western sense and which does not necessarily impose a subject/object alternative on us.

But we have not yet touched on the deeper source of this supersession, in which form and content are once again, for one last moment, indistinguishable in Angelopoulos. This is, to be sure, the age of new waves; but it is not with the French that the Greek filmmaker has his affinities, despite the film theory he absorbed in Paris, but rather the Mediterranean and Italian auteurs and above all with Antonioni and Fellini. To ask ourselves why he is not just another grand filmmaker of their type is then to penetrate to the very heart of the matter and to understand why the frequent thefts and borrowings—such as the great head of Lenin in *Ulysses' Gaze* which so insistently recalls the aerial Christ of *8½* (1963)—are not mere allusions, mere influence or simple intertextuality.

Provincializing Europe, someone suggested;[14] but it would have been better to talk about provincializing Western Europe, for it

---

14   Dipesh Chakrabarty, *Provincializing Europe: Postcolonial Thought and Historical Difference* (Princeton: Princeton University Press, 2007).

is the latter that housed a cultural-imperialist centrality only later taken over by the United States. The presence of General Scobie's occupying army in *The Travelling Players* (not to mention the GIs who relay them), the unclassifiability of the Balkans in our various Western capitalist-historical schemes, not to speak of the "former" Soviet bloc, ought to be enough to suggest some broader "orientalist" prejudices here, and to alert us to the possibility of some more fundamental differences, which the much-abused word "cultural" already trivializes.

For what we want to notice in Angelopoulos's Antonioni side is the absence of the neuroticism and narcissistic anguish of his heroes (and of the hero of *8½* as well), the absence of the obsession with male impotence which has become a figure for Italy's political paralysis. None of that is to be found in Angelopoulos (at least in his first two periods), despite the melancholy tone of so many of the images; indeed, it is often difficult in these works to find an individual protagonist to whom to attribute such subjectivities in the first place; and this despite the commonality of political defeat in both countries and the ultimate failure of politics itself and of revolution. The fact is that the Western political despair in these Italians and their characters is not political in the deeper sense and reflects the absence of politics rather than its failure. In Angelopoulos even the latter remains political, because it remains collective and only the collective is truly political. This is what distinguishes Angelopoulos's long takes and the envelopment of the characters and their acts and experiences within them as somehow beyond any traditional subject/object split: they are not the point-of-view shots of individual subjectivities but rather a collective dimension in which the individuals exist despite their individuality and their individual passions. The collective is the extraordinary lesson that Angelopoulos has to teach us.

In this play of forms and categories, then, and despite the male protagonists of *La Dolce Vita* and *8½*, as I have said, it would be Fellini to whom we would normally turn for some exemplary instantiation of the object pole of the fateful opposition: his great bravura set pieces, indeed, suggest a triumphant mastery of the image as such which might well account for their euphoria and their joy at enfranchisement from the subjective and its alienated miseries. And it is certain that we rarely find such joyous formal production in Angelopoulos: rather the latter's monumentality, like much of

Eisenstein, lacks the extravagance of the master craftsman's gestures. For in Angelopoulos the images are icons rather than symptoms: they have not been formed in the excess and exultation of the individual creator, but rather proposed in advance by reality itself, whose internal forms and unities the camera discovers. So it is that the yellow-clad electricians mounting their poles at the end of *The Suspended Step* like the crucified slaves arrayed along the Appian Way in *Spartacus*—these extraordinary figures do not make up an image that means something beyond themselves, whether that be hope, or community, or simply communication across the borders. They are not symbols, they do not stand for something else or for concepts, they speak an autonomous and self-immanent, self-sufficient epic language. And this why the epic is episodic as well, an iconic series, a veritable iconostasis in time which authenticates that collective ontology with which Angelopoulos has been able to put us in contact, however briefly and in whatever alien national history and experience has enabled it.

Still, a final uncertainty remains, and it is that of theatricality as such; for is not the very possibility of self-exhibition in however neutral and collective a form necessarily what we call theatrical? And does not the new medium of film itself, despite the omnipresence of theater in Angelopoulos's films, necessarily rebuke that other, older and very different medium?

Something like this, indeed, is played out in the opening scene of the *Voyage to Cythera*, in which the son (Giulio Brogi) seems to be rehearsing a script of some kind. (Indeed, he seems to have before him the whole script, as in a film, indeed the film we are watching, of the return of his partisan father [Manos Katrakis] from exile and subsequent disgrace here): a seemingly endless lineup of elderly male extras waits against the wall (as for an execution), in their dark suits and hats, who are called to the podium one by one to try out for their single line in the play: "It's me!" When the director and son leave the building—a wonderful touch and so characteristic of the way in which Angelopoulos never gives up, always deploys all the multiple dimensions inherent in his raw material—he comes out into a crowd of the same extras, each having made his individual tryout and now clustered in the back alleyway of the theater and the street in small groups or individually, smoking their cigarettes, as though in rehearsal and in preparation for the great historical crowds and demonstrations which will be Angelopoulos's fundamental Event, and for which these hopeful nonprofessionals are also now expectantly waiting, without much hope at all.

An unusual, an unexpected episode: but now son and mother (Dora Volanaki) set forth for the main event, the ocean liner arriving from Russia, the lone figure advancing through the waiting room, holding the inevitable, the eternal suitcase, a tall gaunt bearded figure who, when close enough to them to be recognizable after thirty-seven years in exile, pronounces the same words, this time definitively (he gets the part!): *Eγώ είμαι!* ("It's me!"). Is this repetition or the fold? Is it reality and illusion, or mimesis and the mimesis of mimesis? It is certainly a minor bravura piece in this film, whose great scene is the aged exile's dance in the empty village, in the graveyard of his dead comrades, the traditional Greek dance, turning on himself with arms outstretched and hands marking these rhythms: a vision of absolute grief, absolute joy, and of the non-place of place, the non-time of time. The other is the image of the raft, on which the expelled exile and his now reconciled and aged spouse are once again sent out to sea, passing into the mist and into invisibility: death, failure, history, all transcended and masked, veiled, blotted out by the eternity of mist they have become.[15] Here what is monumental in Angelopoulos—the eidos which needs no commentary or interpretation, and yet which bears the entire narrative situation within itself, motionless—is revealed to us in all its untimely originality.

The Travelling Players stages theater as a different kind of repetition, the popular melodrama the same from village to village, its roles, over-identical, yet spoken by ever-younger generations as

---

[15]   I do not wish to understate the role of a different kind of politics in this first of Angelopoulos's allegedly postrevolutionary films. Despite powerful political moments, such as the refusal of the returned exile of *Voyage* to surrender his part of the village common lands for a shopping center, this is now always a politics that confronts international consumerism, the market, and universal Americanization as its target, and no longer fascism or anti-communism. The penetration of the market at home, then, and its corrosive effect on the immemorial lifeways of the village, make of everyone an exile: yet the category (seemingly archaic in the immense population transfers and multinationality of the new world system) in fact awaits its genuine content for another ten years, until the upheaval of the Yugoslav civil wars allows Angelopoulos to transfer his new forms onto a fundamentally modified and enlarged dimension which it would be ironic indeed to call "postnational" space, but which is certainly already that of the world system.

history passes, taking the older ones with it.[16] The play, however, is ultimately concluded in the course of the film, the repetition of its well-known opening lines joined by the assassination of the "Aegisthus" figure and ultimately by the death of the protagonists of the young lover, shot in the person of a British soldier who has, by virtue of historical repetition, momentarily assumed his place. One would do wrong, I think, to insist too strongly on the jigsaw-organization of chronology in this film (whose action runs from 1939 to 1952): this is not *Last Year at Marienbad* (1961)—the historical movement is palpable enough, despite a few easily identifiable displacement of episodes out of order; and the famous opening and concluding scenes and lines—in which the players repeat their arrival in Aigion but in 1939 rather than 1952—do not at all suggest some eternal return, some Viconian or Joycean cycle of history, but rather simply ask us to review the events, to gather them together in one unique memory, beyond pathos or tragedy: they ask us, in other words, to think historically about the nature of this collective destiny by pulling all the episodes together in a continuity the film itself is unwilling to construct for us. In other words, they construct a past.

Otherwise, it must be said that *The Travelling Players* is closer to Eisenstein's montage of attractions than anything he himself ever produced (*Strike* [1925] came closest, perhaps). It is a kind of musical, in which each segment is introduced by the omnipresent accordion and in which there is finally fairly little dialogue, as though dialogue belonged to some other form or medium, namely the stage. The internal drama of the film is secured by the integration of the villain into collectivity itself: "Aegisthus" is necessary for the function of the troupe, indeed later he holds it together, and this professional solidarity stands in structural contrast with the absolute divisions and polarities of the political wars themselves. Yet the περιπέτειες (peripeties) of the family drama are as simple in their conflictual form as those of the external political history; and the exchange of these simplicities and their play with each other is obviously required for the intelligibility of a work that covers so long and complex a period.

But that whole period must be dealt with in a radically different

---

16 Nor should we neglect to mention the implicit theatricality of his first film, significantly entitled *Reconstruction*, a word which is also used for the re-enactment in situ of the crime in many European juridical systems.

way in *The Hunters*, which takes place after the "normalization" of 1952, that is to say after the effective victory of the Right and the end of the Civil War. The events of *The Travelling Players* are now over and indeed long past (the troupe itself being dissolved into the rather sentimental reprise of *Landscape in the Mist* [1988]), which is not to say that there cannot be a return of this repressed. Indeed, if there is anything "experimental" in Angelopoulos besides the occasionally confusing interpolation of different historical epochs in *The Travelling Players*, it is his solution to this problem here, which it would be truly meretricious to compare to "experiments" like Lars von Trier's *Dogville* (2003). For here there are no genuine flashbacks, but rather moments in which, as on stage, people and events from other moments in history suddenly intrude upon the set and take it over, reenact their historical roles again and just as inconspicuously withdraw from this present, in which a group of profiteers and counterrevolutionaries celebrate New Year's Eve 1977, thirty years after the bloody defeat of the Greek Left (assisted in that by British and later by American anti-communist forces). These people—lumpen and petty bourgeoisie, Zola's *La Fortune des Rougon* (*The Fortune of the Rougons* [1871]), or the Russian oligarchs, or the racists of the Wilmington uprising, are the opportunistic scum who seize the spoils of a victory they have not themselves fought.

The fly in this celebration's ointment is discovered in the bravura opening of the film, in which a group of hunters is glimpsed across an expanse of snow, approaching slowly, and then beginning to run as a mysterious object—a black speck in the white blankness—is sighted. I see a black which is not in nature, cried Cézanne, as his party searched for a lady's lost umbrella. This particular spot is "not in nature" in a far more decisive and prodigious way: we may not call it embodied guilt, for these characters feel none, but rather the very past itself, and lost opportunities, alternate possibilities, searing memories and (for the others) the experience of defeat all here rises inexplicably to the surface and materializes.

So it is that we observe a snowy waste, immense across the wide screen: dark figures slowly appear on it, scattered out widely, slowly advancing from over a great distance. They are hunters, and the camera bides its time, as though it knows how laborious it is for boots to disengage themselves in snowfall, but with the certainty that an event is worth waiting for. The viewer has more difficulty isolating the exact moment of transition between a leisurely approach and the quickened pace whereby, unevenly, some sighting it before others, the hunters begin to converge on a dark place on the snow hitherto unidentified. This also takes time, but it is now the temporality of excitement, of anticipation, of awakened curiosity: for these people too, an event, something unusual is about to happen. The viewer of *The Hunters* already knows what it is: the dead body in the snow of a partisan in this pacified Greece where even live partisans have not been sighted for twenty years.

But "they are extinct," cries one of the party-going hunters; and indeed this corpse will lie in the midst of the festivities throughout, a living reproach, one is tempted to say, for which the only feasible answer is to rebury it, to sink it out of sight as deeply as possible, and out of mind. But this conclusion will not preempt the inevitable imaginary scène à faire, in which the partisan returns to life and with his equally long-dead (or exiled) comrades executes the whole lot of these execrable victors. The technique is then a dramatic rather than a filmic one, and perhaps more redolent of O'Neill than of Brecht: as the memory scenes commence, the remembered actors, oppressors and victims alike, slowly reinvade this festive space, whose "real" and current, living inhabitants step quietly back out of the way in order to let the past for a moment revive (in historic moments of revolt or repression whose dates are vividly burned into the memories of the living, if not of the non-Greek audience). The occasion is a police inquest on this peculiar corpus delicti, if it is one, before the pleasure boat bearing the New Year's Eve guests and notables arrives at the dock below. Yet it is the locale itself which has ominously enough stirred this political and historical visitation of ghosts, inasmuch as it used to be a partisan headquarters, bought for a song after the defeat by one of the more ignominious and active conspirators.

New Year's Day arrives in another form in *Megalexandros*, at the very beginning of the new century (this time the twentieth), in which a group of supercilious British hellenophiles, disgusted to find that their Athenian hosts do not even know Homeric Greek, set out to witness the new dawn from a Byronic vantage point. Their toast to History is, alas, singularly mistimed: for in one of the most remarkable emergences in all of cinema—and emergence, apparition, *surgissement*, was for Adorno one of the crucial categories of art itself—their view out over the bay is abruptly interrupted by an apparition, as though ancient Greece itself rises up from out of the depths of a shallow modernity: the crest and "waving feathers"

(Homer) of an antique helmet, then the whole body of the warrior as it is lifted on its heroic steed: Megalexandros himself as he mounts out of History into a present in which the philhellene tourists are to be taken hostage and condemned to a miserable confinement and then to death. This is the eponymous Alexander the Great, a rebel who has collected an entire army of the dispossessed and the disenfranchised around him to stage a powerful and alarming revolt against the legal regime, itself in the meantime idly celebrating the New Year in its palaces in the capitol. Angelopoulos seems here to renounce his earlier radicalism, for this false Alexander, this deranged imposter, who has an entire village in his thrall, is by the end of the film denounced as such and in another memorable moment, surrounded by the populace, and metamorphosed into a broken statue; but not before he has resuscitated ancient Greece and modern revolution before our very eyes.

Chapter 5

History and Elegy in Sokurov

Sokurov's is thought to be a gloomy and death-ridden oeuvre by those who do not know *Days of Eclipse* and the transcendental smile of its dual ending—Malianov remains behind, faithful to his vocation, while in second shot human history ends and the planet returns to an untouched nature. I want to retain this perspective, while posing the question of death as follows: Is it possible for the fascination with corpses to coexist with such brilliant and idiosyncratic characterizations? Does the grotesque simply mark those who distract us from the fact of dying; or are the misshapen and bizarre comic figures (like the Hitler of whom Eva Braun says that he is alive only when performing in front of other people) themselves simply dead men who are not aware of it, the dead seen from the standpoint of life and vitality, of the sun coming out again over this grim world after its eclipse, the young doctor frustrated but alive and active among his malnourished and handicapped patients, in the backward countryside of the non-Russian republics? (Perhaps indeed these grotesques are the equivalent of eccentric objects in the documentaries: the woman's shoe left behind as the enthusiastic crowd surges after Hitler; the chair on its back and in motion, as the departing airplane's exhaust propels it across the field.)

But what the fiction films represent as corpses, the documentaries register as history, the decay of whole generations of individuals, the dissolution of the historical process itself in time. The documentaries show us what can only be allegorical or symbolic in the fiction films: Russia itself in the stream of time, given over to its multiple entropies: the graveyards full of the dead of whole generations, the increasing hardships of the peasantry, the flight abroad of the great artists (Chaliapin), the suffering of Russia during World War II (*And Nothing More*), the passing of the Soviet Union itself (the

Yeltsin documentary is still an "elegy," despite the fragmentary echo of the word "hope" at the end); while even the nationalistic effervescence of *Russian Ark*, perhaps a little too shrill and unmotivated (save by the paintings it was commissioned to celebrate), marks a nostalgia and a falling off.

This opposition—between historical and existential decline—is best seen, however, as a difference in the representational capacities of the two genres—documentary and fictional narrative—and goes a long way towards accounting for Sokurov's virtuosity in both forms. The resolute political neutrality of his works (or if you prefer, their political "degree zero") makes it unnecessary to decide whether the two versions of time express a vision of history or simply metaphysics of life and death.

For the moment, let us pursue the matter of history itself further, particularly since Sokurov's recent work—the tetralogy of the dictators—is far more decisively a historical representation than anything he has done hitherto. Lukács taught us that there were two different ways of imagining history, distinct in content as well as in form. In the one, the historical drama, we see the great world-historical figures in person, on stage, larger than life, making the rafters of the playhouse ring with the heroic expression of their decisions and their will, the anxieties of their power and of their mission. In the other, the historical novel, we come at all this indirectly, by way of the mediation of an average character, who is given the opportunity to glimpse the great personages from afar and only for a moment to intersect their fulminating trajectories.

Sokurov's historical films fit neither of these categories; but they are fully as much serious historical commentaries as the other two genres, for which we must no doubt also credit Sokurov's brilliant scenarist, Yurii Arabov, who would deserve a whole study in his own right if one could separate filmmaker from scriptwriter in such a symbiotic medium. No doubt the films' aesthetic framework overlaps that of drama to a certain degree: particularly inasmuch as they also answer historical drama's secret fascination with the primal scene of history, and satisfy its longing to see with our own eyes, to hear what the great ones (as Brecht called them) said and did in private, behind those closed doors the historical drama promises to open for us, if only for one brief peeping glimpse.

So it is that *Taurus* rises stunningly to the occasion, and persuades us that yes, it must have been precisely in this way that Stalin handled the dying Lenin, crying out with obsequiousness, "It's me!"; stroking the great leader's jacket with soothing and false affection, while systematically evading his anxious questions and complaints. This patently insincere heartiness—as when, contemptuously, he pinches Krupskaya's cheek and comments on her pallor (his insults to her were famously among Lenin's last complaints)—contrasts sharply with Hitler's grotesque courtliness with his staff, as he ritually shakes their hands and seems to obey some fantasy image of courtesy rather than any spontaneous human feeling.

But in Lukács's idea of history the private life of the great public figures is still in some sense public: better still, they are defined by the unique identity of public and private in their persons, which is why until very recently scandalous revelations and the whole operation of debunking can be so disastrous for their reputations and their ultimate "place in history." Here, however, in these films there seems to reign an utterly different conception of private life, one of a kind of schizophrenic dissociation, in which the great and powerful lapse back into senility or second childhood. This is the "private life" of the so-called split subject, which never did exist as a full personality, a unified psychic reality, whether in public or in private. So we observe them at lunch or on a picnic, muttering idiotic jokes in their private language and occasionally stricken by the intermittent access of fury or dementia you do not want the "public" to know about. Hitler at play: it is no doubt an obscene spectacle—the vegetarian joking about the corpses devoured by his guests; but this infantile banter does not exactly "unmask." Hitler's hypochondria, his self-pitying sessions with Eva Braun, his alarming vacancies and drops in psychic niveau, these do not make him any less a monster; nor does one encounter any of the tragic or Shakespearean overtones of Oliver Stone's *Nixon*. Perhaps this peculiar space—neither public nor private, nor their synthesis—is to be juxtaposed with that of the *Sonata for Hitler*, which, opening on the image of a reflective, perhaps fatigued or even defeated Hitler, with folded hands, exfoliates this public portrait into newsreel, the famous speeches, refugees and victims, the space of the war, all of which are implicit in the public Hitler but oddly, mysteriously disjoined from the Hitler of *Moloch*. If he is humanized at all in the latter, it is by way of Eva Braun: the true protagonist of this film, compassionate for all her frustration and her solitary exhibitionism (as Aryan as Wilhelm Lehmbruck's statues), and sharing with

Magda Goebbels a feminine position of power vacated by the grotesque and incompetent males. Krupskaya's role in *Taurus* is no less *sympathisch*: but the Soviet context is paradoxically a good deal more sinister than that of Berchtesgaden, the latter enlivened by the stereotypical Wagner and Liszt and (on Bormann's orders) devoid of political discussion.

Both films are, to be sure, haunted by death: Hitler is obsessed by his fears of mortal illness (indeed, historians tell us that the war, originally planned for 1943, was advanced several years on account of them). But Lenin really is dying, and it is his distance from history, rather than his presence within it, that is represented here. Not only the stroke which has paralyzed Lenin's right side, but also the systematic isolation of the manor house in Gorki village, reduce Lenin to the raging helplessness which is the inescapable fact of *Taurus*. He hobbles about, struggling up and down staircases and in and out of his chair, and pushing away the assistance of servants and family with the recurrent shout, "By myself!" It is a musical leitmotif, and not the least of the small details of this beautiful composition can be appreciated at the lunch, when Krupskaya, desiring to serve her own soup, solicits from Lenin the murmur of grim satisfaction, "By herself!" The obsessive outpouring of fantasies of torture and punishment, however, which seem to confirm the current revisionist view of Lenin as the true originator of Stalinist terror, can just as well be explained by this physical impotence and isolation in which a hitherto active and energetic leader, imperious and accustomed to making decisions and having them acknowledged, is here confined. Indeed the assignment to Gorki village is a virtual sequestration: only Stalin serves as the intermediary with the outside world and the Politburo, and carefully monitors and censors Lenin's messages (including the famous Testament).

It is a situation which suggests further refinements of the hypothesis of a third historical genre in films like this. For in both cases, in *Moloch* by choice, in *Taurus* by necessity, the "private life" recorded by the movie camera is also a kind of helpless imprisonment in its gaze: both psychic immaturity (in the Gombrowicz sense) and physical incapacitation are remorselessly registered, and the screen becomes an experimental laboratory, an isolation chamber, in which we follow processes that are neither public nor private in any traditional sense. The physical buildings then, the Berghof or the manor house, become the experimental maze in which these world-historical figures are trapped; and the spatial becomes a kind of unexpected third term here.

But to this space corresponds a new kind of temporality as well: it is the time of *l'emploi du temps*, of the routine and the schedule, the hours of the day. Both historical films obey a modified version of the unities of time and space: as do *The Second Circle* (driven forward by the urgency of burying the father's body) and *Mother and Son,* in which the mother is inexorably dying. But *Days of Eclipse* also presents a relative unity, one further underscored by the routine visits of the young doctor to his patients and friends (one of them a dead man). The pressure of this temporality of the day's routine is not so much antinarrative, as it seemed to be in the immense inaugural work in this new tradition, Joyce's *Ulysses*. Rather, mediated by film, it marks an approach to real time which now returns us to Sokurov's unique dual talent, as a fiction-filmmaker and an extraordinary documentarist. The camera has in any case an "elective affinity" with the real or the referent which none of the other arts (except photography) can claim, as though what counts as reality is precisely this succession of temporal presents that can do without the great events or the dramatic moments of happening, this never-ending sequence of daily cycles and physical preparations, of going about your business, which the camera registers without comment like the passage from morning into noon, and from afternoon into evening (just as film history registers it in the passage from Lumière to Warhol).

The commander in *Confession* most openly expresses this experience of time: it's the same today, and it will be the same my whole life, he reflects; and indeed the daily routine of the Arctic fleet is the very paradigm of a repetitive temporality in which nothing happens, and in which the outside world is virtually extinguished, by the cold and the gray air, the snow. He also most explicitly makes the connection with metaphysics: the "meaning of life" would be found in your ability to organize it day by day, like the ability to organize an army. But this is not a utilitarian matter or a question of management and efficiency: it has to do with the meaning of the social and collective institution itself. The commander compares himself unfavorably to the nineteenth-century Russian officers, who had a real vocation (that of empire) instead of the routine patrol he shares with his sailors.

No doubt one should also observe at this point that despite the interest of naturalist novelists in the workings of such complex social machinery, the filmmaker is in a better position to observe them than the writer, insofar as he is himself part of a complicated collective machine in which material knowledge and logistics are somehow inseparable from morale and motivation. The ship, with its crew and its routines, its rule book, its pedagogy and its logistics, is not only some metaphysical allegory of life (like the legendary Ship of Fools, or like Melville), it is an autoreferential allegory of filmmaking itself, and a representation of the dynamics and dilemmas of art today, of modernist art, one would think, rather than a postmodern Russian kind with which Sokurov seems to have little enough in common.

The modernist conquest of daily life and its temporalities indeed was an appropriation of hitherto unrecorded dimensions and details: the "universe in a grain of sand," Benjamin's "optical unconscious" of the habitual and the microscopic. Here however the central fact of death reorganizes such detail into a new temporality of the absurd, about which Sokurov himself has said: "my strongest belief is that the most complex and inconsistent circumstances which exist in anyone's life are always dissolved in everyday life, because each morning we begin by brushing our teeth and at night just fall with our face in the pillow, without having learned any better how to live." But the moments of daily life also distract us from their absurdity by virtue of the very necessity of living through them; or, in film, of watching them frame by frame on the screen without being able to speed up the process: thus, the son is bewildered by the fact of the father's death and the strangeness of the world and the daily life in which the latter died, but he must also go through the bureaucratic red tape and prepare the body for burial and is in that sense the allegorical representative of the viewing public itself as it sits through the films.

Yet this is not a daily life that belongs to any of Sokurov's characters. All are in exile: the soldiers on the Tajik border, Malianov in his central Asian town, Eva Braun in the Berghof, Lenin in Gorki, the son in *The Second Circle*, and the son of *Mother and Son*. But "exile" and "the absurd" are old words for past historical situations which do not quite suit this new one or correspond to Sokurov's representation of it either. What we witness over and over again in his images is in fact the representation of the inside of a situation of closure or helpless imprisonment whose outside is inaccessible yet constantly makes its presence felt as pressure and as strangeness.

It is tempting to interpret Sokurov's works in terms of that trauma theory and post-Lacanian melancholy which interests so many people today, and which seems to have replaced the ennui of the nineteenth century and the anxiety of the existential period. And there is certainly something plausible in this theoretical reference: "encrypted"[1] is above all, in my opinion, the dead boy in his first documentary *Maria*, the peasant youth we glimpse on horseback in the early footage and whom the later footage, ten years after, reveals to have been killed by a drunken truckdriver. The boy would have gone to school, his mourning family tells us, he would have had technical and professional training. This dead boy, far more than the dead father (of *The Second Circle*) or the dying mother (of *Mother and Son*) is the true place of mourning: he is the sons of those two other movies as well, alive in death and without their own lives. But he is above all Malianov, the one vibrant protagonist of Sokurov's films, and the fulfillment of what the dead boy might have become, had he lived.

And had communism lived as well, and fulfilled its promise to him and to Russia: for it is important not to reduce trauma theory to the merely psychological. Collective mourning is also at stake and historical tragedy is also a necessary dimension of this new affect. Malianov is the medical doctor the peasant boy might have become; and the melancholy of trauma theory is the resonance of the experience of defeat, as Lucien Goldmann already analyzed it in *The Hidden God* (1959), in which French classical tragedy is grasped as the expression of the Jansenists' failure to come to power as a class, and of their missed rendezvous with history. Russian melancholy is thus not only the tragedy of space, the distance from the center, the tedium of the provinces, it is also the tragedy of time—the passing of the Russia of expansion and the empire (as celebrated in *Russian Ark*), the passing of the Soviets as well and their heroic war, and even of Stalin (Churchill is quoted as saying, choosing his words carefully, that the latter will certainly have his page in the history books). The melancholy of Sokurov (born 1951), who lived through the

---

[1]   I take this notion from Nicolas Abraham and Maria Torok, *The Wolf Man's Magic Word: A Cryptonymy* (Minneapolis: University of Minnesota Press, 2005); and I associate Sokurov's figure here with Mahler's song, "Ich bin das Leben abgekommen," in which the dead boy, at heaven's gate, refuses to be turned away: itself a reminder of Rimbaud's *Enfance*—"il y a enfin, quand l'on a faim et soif, toujours quelqu'un qui vous chasse."

"era of stagnation" only to emerge into the current post-great-power Russia, is that of an Arctic routine in which cold-benumbed teenage Russian sailors watch American youth-culture beach movies for bemused distraction.

Days of Eclipse is once more paradigmatic of this situation, which it borrowed, with much modification, from the novel of the Strugatsky brothers called *A Billion Years to the End of the World* (*Definitely Maybe* in English). In the original science fiction a group of unrelated scientists are mysteriously disturbed and interrupted in their work by all kinds of fortuitous accidents, pleasurable distractions as well as annoyances or even warnings of various kinds. It transpires—we are led to understand—that the universe itself (the so-called Homeostatic Universe) is taking a host of unrelated yet analogously motivated precautions to break off scientific investigations which eventually (in the "billion years" of the title) will fatally lead to its own destruction.

Sokurov and Arabov have removed the science-fictional scaffolding and retained (and intensified) only the mysterious interruptions, in the face of which the various protagonists give up, commit suicide, get themselves shot by the army, retreat into a humdrum life without ambitions, witness enigmatic explosions, or simply leave town. Only Malianov himself remains true to his vocation (also a change from the novel), a persistence reinforced by the alleged experimental associations in his research between religious belief and physical resistance to disease, a belated version, no doubt, of the great modernist conception of the Absolute. What is however postmodern is the representation of the unrepresentable, namely the forces which impinge on our monad from the outside. The Strugatskys' theme was no doubt the shift from "hard" to "soft" totalitarianism, as in *The Second Martian Invasion*, where the new overlords deploy bribery and propaganda instead of the horrendous physical violence of Wells's first one. In the context of a now universal consumer society the role of the media thus designated will seem even more persuasive; but it would seem that globalization and Americanization in this sense is only indirectly Sokurov's central preoccupation in his historical films.

Is Sokurov then to be seen as the last modernist, the last great modernist auteur? If so, he is generationally very belated indeed, born decades after Parajanov or Tarkovsky (with whom it is always worth insisting that he has nothing in common) or still living filmmakers like Alexander Kluge; only Victor Erice and Béla Tarr share something of his untimeliness, and also—what Sokurov has in common with all these artists and what would seem to account for our lingering impression of a modernist survival—his commitment to the idea of "great art" and its autonomy. It is an idea and a value whose fundamental renunciation constitutes the postmodern. The latter, indeed, would seem to have sacrificed the eternal, and posterity, for the ephemerality of mass culture, for a devil's pact with the commercial, and for an integration into fashion and the most febrile attention to fads and marketable novelties, to the invention of new brand names and of a nostalgia sensibility comparable only to a neo-classicism two centuries earlier, capable of simulating all previous styles, including that of modernism itself.

But perhaps *The Sun* (2004), the third film in the Tetralogy, offers a kind of compromise with Hirohito's little dance in imitation of Charlie Chaplin, enormously popular in the Japan of the period, with whom the emperor himself bears some distant resemblance.

Its final film, however—a version of Goethe's *Faust* (2011)—is hard to classify, either in the so-called Tetralogy of Power, or in Sokurov's work as a whole. It reverses Goethe by having Mephistopheles lose the bet (he tells the instant, You are *nicht so schön*—not so beautiful, not worth delaying). Sokurov has given us one of the most repulsive Mephistopheleses on record, in the midst of a medieval village which packs the screen as oppressively as anything in his great contemporary Alexei Gherman, of whom this film may be taken as a kind of postmodern pastiche, if not a tribute.[2] Nor does this mature Faust need any rejuvenation: but homunculus is here if not the Empire, or Helen of Troy.[3] But the Tetralogy was never really about power, anyway, but about everyday impotence, even in the powerful. We are all condemned to the border of frontier patrol.

Perhaps this is why, after the relative failure of the ambiguous *Father and Son* (2003), in which the roles are reversed and it is

---

[2]   Pauline Kael is supposed to have said, on the occasion of John Travolta's scientology epic, *Battlefield Earth*, "If it's not the worst film I ever saw, then at least it's the ugliest." If one could modulate this judgment into a frisson of the sublime, something like that would express the awe one feels before Gherman's two final masterpieces, *Khroustaliov, My Car!* and *Hard to Be a God*, about which I hope to write something elsewhere.

[3]   For a more positive view of *Faust*, see Jeremi Szaniawski's remarkable *The Cinema of Alexander Sokurov* (New York: Wallflower, 2013).

the son who becomes the protagonist, the most joyous Sokurov is the one who reverts to pseudo-documentary in the more recent *Alexandra* (2007), in which both parents, along with the live or dead son, disappear, and it is the grandmother who visits her nephew's military camp in Chechnya. None of Sokurov's actors have ever been so mesmerizing and vibrant as Galina Vishnevskaya in this remarkable portrait.

Sokurov shares several features of the last high modernists, including the dilemmas of financing (see Godard, Kurosawa, Altman, and even the Soviets, if one understands that there the material difficulties of funding and distribution are in the West called "censorship"). The status of art in his works is first and foremost registered in the role played in it by music, whose presence in the soundtrack offers a perpetual counterpoint to the image. The Arctic commander is here rather disingenuous: I deal with present-day reality, he tries to tell us, by finding escape in long nineteenth-century Russian novels. Yet Chekhov, the central literary figure here, is scarcely long-winded; and it seems to me that these references have rather as their function the setting in place of a quasi-religious solemnity (on the order of Arnoldian "high seriousness"). In my opinion, it is no longer a question here of the religious mysticism that marks Tarkovsky's films; here, as elsewhere in the present period, and despite the religious obsessions that have so often gripped the Russian (and Russian-Jewish) soul, religion is to be grasped as a stand-in for the religion of art: the latter's smuggling past the anti-aesthetic atmosphere of post-modernity under the cover of something the neo-ethnic sensibilities of the present age are far more willing to tolerate.

It is also, in my opinion, the smuggling in of another theme and value which seemed to have disappeared from the Zeitgeist, namely nationalism. It does stand to reason that if art is to constitute an Absolute or a supreme value of some kind, it must also somehow express a whole people as such. What could a genuinely Russian art otherwise be, in a globalized or post-national situation? To be sure, religion (and language) can also sometimes serve as badges for some properly postmodern small-group ethos, but only if the latter is a minority. The great surviving modernist art however must bear within it some lingering sense of the nation and its destiny. So it is that Kluge's work (however ironic and formally postmodern) still rehearses the ambiguity of German history as such, and scans it for elements productive of a utopian future. So also Angelopolous (at least until his recent Balkan and regionalizing turn) was haunted by the trauma of the Greek civil war and its historical exceptionalism. Sokurov's elegies for the even more unique historical destinies of Russia, inseparable from his melancholia and his aestheticism, mark an uncommon and untimely artistic enclave within the global warming of an international postmodern public sphere.

Chapter 6

Dekalog as Decameron

It is always wise, when confronted with a mass frenzy of interpretation, to sober up on purely formal problems. I will therefore approach Kieślowski's philosophical enigmas by way of a little structural analysis, of the now old-fashioned kind. Actually, it is to the Russian Formalists that we owe what is perhaps the most dazzling narrative analysis in the canon. To begin with that would constitute an acknowledgement of the peculiar kinship of the episodes of the *Dekalog* with the short story as a form, radically different as they are in temporality and in plot resolution with the standard-length feature film, about which one does not want to decide whether its kinship lies with the novel or not, but which at least arouses very different generic expectations, which any perceived kinship with short-story form tends to frustrate (just as it is frustrated in another way by theatricality and the sense of the filmed play).

"The Hawk" is the shortest story in Boccaccio's *Decameron*: it tells the story of a very poor young nobleman, whose only possession is a hawk as legendary throughout the region as is his own skill in maneuvering it. Pining away for love of a neighboring heiress, he invites her to his modest dwelling. She accepts, because she has become fascinated by the stories about the hawk and the expertise of its owner. But he has had to serve the hawk to her for lunch, having no money for anything else.

It is one of the most fascinating stories in the archive, and not least because it is about fascination as such. If it seems to promise to reveal the very secret of the short story itself, this is probably accounted for by the fact that the central experience of the short story, namely chance—Goethe's *unerhörte Begebenheit*, or unparalleled event—is here for once internalized within the narrative as such, and motivated. Chance here suddenly becomes revealed as what people themselves do, as part of their destiny.

So this is what the Formalists said: "The Hawk" is a paradigm of the short-story genre in that it offers two distinct plotlines or centers: the hawk and the love-passion. But these are like the empty shells of the shill game: we think the telltale pebble is under the one; it is in reality under the other. The hawk unexpectedly passes from its plotline over into the other one where it becomes a dinner fowl. And this abrupt displacement unites the two plotlines, but against all probability: their sudden unification is the paradigmatic event of this genre, and after it happens, nothing more remains to be said.

Of course a great deal might still remain to be said in the way of interpretations: Is not the lover himself, all skin and bones and eternally fasting from love, indeed, devoured by it, is he not himself the bony carcass he serves up in honor of the noble lady? Or we could talk about thirdness, and the way in which the hawk makes a third in the process of producing a couple, and emblematizes the inevitable foreign body that intervenes to prevent any face-to-face immediacy, an absolute transparency of communication. Or we could relate the consumption of the hawk to the consumption of the tale itself, as though the author pined for his reader and found nothing better to give. We could talk about class dynamics, or we could talk about tragedy or fate. That is the flesh and feathers of the hawk, or as it were its vital uses and actions—the bare bones I take to be established in this classical structural analysis of the two narrative lines or series and the prestidigitation of their mutual substitution for one another.

It is this structure which we find again in the first episode of the *Dekalog*, where we confront two alternating lines, that of religion and that of science. At the center of this episode stands a computer, whose status has always surprised and fascinated me, in its strange formal isolation as some postmodern technological artifact, in the midst of a still essentially modern or even nineteenth-century life-world. (In hindsight, we may recall that diagnosis of the Soviet collapse that highlighted the failure to computerize their economic system.) At any rate, mysterious green light and enigmatic unprogrammed messages underscore the duality of this technological object, which in its Polish setting speaks with a strange and isolated voice from out of the silence of an otherwise old-fashioned and seemingly familiar bourgeois context. The computer here speaks with a strangely silent yet urgent piercing voice, much as God is supposed to have spoken out of the burning bush. The computer is the voice of science, absolute, like Lacan's *sujet supposé savoir*; no wonder the father imagines it to be God. And as for the other line, the boy's vague religious and metaphysical questionings, one has to suppose that they simply reflect standard primal mysteries and sexual confusion, particularly in the situation of parental separation. The boy is then the swap or substitution between these two lines, which officially identify themselves as science and religion.

I must say that, although, like everything in the *Dekalog*, every moment here is mesmerizing, this is for me a bad beginning. I don't like the religiosity, although I am willing to agree that it is far worse in the later films. But I very strongly object to the author's decision here to kill the boy: and this is certainly the author's doing, and not God's. Lionel Abel floated the weirdest theory, many years ago, that when a character is made to die in a fictional narrative, the author ought to be made to assume responsibility for his death, for it is the author who is guilty of the murder. As far as God is concerned, one need only quote Sartre or Camus (I don't remember which), who said that God, having invented death in the first place, was the first murderer.[1] Yet on some more restricted level, I think we have all had the feeling, faced with certain kinds of plots in which things could go either way, that there was something intolerably arbitrary about the decision to choose the tragic ending (or a happy ending either). There are some plots—the good ones, perhaps?—in which the ending has some real inevitability about it, and by this I don't necessarily only mean death (happy endings can also be inevitable, as in Jane Austen). Thus, in retrospect, it was clearly inevitable that Boccaccio's protagonist kill his hawk. But for Kieślowski or Piesiewicz (his screenwriter) to kill off the little boy seems somehow unforgivable, although I am willing to entertain the possibility that my very indignation is the aesthetic effect desired here: the substitution of some properly aesthetic transgression for religious ones that are no longer operative.

At any rate, my thesis lies elsewhere and is more formal, namely that Kieślowski is essentially a short-story writer; where his films, which constantly, as we shall see, push the limits of that form,

---

[1]   The published scenario in fact offers a naturalistic or scientific explanation for the disparity between the father's prediction and the temperature of the lake: what is significant is that this explanation has been removed from the film.

manage to transcend those limits altogether, they are, for me at least, much less interesting (and also far more "philosophical"). Thus my canon would include his wonderful early work *Personnel* (1975), any number of documentaries (in particular *Curriculum Vitae*, from the same year), the official first "fiction film" *Amator* (mistranslated as *Camera Buff,* 1979), and *White*, the only Polish sequence in the so-called color trilogy and in my opinion the best of the three. But in this last the color motif does not function as a metaphysical clue or an incitement to interpretation. Rather, it becomes an ambiguous word, which, like a pun, or Saussure's paragram (or indeed Raymond Roussel's "method") gathers up the various substitutable plotlines into a single portmanteau figure: *mariage blanc* (unconsummated marriage), *nuit blanche* (sleepless night), the blank of a blank cartridge, and so forth.

The other color films all express the perplexity of the Polish director in the new situation of Europe, or in other words after the end of communism, the Cold War, and "dissidence" itself. *The Double Life of Veronique* is paradigmatic of these works and their fundamental form-problem, in the way in which it gives us two versions—East and West—of everything, following a principle of narrative variation we have yet to examine.

As for *Camera Buff*—the hawk that hangs across its opening shot is almost too coincidental for my purposes here—it is not easy for the foreigner to decode. Encrypted messages make up the relationship of such works to the ever-changing day-by-day situation in which Poles then lived and which would need no explanation for the Polish public, while remaining opaque to nonparticipants. But in one sense this is the very theme of *Camera Buff* itself: a politics in which what looks like evil, that is to say, bureaucratic abuses, corruption, inefficiency, is in reality good and a positive community program. My understanding is that it was precisely in this way—at least in the period in question—that Polish communism and the party functioned: paying lip service to Soviet models while pursuing its own program behind the scenes—in this case, as the director of the plant explains, neglecting to fulfill a quota which would in fact have resulted in the unemployment of several hundred workers. In this kind of reversal (which is of course formally the short-story narrative mechanism I have already referred to), the director, who has come before us as the very essence of the bureaucrat and (what is worse for intellectuals) the censor, is suddenly unmasked as the agent of collective wisdom and the good of the community; it is a reversal familiar in the West in what I'm tempted to call the Anglo-Catholic model of the spy story, as in Graham Greene, where the wicked Stasi agent turns out to epitomize the good, while the naive, well-intentioned Westerner (generally an American and a Protestant) turns out to bring nothing but evil and destruction with him. But in these Western works, the emphasis is on ethics and the ethical binary as such—the way good turns into evil and vice versa—and the ethical abstraction finds itself grounded, not in the sociopolitical but in religion. They offer as it were a reverse image of the concrete Second-World raw material, and may be said to bear the traces of Second-World influence (nothing of the sort is detectable in the older Nazi-based spy stories, for example).

I want to posit a specific Second World form here, something one might call the dialectics of the Comintern, and which one finds in the West at certain moments of Sartre's work and belatedly, but full-blown, in Peter Weiss's *Äesthetik des Widerstands*. This dialectic draws its paradoxes from the incommensurability of the collective and the individual, the politics of the party and the personal intentions of its members or opponents. In Poland it seems to me very centrally developed, with great originality, in that filmmaker deliberately placed at the center of Kieślowski's *Camera Buff*, I mean Krzysztof Zanussi, whose subtly ambiguous conversations rehearse paradoxes which perhaps have their equivalent, but only in the realm of love and pure subjectivity, in the West, in the films of Eric Rohmer. But this is only a passing phase of Kieślowski's own work, which clearly enough evolves with the Polish '80s, even though it continues to remain ambiguous in this good and formal sense.

Kieślowski himself foregrounds what he thinks of as his central theme in the title of his second film, *Przypadek*, which does not mean blind chance but simply chance as such. For is not chance always blind, and what would non-blind chance mean? These are the kinds of stupid questions we don't want to find ourselves entangled in, particularly since they lead us away from the essential formal meaning of this theme. You will remember that the film offers three versions of a life: the first as a party member, the second as a dissident and a Catholic, the third as someone who avoids either commitment, but in an honorable way. The theme of chance is supposed to be linked to the protagonist's catching or missing the Warsaw train (and if you like, to the completely gratuitous ending to which you are welcome to apply all the things I said about the arbitrary ending of the first episode of the *Dekalog*).

I call chance a theme here rather than a concept: this does not strike me as a philosophical film (whatever that might be, but perhaps Zanussi's work qualifies); and I also tend to feel that philosophically the very notion of chance is bound up with its opposite, namely providence, and that you can't really have the one without the other. Is chance then related to contingency as such—for example the rabbit falling out of the sky in the *Dekalog*, or the car-wash rags similarly falling out of nowhere in the episode about murder? But maybe contingency (certainly a medieval concept) also has to be staged against a background of meaning; and I have always found it very interesting, in connection with the existential sense of contingency, that Sartre relates the concept to his early movie-going experiences as a child. Everything in films was meaningful (even when the filmmaker tried to introduce something contingent); and therefore, Sartre says, when you came out of the theater you were all the more intensely aware of the fundamental non-meaningfulness of the real street and the real world.

Be that as it may I want to argue that chance here has a functional role as the operator of variation. Chance is the formal peg upon which the variant outcomes, the variant lives, the three variant tales, are strung: chance converts the limitless and formless area of sheer possibility into the structurally constrained and delimited number of variations; it gives form and number to possibility, carrying it even beyond sheer potentiality into a precise combination scheme. And this is where our generic topic of the short-story form returns: for without the structural variation achieved through chance, each life is simply a set of unrepeatable empirical facts. Indeed, there is no life or destiny anymore but simply experience, of whatever kind— personal, political, historical, professional. Without variation we are simply in the world of being. The mechanism of chance now allows us to transform that incomparable realm of experience into so many alternative short stories or *récits*. But these are stories that are as it were produced laterally, in place of each other, synchronically, rather than one after the other. It is as if the short-story form suddenly developed some new structural dimension: a machine, a combinational apparatus, that not only produced narrative differences, but differentiation within narrative identity. It is difficult to work this out theoretically, but what I want to show is simply that with the theme of chance and its effects of variation we also touch the matter of the short story, but from a rather different formal angle.

In fact, in *Chance* Kieślowski does not want to give us a novel, the ontology of a life or a situation; he wants to offer us an anthology of tales. The gimmick is very specialized, to be sure; and like related ones, whether adorned with hyperintellectual structuralist theoretical slogans or simply taken as an "experiment," it would not seem very promising. Indeed, the next film, *Bez konca* (*Without End* rather than *No End*) fails in its effort to produce variations by way of a ghost: which should also have given us three possibilities—what the tale would have been like had the protagonist lived; what it was like after his death; and what it was also like when he was neither dead nor alive but always present as a ghost. The variations are then— in anticipation of the *Dekalog*—organized around a trial: which is naturally enough the form most suitable to structurally precise and delimited alternate outcomes. There is certainly some wonderful acting here, and it's good that Aleksander Bardini gets the chance to return in force in the *Dekalog*; but the film's incoherence heralds that of *Blue* and *Red* later on; and you can probably already guess what I think of the ending. But now let's try to confront the *Dekalog* itself, which is surely Kieślowski's true masterpiece, and something without equivalent anywhere in world film. Is there any way to deal with it without simply taking up one episode after another?

Well, he himself does, in a whole variety of ways. I had originally thought of making a comparison between this short-story collection (as it were) and Altman's *Short Cuts* of 1993, based on a number of stories by Raymond Carver. But the principles are completely different: Altman's work has often been Dickensian in the formal sense I alluded to earlier, in which crosscutting between various narratives produces an entanglement of plots (in Dickens also motivated by serialization): the short stories lose their autonomy as separate episodes and become a kind of totality which moves forward towards some final complex interrelationship (in the case of *Short Cuts*, the earthquake, but many other things as well). This marks the tying together of all these narrative lines and is a very specific aesthetic effect, which we find selected on the basis of themes or motifs in Joyce's *Ulysses*, where virtually everything reappears in the Nighttown sequence. The same is true in Fassbinder's *Alexanderplatz*, with its long and nightmarish recapitulation; and oddly enough it also happens at the end of the trilogy, in *Red*, where any number of individual destinies shoulder each other and come to their ends in the sinking of the ferry boat.

But this is not at all the organizing principle of the *Dekalog*; and although for many of us the final stamp-collecting sequence may be the most glorious and comic moment of the whole series, it certainly does not tie anything together. Perhaps indeed the motif of the stamp collection may serve as a veiled comment on precisely this lack of closure: the individual stories are collected together like so many precious stamps, of varying value; but then the entire collection vanishes without totalization or conclusion. When you are robbed, indeed, there is always that strange feeling that something more ought to happen; the lost object's destiny ought at least to come to your knowledge, the story ought at least to be concluded. But nothing is there, even the lack or absence is somehow missing, and you wander about, confused and somehow incomplete; the very event of the robbery has itself somehow been confiscated.

Still, there are some other principles of organization that ought to be mentioned. The Man in the Macintosh, for example: this is the meaningless designation for an enigmatic figure whose appearance throughout *Ulysses* is noted but never clarified. Is it the author, or some mysterious angel; an IRA gunman; the reader; an English spy? We never know, and no one has ever identified this character: so that we are obliged to fall back on a purely formal description, namely, that the Man in the Macintosh is the very allegorical personification of interrelationship and repetition itself, the anthropomorphization of the urban totality, the being-seen of the whole. In Kieślowski, an analogous figure appears warming himself at a fire by the frozen lake, carrying something through the woods, riding a bicycle. The important interpretive question is then whether this figure marks the presence of destiny (which as we have seen is the same as chance) or whether, as I have been suggesting, he marks the interrelationship of all these destinies, a very different matter indeed and a formal one rather than a metaphysical signal. But what I am calling formal here, and what I clearly prefer as a reading, is itself the reflex of the social as such: in this sense, this particular genius loci can be thought to be the dialectical counterpart of the apartment complex, which itself stands for the city and ultimately for urban society as such.

I think that what in Balzac is called "le retour des personnages" is a little different from this: to glimpse in one episode a character from another one is a kind of supplementary bonus of pleasure, as Freud liked to call secondary elaboration. It reminds us that all these episodes belong together, something less imperative in the *Dekalog* than in the color trilogy, where the brief incursion into the French courtroom (in the middle of a speech in Polish) comes as a shock which at the same time reassures us about the deeper interrelationship of the three episodes (but which will only be definitively confirmed at the end of *Red*, with the tragic *fait divers* I have already mentioned). But these are, as it were, reassurances about the author's intentions and his trustworthiness: so he does mean them to be interrelated after all, we think. And otherwise they can simply count as chance: but a chance that means nothing, that marks another narrative no doubt; but that mainly contributes to the surface appearance of the whole, namely the impression and the illusion that it is about chance in the first place.

I want rather to underscore a different organizational principle, one also based on lies as it were, or if you prefer on illusion; but an illusion of an altogether different type. This is the very frame itself, which encourages us to think that these ten episodes are somehow to be thought through in terms of the Ten Commandments, that is, somehow as modern versions of the biblical injunctions—whereas as everyone ends up admitting, the connections are for the most part tenuous indeed and the search for parallels a truly frustrating and unrewarding task. Even Joyce's *Odyssey* parallels are more satisfying and fully executed than this: yet even this comparison may be misleading to the degree that in *Ulysses* two narrative lines can be set in juxtaposition with each other, whereas here we have the formal disjunction of a narrative on the one hand and a law on the other.

What can the relationship between two such different forms of discourse possibly be in the first place? It is clearly a different one from, say, the way in which a maxim (like those of La Rochefoucauld) is somehow illustrated (or disproven) by a story; or the way a story proves to have a moral, as in a fable or a parable. This is then the moment to mention a neglected work I consider to be one of the great books of modern literary theory, namely André Jolles's *Einfache Formen* (Simple forms), which first appeared in 1929 and has to this day still not been translated into English. Jolles's premise is that there exists a certain number of simple or primitive speech genres—he analyzes nine of them—which serve as something like the kernel or core of more complex and artificial literary genres. They are as it were the most fundamental gestures of language itself, and like Heidegger's etymologies vouchsafe a glimpse into older and simpler forms of life (thereby sounding an ambiguously primitivist note in the historical context in which both theories appeared). His first forms seem already fairly elaborated: legend, saga, myth; but then we find riddles, proverbs, fait divers, and jokes (or witticisms, as in Freud it is difficult to distinguish the two in German), alongside the equally elaborated fairy tale. But it is the ninth form that interests us here, besides being relatively original and unusual in this double sequence: this is what Jolles calls the "Kasus," and is as he himself admits a hitherto relatively uncodified figure to which we are normally accustomed only in the specialized context of the law. Indeed, the trial, if it is to be thought of as a more elaborated literary form, may be thought to have as its simple form, or its primitive kernel, very precisely the *casus* as that mode in which we compare an anecdotal narrative with an equally reduced and simplified legal injunction. Nor is it merely a question of weighing evidence or deducing motivation: there is some first question to be resolved, of universals and exceptions; as to whether the act falls under the purview of the law in question; even whether the law in question has any validity in the first place. I quote Jolles:

> In the casus itself the form derives from a standard for the evaluations of various types of conduct, but in its fulfillment there is also immanent a question as to the value of the norm in question. The existence, validity and extension of various norms is to be weighed, but this very appraisal itself includes the question: according to what measurement or what norm is the evaluation to be performed?[2]

As in the fable, two types of discourse are juxtaposed; but in the more familiar form we attempt to subsume the one under the other, whereas here the two radically different types of discourse interrogate each other and call each other into question. I want to see the presence of the legal in Kieślowski—the court cases, the judgments in *Red*, and so forth—not as some primacy of moral or legal judgment, but rather the other way around, as projections of this more fundamental speech form which is the casus itself, where what we call judgment is the interrelationship of two types of discourse, each

---

2 *Einfache Formen* (Tübingen: Niemeyer, 1930), p. 190.

of which remains to be determined: is there an event or a fact, an act; and is there a law?

Still, this line of approach would seem to lead us back to the standard interpretation of the *Dekalog* in terms of the Ten Commandments. I mean it to do something rather different, for which the comparison with Joyce and the *Odyssey* parallel remains fruitful in a different way. I want to argue that these parallels have no content, but simply designate closure and uniformity. Homer lends Joyce a specific number of episodes, after which his book can be considered as finished and closed: it is this famous thing, about which so much that is sensible and so much that is idiotic has already been said, namely that the form resists and allows a genuine free play of invention within and against itself, a freedom that would not have been possible if everything and anything had been permitted in the first place.

Here, in the *Dekalog*, I think we can be more precise than that: the fact that these are all commandments means that they are considered to be all alike, and of the same form: they thereby solicit a reading which is programmed in advance—the specific form of attention and interrogation determined by the *casus*—and at one and the same time a constant comparison back and forth between episodes considered to be more or less "the same" in their general form and the type of meaning they are supposed to carry. Meanwhile the traditional cultural and scriptural fact of "ten" commandments gives us closure, and assigns a term and a limit to Kieślowski's work. It does not have to be indeterminate, let alone infinite—ten is enough, the task is completed, and so forth: but this limit is more powerful than Boccaccio's traditional numbers, since it is also doubled by history.

It is this double structure—closure and formal replication—which gives the *Dekalog* its fascination and launches a rich and inexhaustible interpretive process: for however finite the interpretation of any given episode may be, it always ends up in an activity of comparison which can virtually by definition never know a limit (and at the same time never arrive at any truly satisfying solutions either, which is another way of saying the same thing).

Let's try it anyhow, and begin with the obvious. This is a film or a series about daily life, but about daily life of a very special sort. I am tempted to say (however anachronistically) that this is a middle-class daily life led by professional or managerial people. The two taxi drivers are the exception; but, as mobile as the camera itself, they do not tend to give us any sense of working-class life either. Moreover, seen from the standpoint of the various apartments in the complex, and despite the yuppie overtones of skiing and mountain-climbing and the like, this seems a rather old and stable, a genuinely traditional kind of bourgeois life. But we are, after all, in a preeminently political country, and in a period in which convulsive political struggles are taking place and will continue. None of that enters the series; the only political note is the ancient politics of resistance to the German occupation in episode 8. Not a trace of socialism and its problems here, but also not a sign of the heroic stereotype of the dissident, as it was galvanizing an anti-communist Europe during this same period. I believe that all this has been excluded symbolically by the first episode, where we have two disembodied forces pitted against each other starkly: science and religion. Surely these are the ideological forces appealed to politically on the one hand by Marxism and on the other by the anti-party movements. These two forces turn into each other in effect and each deconstructs the other if you will, with both eliminated in the process in the first episode. This inaugural act of the series thus removes politics altogether, in either of its forms: no heroism of protest, no dialectic of the party. What is thereby opened up is an appearance of bourgeois life and its temporality; but only an appearance: for this utopia is in reality that of socialism itself, it is a Second-World utopia, which has here found expression thanks to the bracketing of the political as such. It is the utopian daily life of the future returning to us in the guise of Eastern European middle-class life in the past. I will briefly quote a remark of Slavoj Žižek about this phenomenon (which deserves to be examined and quoted at much greater length):

> What we are dealing with here is the old structural notion of the gap between the space and the positive content that fills it in: although, as to their positive content, the communist regimes were mostly a dismal failure, generating terror and misery, they at the same time opened up a certain space, a space of Utopian expectation which, among other things, enabled us to measure the failure of really existing socialism itself.[3]

---

3   Slavoj Žižek, "Suicide of the Party," *New Left Review* I/238 (November–December 1999), p. 46.

Kieślowski in the *Dekalog* manages to project the latent utopian content of bourgeois life itself. It is as though an essentially nineteenth-century cultural tradition and mode of life had been lifted out of its own historical infrastructure into a different one, characterized above all by the silence of the commodity form. No doubt, the *Dekalog* gives us glimpses of the arrival of the new image culture, the new commodification; but its interiors strangely express a kind of repressed utopian content of nineteenth-century bourgeois life which surfaces for one last moment in actually existing socialism (as a ghostly parallel to Lukács's recommendation of the incorporation of "great bourgeois or critical realism") before being eradicated East and West alike, and swept away by globalization and postmodernity, by late capitalism as such.

Perhaps this fleeting utopian glimpse has something to do with what Deleuze calls virtuality: if so, then we must grasp the latter's operations in a very peculiar space indeed. In fact, I tend to agree with those who have concluded in some exasperation that the *Dekalog* has little enough to do with the original Ten Commandments but very much to do with the matter of lying[4] (not particularly mentioned in them, as I recall). On the other hand, Lacan thought the biblical injunctions all had to do with the emergence of the Symbolic Order, or in other words language itself, where lying and the very possibility of lying plays a primordial role.[5] Eco also observed that speaking is not the precondition of lying as rather the other way round: you can't speak unless you can lie.[6] At any rate, in the *Dekalog* it is precisely lying that enables a kind of Deleuzian virtuality. Lying produces multiple narratives, the possibility of narrative variations and the coexistence of fictive or imaginary alternative story lines.

Thus at once the second episode presents us with a wonderful *casus* and a dramatic if pseudo-Solomonic judgment: the heroine will have her lover's child if her husband's illness is considered fatal; and have an abortion if he is likely to live. The doctor's lie combines the narratives into a new one, which is unexpectedly successful.

---

4   See for example Annette Insdorf, *Double Lives, Second Chances* (New York: Hyperion, 1999).

5   Jacques Lacan, *Le Seminaire*, Livre VII ("L'éthique de la psychanalyse") (Paris: Seuil, 1986). See also Kenneth Reinhard and Julia Lupton, "The Subject of Religion: Lacan and the Ten Commandments," in *diacritics* 33: 2 (Summer 2003).

6   Umberto Eco, *The Search for the Perfect Language* (London: Blackwell, 1997).

The salvational motif proves that you can and must play God: and that lying is a rich force of invention and of creativity. And perhaps this power of the lie sheds retrospective light on *Camera Buff*, where the will to tell the truth is destructive in a more than Nietzschean sense.

But now I find myself wondering whether I have not painted myself into a corner I would rather not be in: for one of the motives of praise with which I wanted to conclude here was that, at least in the *Dekalog* we were spared the usual postmodern glorification of art and aesthetics (normally accompanied by this or that religious motif) which tends to mark the absence of concrete content of the worst kinds of contemporary artistic production (and which can of course also be found ad nauseam in Kieślowski's final trilogy). But, it will be objected, is not the motif of lying itself a kind of celebration of art in the form of fictionality? And does it not precisely emerge in what you have called a utopian space opened up by the exclusion of that concrete social content we call politics?

This is at least certainly true enough for the next two episodes, in which narrative multiplicity is achieved by the coexistence with a dream life, with a fictive existence either told to oneself (as with the incest-prone father and daughter of number 4) or the mythomaniac temptations of the taxi driver's old flame in 3. These episodes tend to tilt powerfully towards the purely subjective and its seemingly shapeless fungibility, held only in check and given precise definition by the requirement that it offer a narrative alternative and not merely a vague daydream.

The episode of the false mother (number 7) makes this particular formal issue a good deal clearer: for the grandmother's alternate narrative (that she is the real mother and not her hapless and maternally incompetent daughter) is socially objective: that is to say, it is a public lie in which everyone else believes, and not some mere figment. As for the holocaust episode (8) and the impotence narrative (9), in these cases narrative options take the form of historical mysteries, or the reconstruction of missing causalities; the Jewish child was refused, not because the couple suddenly changed its mind and became more hard-hearted, but because of a crisis in the resistance network and the possibility of a traitor. In 9 the husband believes the wife has taken a lover because of his incurable impotence, whereas she had the lover beforehand, and thus, I'm tempted to say, in reality there was nothing personal about this passing infidelity.

That leaves us with three missing exhibits: the two central ones, important enough to be extracted and turned into feature films in their own right: on death and on love—the murder sequence and the voyeur episode; and finally the last one, the stamp collection.

In episode 5 it seems clear enough that the real narrative option at stake here is not whether the taxicab driver lives or not, nor even the struggle between capital punishment and something else, but rather the alternate life that might have been possible had the boy's little sister lived. A classic short-story-form chiasmus is then set in effect where the narrative virtuality is transferred from the victim (and also from the lawyer, the third party in all this) to the killer. It is a painful, moving, maybe even sentimental casus.

As for six, the voyeurism episode at least has the merit of doing away with the opposition between love and sex. The boy loves his fantasy image because of the sex involved: this is a case in which pornography has the most uplifting and morally inspiring, even spiritual results. The swap here is that the victim becomes the aggressor, making the most offensive physical advances to the boy, while the latter, the pervert and aggressor, is the truly pure and innocent victim of this aggression. Meanwhile the "rear-window" situation would seem to place this episode squarely within aesthetic reflexivity, as an exploration of the camera and of film and the latter's exhibitionistic immorality: where does that leave us as the audience of this television series?

From the dead son to the dead father: the sons of the final episode indeed can stand as two very alternate narratives, into which pop or punk music intervenes with something of the old meaning of bourgeois or Western degeneracy it had in Soviet times (as Perry Anderson has observed, the lyrics invite us to break virtually every commandment on the books). The old utopian bourgeois or Victorian traditions of the apartment building are coming to an end; the uniqueness of People's Poland is about to give way to the unknown quantities of some new market-oriented Europe. This is the point at which the discovery of the dead father's narrative is climactic. For it is not only the discovery of a secret life, nor even of the value of objects to which you had never given a thought before. Parenthesis: following Stanley Cavell's principle that what you remembered wrong in a film is part of the film, I will make a confession; namely, that my favorite part of this episode is something that does not take place in it, namely a misrecollection on my part, in which the two sons go back to the dealer who has managed to appropriate the Penny Black by guile and misrepresentation. He says calmly, I was expecting you; I didn't really expect to keep it; I only wanted to have it in my possession for a few hours, have the enjoyment of it for a day or so, temporary or provisional private property: it strikes me still as an interesting alternate version.

At any rate what the sons really find is a whole other world, a secret society within this one, unnamable, unmentionable to outsiders, ignored by the great social institutions; it is like a secret league of foot-fetishists from all over Eastern Europe, or like the child pornography rings hidden away in the Internet. This is the secret society of philatelists: it has its classes and its gradations, its officers, president, local dignitaries, and the like. It also has its traditions, its history, its legend: the father is one of those, a dead partisan, a hero of philately even in his own lifetime. This is the older utopian world hidden away and promised within the dissolution of the old one, the supersession of individual crises and stories by the collective. It is a joyous and salvational ending, with something of the gaiety of an Irish wake—something it was worth losing the stamp collection for.

We have tried, in this discussion, to minimize the importance of metaphysical or religious interpretations as much as possible. But in conclusion we must confront the issue of ethics as such: Can it be so easily evaded as an interpretative category? And are not the various suspended endings so many Brechtian appeals to choice and to an essentially ethical form of judgment? I would prefer to follow Slavoj Žižek in identifying the ethical in Hegel's or even in Lacan's sense; from which it would follow that the fundamental theme of these films is not ethics but rather morality: or, if you prefer, that we have here to do with the critique of morality by ethics itself (rather than the expression of any ethical position in its own right). This is in fact the very space of Kieślowski's politics as such, restricted to precisely this ethical critique and thereby marked historically by the Eastern European situation in the 1980s—the dialectic of "honesty," for example, the ambiguity of dissidence but also of communism itself, and so forth. But this particular situation comes to an end in 1989, and is therefore no longer available, either as theme or situation, for the later works, which must transform it into transnational paradoxes.

As for the form, it emerges from the construction of chance, from the restructuring of daily life into coincidence: that is to say, into enigmas that solicit interpretation without confirming it. The enigmas are those of narrative variation, of the proliferation of alternate narrative lines and worlds (a "virtuality" perhaps itself enabled if not generated by a historical moment in which alternate economic systems still existed).

PART THREE

ADAPTATION AS EXPERIMENT
IN THE POSTMODERN

Chapter 7

Eurotrash or *Regieoper?*

The opening of a new Danish production of Wagner's *Tannhäuser* would not be the occasion for extended theoretical comment were it not for a worldwide Wagner revival, in which the sheer number of new stagings of Wagnerian music dramas has overtaken, we are told, the revivals of virtually all now-classic twentieth-century (or "modern") operas. Perhaps the career of its director, Kasper Bech Holten, director of the Royal Danish Opera at the age of twenty-seven, and soon to join the new cultural globalization of internationally mobile conductors, virtuosi, multilingual actors, and soccer players, can add an additional perspective to what looks like the development of a new historical phenomenon, which neither Wagner's genius nor Holten's talent are sufficient to explain.

Tannhäuser may indeed seem to offer a merely peripheral occasion for examining such developments, since it was something of a transitional work in Wagner's own career, and one whose libretto was flawed in ways that tormented Wagner throughout his life. Indeed, a week or so before his death he told Cosima, I owe the world a *Tannhäuser*; this, when after the bitter disappointment of the first Bayreuth *Ring* he had decided to abandon opera for purely orchestral compositions. But *Tannhäuser* (first performed in Dresden before the revolution, but still a "romantic opera" and not a "music drama") remained unfinished business: an amalgam of two medieval sources which was too big for its rather conventional and rigid theatrical form (choruses, theatrical set pieces, lack of stage machinery, summarily reported offstage action), the space for traditional arias not yet effaced by the theory and practice of the leitmotif, yet not really serving any longer for full-blown Bellini-style virtuosity.

There are some foreshadowings: the singing contest between the *Minnesänger* will be fully realized, for example, only in its more bourgeois form by *Die Meistersinger*: and Tannhäuser's prizewinning song will never quite take on the centrality of Walther's, even though it exemplifies the autoreferentiality, the music about music, which is always implicit in opera and lurking beneath the surface of the form.

The great song duel of the Minnesänger on the Wartburg—a seemingly legendary event supposed to have taken place around 1216—is attributed to real historical figures (with the exceptions of Tannhäuser himself), and was fictionalized by E. T. A. Hoffmann well before Wagner. The other medieval legend combined with this one in the opera has to do with humans enticed into magical or diabolical realms from which they are then unable to escape: in this case the realm of Venus, who was absorbed into Christian culture along with the other pagan deities, there to be transformed into a demonic agency (as documented by Jean Seznec in a classic work). The Venusberg—mons veneris!—into which poor Tannhäuser has been tempted and which henceforth holds him in thrall, is just such a pagan space, which inspires horror in the Christian subjects of the aboveground daylight world, very much including the court of Eisenach. This is clearly a first and virtually overt dramatization of what is today clinically (and comically) termed sex addiction: and of course it also slips effortlessly into the conventional romantic motif of the two lovers—dark and fair, but more significantly physical and spiritual, whore and mother, prostitute and wife-and-family. For Tannhäuser knows a pure and spiritual love for Elisabeth, the sister of the Elector Heinrich and the patroness of the song duels, as it were the judge and poetic emblem of *Minne*—courtly love—itself. In Wagner this purer face of love (which has its carnal one in Lady Venus) is endowed (as is the latter) with its own characteristic music, and yet that music is also identified with the pilgrims and the Christian religion in general in such a way that we confront three positions rather than two, and everything is thereby irredeemably confused and confounded.

This was surely one of the flaws that bedeviled Wagner in hindsight: for it is not at all clear why the spiritual purity associated with Elisabeth, and with courtly love generally, should be identified with the church and with religion as such. The sex drive, and whatever relief (chastity, sublimation) or release from it, are libidinal affects which do not particularly require the Western theological ideology of sin and redemption for their justification. When the drama of erotic temptation is repeated in the much-later *Parsifal*—where Wagner in his old age takes a decided position for chastity—the religious solemnity need not be read as Christian at all, and many believers have refused to acknowledge the work as theologically orthodox. Wagner certainly meant it to have a ritualistic and cultic flavor: it was not supposed to be performed anywhere but in its temple, Bayreuth; and yet—and despite his professed anti-Semitism—he was perfectly content to have it premiered by a Jewish conductor.

What is more interesting about the relationship between *Tannhäuser* and *Parsifal* is their deeper and less visible kinship through the sources. Wagner certainly knew the Hoffmann novella, where the demonic poet-figure is called Heinrich von Ofterdingen, a name also consecrated by Novalis's novel: indeed Tannhäuser is occasionally addressed as Heinrich by careless colleagues in Wagner's opera. Hoffmann's poet is not, however, tormented by sex, but rather by the quality of his verse, and appeals to a magician to endow him with heightened talents, ultimately derived from the devil. This magician is named Klingsor, and Wagner will transport him to Spain in *Parsifal* where, as a fallen Grail-knight, he exercises his powers of temptation in the magic Moorish garden that explicitly offers sexual bliss; and which Parsifal, in his innocence and purity, his refusal of temptation, reduces to dust. Klingsor's garden in *Parsifal* and the Venusberg in *Tannhäuser* have much in common, including extraordinary music; but the opposition is more convincing and dramatic in the later music drama, where Klingsor has paid for his magic by castrating himself—much as Alberich does, albeit symbolically, in the *Ring*.

I would also hazard another, more "scholarly" hypothesis, which bears on Wagner's development in a different way. In the early 1840s, the German operatic tradition was inauspicious, and the outstanding contemporary practitioner of opera anywhere was still Bellini, whom Wagner admired. The motif of selling one's soul to the devil, however, was at the center of the one truly successful German opera of the period, namely Weber's *Freischütz*, with its deep Teutonic forests, magic bullets, hunters and their competitions, although here shooting, not singing. This work not only set a glorious musical example for Wagner, it also pointed the way to that use of Germanic material which he will so triumphantly exploit later on. I suggest then that the Hoffmann novella is the key to the meaning of Wagner's synthesis in *Tannhäuser*; Venus and the motif of paganism in reality conceal the ur-Germanic motif of the devil which, given Weber (and to be sure Goethe's *Faust*), Wagner could not use without an obvious confession of unoriginality. At the same time the link inspires further work in the Teutonic vein, whose variety will become apparent in all of Wagner's successive works.

So how does Wagner handle the representation of the spell of Venus? The addition of a Venusberg ballet for the Paris production (1860) is too well-known a story to be repeated here: the Jockey Club audience of the Second Empire required a ballet in the final act; Wagner told the authorities—the production had been ordered by the Emperor himself—that they would have it in the first act or not at all. The performance was a failure, but one that vouchsafed Wagner European fame and ourselves Baudelaire's great essay. True: Wagner and the traditions of operatic ballet go poorly together, and productions of *Tannhäuser* are about as successful in solving the problem as are those of *Parsifal*'s flower maidens in Act Two, orgies apparently requiring lots of dancing.

But now we have Kasper Bech Holten's solution, prodigious as always. We are not in a dimly lit (but reddish) grotto with, "in the distance," as Wagner specifies, "a bluish lake" filled with "the swimming figures of Naiads"; but rather in the interior of a large mansion with many different staircases, whose foreground is furnished only by a writing desk at which Tannhäuser is at work. I should pause here to underscore the peculiarity of this "reading," which seems to require the doubling of Tannhäuser's musical vocation with that of another art, namely writing. This seems to be a favorite conceit with Holten, as we shall see, which we should perhaps none too quickly associate with the old sixties proto-structuralist thematics of *écriture*, even though the troubadours were poets as well as composers and Holten's Tannhäuser is clearly a *graphomane* as well as a performer. Holten's reading of the opera's final act testifies that the hero keeps journals and writes narratives fully as much as he does verses. I am tempted to generalize this doubling in the light of the twenty-nine-year-old Katharina Wagner's sensational Bayreuth *Meistersinger* a few years later, in which the competing singers are also staged as painters, as though it were necessary to superimpose several arts or media in order to disengage the plot from an old kind of opposition between tradition and genius.

Holten does, however, retain Wagnerian orthodoxy to the extent of insisting on the fundamentally sexual inspiration of Tannhäuser's art, exaggerating it only by the seeming affirmation that it is solely under Venus's spell that he can write anything at all.

Be that as it may, however, what interests us is first and foremost the set. Frau Venus's red wig suggests that we are observing an upmarket bordello of some kind, and there are to be sure a few courtesans wandering through. But so far the whole thing is decent and well-behaved; and the space is mainly peopled by domestics: young women in Victorian costumes, young men in the formal attire of butlers or valets. The curtain has indeed risen on the famous Overture (the moment Wagner insolently designated for the Paris ballet). Sedate and pious opening bars accompany the lady of the house—not Venus; Elisabeth!—and her young son; they approach the industrious writer and encourage him, then retreat to be the horrified witnesses of what follows, from which they quickly withdraw. For Holten has staged, in concert with the bacchanal tones that begin to infiltrate this overture, an extraordinary awakening of frenzy, which seizes on the servants, men and women alike (it may be the first time, in this Venusberg delirium, that men have been given an equal role with women, at best normally accompanied by a self-effacing male dancer). The Dionysian music—I don't know whether Nietzsche ever recorded his thoughts on this particular exemplification of the god—may well reflect the evolving subject-matter of *Tannhäuser*'s inspiration, or the latter indeed may itself cause it; the ambiguity is worthy of the later "music dramas" and their new aesthetic.

The director succeeds in staging an extraordinary pandemonium, which rises in crescendo along with the score: in an infectious frenzy the men tear their shirts off, the maids begin to pour buckets of water over themselves to cool the fever, acrobatics take the place of classical ballet moves, the participants flinging themselves back and forth across the stage and eventually drawing Tannhäuser himself into this frenzy in which he participates only to the degree that he begins to write (frenziedly) upon the increasingly naked bodies of the dancers (shades of the poststructural theories of écriture and tattoo!). Finally, and coinciding with Tannhäuser's increasing disgust with the orgy, and with sex itself, a transcendental moment is reached in which one of the participants—they are now running up and down the multifarious staircases—can be observed to mount the highest story of these crisscrossing flights of steps *upside down*! Calmly hanging in midair, he scales these grades without effort, as though it were the most normal activity in the world; indeed the audience only gradually becomes aware of him, so insignificant and prosaic does this detail seem in the chaos in full movement all over the rest of the stage. It is an O altitudo! you can find occasionally in the words of literature, or the sounds of music, perhaps even in that "frozen music" which is architecture; but not onstage in this fashion, not in this disbelief of eyes too stunned even to feel surprise!

Such are, however, the sublime moments of the high style and expressivity of *Regieoper*, of postmodern staging, and of Holten's extraordinary imagination (as when, to take one minor example, he has Sieglinde rather than Siegmund pull the invincible sword out of the tree in which Wotan has plunged it).

There is to be sure a purpose in all this, or rather a point Holten is making. This bit of staging composes a sign—in the hieroglyphic or ideogrammatic sense, rather than the linguistic one. Holten wants us to understand that at this moment Tannhäuser is undergoing a transvaluation, so to speak, a swinging of the pendulum of values back to purity and chastity, or faithfulness, and away from the exhausting frenzies of the "Venusberg" itself: in other words, his ideals have been utterly turned upside down. But to put it that way is truly to trivialize an extraordinary language of stagecraft by interpretation: by translating it back into intellectual clichés, into something we might have found in a psychology manual if not a book of ethics. The staged gesture, in all its originality, is to the playbook what Wagner's music is to it in another direction: it draws out unsuspected expression in another language altogether—a *gestus*, Brecht might have called it, albeit an emblematic one. 1 believe that this moment puts us on the track of the secret of so-called Regieoper (and *Regietheater* no doubt as well): it is to break the work down into pieces of meaning and translate each of them into letters, like a rebus, whose collection of signs then unfolds before us.

The translation can of course fail, or fall flat: and then we have the utterly gratuitous presence of Elisabeth in this orgy. A son? Perhaps hidden from the public? Is she supposed to have had Tannhäuser's child, unbeknownst to the court and perhaps even to the poet himself? Such illicit commerce would make a mockery of the courtly love that serves as the ostensible backdrop for this plot; yet it is true that it could be defended precisely on the grounds of the rebus-aesthetic we have already proposed. The son does not have to appear in the later sections because he was merely a part of this particular ideogram: later on, other elements will come into play which do not need to recall him, let alone take account of the seemingly scandalous detail in the first place. Clearly Holten means here to embody the theme of domesticity: the opposite of Venusberg sex addiction is to be grasped, not as courtly love, let alone religious devotion, but merely marriage and family, and the "true love" supposed to be embodied in that institution, at least in the modern Western or individualistic system. Whatever we may think of this quite un-Wagnerian revision of Wagner's original and decidedly rebellious and Bohemian one—and we find Holten's commitment to this theme of domesticity amplified in his changes to the *Ring*, where the happy ending and Brünnhilde's newborn child may indeed be more biographically Wagnerian and at the same time more questionable—I want to distinguish this kind of modification from what is at work in the staging of the bacchanal. I want to call this thematics a matter of interpretation, ultimately organized around the symbol, while the embellishments of Frau Venus's establishment fall under the rubric of allegory in its contemporary or rather post-contemporary, postmodern sense.

The isolated signs of the latter indeed lead a vertical rather than a horizontal existence; and we may conjecture that this documents a more general movement in postmodernity from the symbol to the allegory: the former demanding the transcendental unification of the work, that ideal of the "concrete universal" underway since Coleridge, while allegory—the postmodern kind, and not that ancien régime decoration to which Coleridge and Wordsworth were so allergic—returns to the moment in all its semiotic isolation, spurning the superstitions of modernism's (and romanticism's) "grand narratives," which is to say, their absent symbolic unity. This makes for a different kind of reception—or consumption—than that of the architectonic reading, encouraged by the older "masterworks." It was already prefigured in the taste for individual tricks and bravura set pieces we brought to Hitchcock or Buñuel: waiting for the great oneiric flashes or dream sequences in the latter, for the gratuitous flourishes in the former, such as the tennis match in *Strangers on a Train*, where the public uniformly and obediently swivels its multiple heads from one side to another, with the one sinister exception staring back at you; or the leer of John Dall, fingering the eponymous instrument in *Rope* between two swings of the kitchen doors.

So we do not necessarily witness some new "interpretation" when Holten stages Tannhäuser's awkward return from the unmentionable Venusberg, his mixed reception by old friends and wary fellow Minnesänger, the revival by the reanimated Elisabeth of the old poetry contests—all of which culminate in an extraordinary bourgeois cultural evening, with dress clothes and folding chairs, in which the hero, unable to contain himself, blurts out the secret of his deeper knowledge of "love" and, murmuring an underplayed version of the prize song, knocks the chairs over in his eagerness to take the stage, to the scandalized pandemonium of the distinguished guests and his now hostile colleagues—an uproar suddenly frozen to a painterly tableau of mass gesticulation as he alone hears the renewed strains of the Venusberg music, pardoning and calling to him.

Holten stages the awkward third act in a graveyard, with aboveground mausolea, and gives us the satisfaction of an onstage death for Elisabeth, whose frantic search in the twilight does convey some sense of the illicit nature of her love for the poète maudit. The latter, however, fulfills Holten's program by reciting the story of his unhappy pilgrimage to Rome, rather than improvising its music: a large notebook testifies to his vocation for writing and is insistently held under the eyes of his last unwilling witness (Walther). So this textualization turns after all into an overall "interpretation" of the opera: is it persuasive, or has most of the energy gone into the wonderful set pieces?

Still, this Tannhäuser would not particularly seem to offend by any outrageous modernization of its content or message (if anything, the Wagnerian triangle of Eros, religiosity, and poetry or genius would seem enhanced by the modern version). Yet aesthetic objections to this kind of allegorical heterogeneity generally turn out to be moral and political ones as well; whence the term "Eurotrash," which, when it is not simply an Americanism for European cultural self-indulgence, surely vehiculates a distaste of traditional modernists for the more epochal triumph of postmodern and mass-cultural tastelessness.

Yet the more coherent productions of Regieoper do often seem to have an ax to grind: as in the antiwar statement of Kenneth Branagh's *Magic Flute*, surely one of the triumphs of the form. Set in a World War I landscape, this production gives real content to the struggle between Zarastro and the Queen of the Night, the former a pacifist leader in charge of a hospital refuge, the latter a gloriously demonic enthusiast and warmonger whose immortal high notes are rendered from the top of a tank. Her three emissaries are seriously lascivious nurses, while Tamino's coup de foudre is rendered by a wonderful black-and-white "dream sequence" of a high-society ball. Yet perhaps the overture itself gives the best idea of the "matching" mechanisms that, as we shall see in a moment, constitute the very heart of this form as such. A butterfly crossing empty and peaceful fields discloses the first trench, in which we meet crowded and agitated movement (which includes our first glimpse of the male protagonists) and finally settle on a messenger capable of navigating his way to the other end, where he delivers his note to a uniformed personage we take to be a commanding general, whereas he is in fact the director of a regimental marching band, lavishly outfitted and serving to herald the beginning of a new offensive, in which the emerging forces are led melodiously by our hero into the murderous machine-gun fire of the opposing party. The "serpent" is here death itself, from which the scripted rescue launches us into the plot as such. Nothing here annuls Bergman's elegant modernist version of the opera; but the reverse is also true, and the effervescent joyousness of this music also expresses the delights of Branagh's irrepressible inventiveness.

The latter then adds another signifying level to the inoffensive pacifist "message," at the same time that it restores a coherence to Da Ponte which the opera does not always have. But far more weighty reinterpretations are possible, which raise far more serious aesthetic issues than such glorious yet modernist stagings as Losey's *Don Giovanni* or Haneke's *Così fan tutte* (or even Ponnelle's *Tristan*).[1] Nowhere is this more apparent than in Katerina Wagner's remarkable version of *Die Meistersinger*,[2] a provocation to Bayreuth itself surely far more scandalous than anything Leftist about the Chéreau/Boulez centennial *Ring* (save for the nationality of these artists).

For here the problem is internal and it is ideological as well, turning on Beckmesser and Wagner's well-known anti-Semitism.

---

[1] In the Barenboim version, Ponnelle stages the entire third-act return of Isolde as the unreal dream of the dying Tristan: it works and at the same time transforms the opera into something new and different.

[2] For more on this scandalous departure from tradition, see the essays by Clemens Risi and David Levin in Robert Sollich, Clemens Risi, Sebastian Reus, and Stephan Jöris, eds, *Angst vor der Zerstörung* (Berlin: Verlag Theater der Zeit, 2008).

Katerina Wagner has chosen to displace the otherwise unavoidable issue by turning it inside out, and instead foregrounding the nationalism which is its inevitable correlative and which is given full-throated expression in Hans Sachs's closing encomium to "die heil'ge deutsche Kunst" (an evocation perfectly consistent with the drama and its historical period, but which is probably always a trifle unnerving for the foreign spectator, at least in this day and age). All of this is then made possible, as Clemens Risi has shown, by setting the characters in motion, by taking these figures—Walther, Beckmesser, Hans Sachs himself—not as static identities, but rather psychologies in full development and transformation, and in particular as representatives of new and evolving aesthetic solutions to the situational dilemmas of modern aesthetics. So it is that the class differences are at first strongly underscored: the mastersingers are clearly affluent burghers with their lower-class apprentices, and the earnest and unimaginative Beckmesser is their characteristic representative. In this beginning, Sachs remains the eternally sympathetic father figure of traditional productions—something that renders his later evolution even more ominous. Meanwhile, and this is the crucial starting point, Walther is here an arrogant and conceited young aristocrat, complacent in his efforts to break into the middle-class fellowship. It is from these class positions that the evolutions which make up the originality of this production will emerge, but by way of the superposition of two historical situations. For Beckmesser and Walther the changes will be as it were shifts in postwar art: the former attempting to discover himself as an avant-garde performer in the worse sense, the latter seizing the media opportunity and becoming a successful crooner, who wins the celebrity prize. Hans Sachs, meanwhile, the presumable embodiment of the most authentic German spirit, will become a Nazi, his final tirade ominously up-lit by Nuremberg-style flames. This is a remarkable development of latent elements in Wagner's text, and a true critical and hermeneutic act: it does not have to be the last word on *Meistersinger* or on Wagner himself, but it certainly brings out a plausible and coherent alternative reading, which offers its own supplementary pleasures of ingenuity and inventiveness.

What is less convincing in this version is a Johannisnacht festival in which rubber effigies and simulacra of all the great German cultural figures and icons, including Wagner himself, are orgiastically paraded in front of us, in what seems like a ritual act of political transgression. Indeed, the sixties had already accustomed us to a specifically German aesthetic radicalism in which the desecration of the canon was assumed to threaten the legitimacy of the state itself, something less probable in France or England, and certainly utterly meaningless in an anti-intellectual culture like the United States, where highbrow art was already understood to be the province of the upper classes (although the latter were not specified in class terms). At best, in America, this gesture had the materialist value of disclosing the presence of the institution behind a seemingly transparent aesthetic production, as in the work of Hans Haacke. At its worst, however, in German academia, it offered politically ineffective indulgences of bad taste, as in Konwitschny's staging of *Götterdämmerung* (in the already heterogeneous Stuttgart *Ring* of 2002), in which a simpleminded adolescent Siegfried prances around the stage on a hobbyhorse. These excesses, however, can scarcely be said to discredit what Regieoper can accomplish at its best and most intense.

Perhaps, at the risk of oversimplification, we might agree that traditional opera was staged under the sign of melodrama (including the naturalistic varieties)—Sir Walter Scott alternating with Victor Hugo—and delivered with all the resources of silent movie acting. The conversion to what is now the orgiastic gusto of seemingly illimitable varieties of Eurotrash seems to me to have been unleashed by two developments: the experiments in modernizing Shakespeare and (paradoxically) the impact of theatrical realism as a new scenic ideal. This is a dialectical moment in which, in both of these currents, the turn towards a modern or contemporary scene does not develop into a tradition in its own right, but simply works to sweep away old barriers and habits and open theatrical practice to innovations of all kinds, not necessarily in the spirit of the experiments that made them possible.

Modernized Shakespeare cannot really be said to have broken with costume drama but merely to have introduced a whole new wardrobe of essentially historical and political costumes, ranging from Orson Welles's Italian-fascist *Julius Caesar* to the British fascism of Ian McKellen's *Richard III*. One would think, however, that such "adaptations" demand the identification of a historical period, whose style in turn demands to be marked by specific and memorable historical events (and not, for example, the generalized "romantic costumes" reviews and program notes sometimes flaunted as a sign of the originality of this or that staging). This line of exploration leads us on into the more contemporary historical problem of periods and period styles (as in nostalgia film); and it also takes us, via the analogy of the filmic adaptations of novels (whence the significance of that term), in the improbable direction of cartoons and the musical accompaniment they seem to have required since the beginning of the sound era. For it is not widely understood that Disney's essential genius (and the true originality of his productions—for he himself could hardly draw) lay in the discovery that the new genre which was animation had to find its defining form-problem in the matching of image with sound, and of the mutual constraints exercised on each other by pictorial action and musical accompaniment. To be sure, in silent movies the music played by the accompanist needed to match the mood and rhythm of the action as far as possible. Here, however, paradoxically, it is the other way round; and the genius of Disney was to have understood, from the very onset of sound films, that real originality depended on the synchronization of the animated action with its background music. My suspicion is that this requirement ultimately originates in the very nature of the senses themselves: for hearing completes a temporal unit far more thoroughly than sight, and it is said that only a few initial notes are needed for the listener to identify a given tune, while the elements of vision are fragmentary and only gradually completed. Thus, in animation, the initial musical sounds will project a completed unit which the visual equivalent will need at once to follow. The climax of this priority of sound over sight is reached, for better or for worse, in those nature films in which Disney organizes nature itself, and wildlife documentary film is edited to act out the often rather silly musical accompaniment (the viewer, however, receives this the other way round, and assumes that the music has been designed to "orchestrate" the animals' natural antics).

This seemingly far-fetched analogy then helps us to understand the novel kind of synchronization demanded by the Shakespearean modernizations, where the original text takes on the function of the musical score to which the staging must itself adapt. This requirement then adds some rules to what might otherwise have seemed an utterly free and arbitrary exercise, and thereby defines a genre by way of a specific form-problem (a useful term I have from Lukács). Such form-problems, whose role distantly resembles that played by contradictions in philosophy, then confer a kind of historical meaning on the new genre as such.

How this works for Shakespeare may perhaps be illustrated by a minor yet striking example of textual constraint, for no production of *Richard III* can omit a confrontation with one of its most famous, nay immortal lines: "A horse, a horse! My kingdom for a horse!" This ought to be a fatal dilemma for any modernized and indeed motorized version such as Ian McKellen's, which, however, triumphantly solves it by way of the breakdown of the usurper's jeep. A somewhat more general illustration of the way in which modern adaptation can richly exploit hitherto underutilized resources in its original can be found in Branagh's interpretation of Fortinbras as a semi-crazed obsessive whose army, far from heading for Poland, are in reality in the process of laying siege to Elsinore itself, at a moment when as it turns out there is no longer anything to besiege and the throne stands vacant. On the other hand, to find a happy ending for one or another of the great tragedies—as Holten does for *Götterdämmerung*—is in effect to change the script altogether; it is the difference between Helmut Käutner's *Hamlet* (*Der Rest ist Schweigen*, 1959), set in the still-flourishing "kingdom" of a postwar Nazi industrialist, and Tom Stoppard, or Jarman's gay *Tempest*. At any rate, the comparable "modernization" of Wagner will face similar dilemmas, and call for analogous distinctions between symbol and allegory, between interpretation (or reinterpretation) and witty or fanciful embellishment.

The other genealogy here is more paradoxical, for it leads us back to realism itself and in fact to the East German reinvention of realism which was happily consistent with official state aesthetic dogma. Indeed, as we shall see, the theatrical practice of the GDR (from Brecht to opera) involved that reestablishment of artistic continuity called for by Habermas in his notorious slogan of a *Nachholen* or "catching up" far more literally than the provincial culture of a West Germany physically shorn from its metropolis, and more immediately served as inspiration and model for the first great Wagnerian realism in the West with the Chéreau centennial production of the *Ring* at Bayreuth (1976).

I believe that what is here generally termed realism is in fact a commitment to the text and its dramatic content; it is in this sense that Chéreau is, in his way, the logical fulfillment in the West of this development.[3] But it is precisely this attention to the text that

---

3   For more on Chéreau and the relationship of opera to theater, see Chapter 2, above.

opens up the multiplicity of possible versions of the *Ring*—some dozen different productions currently all over the world—and in particular exacerbates that opposition between allegory and interpretation which I touched on above; an opposition clearly nourished by the very multiplicity of forms and genres within the *Ring* itself, as well as the problems and alternatives any new production of this sixteen-hour four-part work must confront and "solve."

Above and beyond the most general decision for drama or for music—an alternative Wagner himself never resolved (Holten following Chéreau in opting for drama)—the score and text of the *Ring* offer numerous levels on which priorities must be decided. In the music itself, of course, harmony versus counterpoint takes the contemporary form of an opposition between Boulez's transparency and instrumental "miniaturism," to follow Nietzsche's insight, and the traditional heroic blare of the great Wagnerian orchestras (no true Wagnerian would want to lose that thrill altogether). The text clearly solicits an option for the archaic and mythological versus the kinds of modernizations we are witnessing here. But it is in the content itself that numerous rich ambiguities are housed, which cannot be so easily dismissed: on the political level, the alternation between the great ruler and individual freedom: on that of the Law, the issue of the runes and marriage laws; on the theological level, the tensions between the gods and Fate, and the matter of foreknowledge or predestination; on the economic level, the existence of gold and the nature of production; on the social one, the clan system, feudalism and modern individualism; on the psychoanalytic level, the split subject, Spinoza's sad passions, love and identity, castration and the will to power; on the cosmological vision of earth, air, fire, and water, and the place of the traditional, of magic and shapeshifting, of the potion and the spell; on the ethical level, the coexistence of trust, envy, and vengeance; and finally, the problem of the End itself—end of the gods, end of the demigods or heroes, end of the world itself? No staging can be of philosophical interest today without positions taken on all these themes; and the point—and Wagner's originality in the history of opera—is that his work makes such a philosophical focus unavoidable. Nor is this exactly a question of didactic or thesis art; or perhaps Wagner allows us to grasp the deeper content of that more superficial question, which seems to turn on what distracts us from art's "purely aesthetic" or entertainment (commodity) value. For here the work is staged as an expression of the Absolute,

take it or leave it! Wagner—and indeed modernism in general—
seeks to renew Hegel's account of that moment (for him, preceding
philosophy) when, after religion, art was the primary vehicle for
truth and for a vision of the world. (The end of art, for Hegel, being
the moment in which it no longer does this, or rather no longer can
do this, and sinks again to the level of the decorative).

But does this not raise the ominous question of Wagner's own
opinions and philosophy, and of the kind of Absolute he wants to
foist upon us? Any number of contemporary scholars and authorities
convince me that he had only one philosophy or value, and that was
getting his own works written and produced; this does not mean that
he was little more than an aesthete or adherent of "art for art's sake,"
but rather that the whole world, including politics, society, revolution, history, should turn and revolve around this crucial center
which was the Absolute itself: whence Wagner's personal fascination
for several generations. But it is a misunderstanding of ideology to
feel that it involves the endorsement of a specific opinion. Ideology
is the symptom and expression of the objective contradiction constituted by the historical situation itself. The older forms of staging
and interpretation felt a commitment to resolve such contradictions
and to transform this or that ideological tension into a coherent
world-view; and in hindsight this commitment to coherence also
dominated much of what we might call, if not modernism, then
at least the modernist approach to Wagner—in theater, symbolism
and modernism being largely of a piece with one other.

Perhaps the "interpretation" tells us a little more about Holten's
personal thematics, particularly since it casts light backwards on his
greatest achievement, the Copenhagen *Ring* itself: the most extraordinary staging since Chéreau's legendary 1976 collaboration with
Boulez, on the centennial of the original Bayreuth *Ring*. In the light
of Regieoper, we might be tempted to call Chéreau's a "realistic"
production, at least in the sense in which he took Wagner seriously
as a dramatist and staged the characters in truly dramatic interaction and dialogue with one another (along with a few "postmodern"
details avant la lettre, such as the Siegfried forest bird—she of the
"forest murmurs"—endowed with a real birdcage).

Indeed, in one of those paradoxical genealogies in which cultural
history is so rich, it seems that we may trace *Regieoper* back to that
East German cultural production which, in the almost universal
obloquy of this state, has until recently been virtually ignored. But

the theatrical practice of the GDR, from Brecht to opera, was in far more lineal continuity with Weimar traditions—Klemperer, the Kroll opera—than that provincial West German culture so memorably encapsulated in Habermas's idea of a *Nachholen* or "catching up" to modernity. Thus Walter Felsenstein at the Komische Oper, or his associate Joachim Herz, or Ruth Berghaus—although from the hindsight of the postmodern their work may seem better characterized in terms of "realism"—all pioneered an operatic realism, contributing to a break with the past and with conventional bourgeois melodrama and opera that released the later freedoms of Regieoper. Indeed many of the later practitioners of these newer innovations were East Germans, or pupils of the first generation of that culture. (I may add that we are only now, with the Leipzig School, beginning to revisit GDR accomplishments in painting; film remains to be adequately assessed.)

To be sure, the GDR conception of realism differed significantly from a postmodern aesthetic, for which it is the articulation of contradictions that counts, and the registering of tensions, formal as well as ideological, within the work. For this aesthetic (if we may call it that) it is the struggle over interpretations that is vital, and the bringing to the surface of the contradictory impulses and forces within the text itself. The remarkable resilience of Wagner's works is thus not the consequence of their greatness before posterity, nor even of their relevance to our contemporary political and aesthetic situations (it is always wise to separate these levels, at least in some preliminary way): even less does it reside in the power of his own answers to the various problems they raise. It lies rather in his inveterate staging of these contradictions as problems to be solved, as situations which require solutions and interpretations in the first place. In the production that interests us here, it is the mounting of the works as dramas and as texts that is most calculated to heighten and intensify such articulations.

Meanwhile, *Tannhäuser* and its maternal and textualizing thematics cast some light back on Holten's interpretive preferences as well as on his extraordinary reinterpretation of the *Ring*, both overall and in the detail or witty embellishment. He seems to have taken heart from Peter Stein's legendary proposal ("Can I change the ending?"), which got him fired from the Bayreuth centennial production, thereby inestimably placing us in debt to him for Chéreau. I hope it is not a spoiler to reveal that in the Copenhagen *Ring*,

Brünnhilde survives, and gives birth to the child who may well become the superman Siegfried failed to be. Is this so inconsistent with the multiple endings Wagner toyed with—that of Feuerbach and that of Schopenhauer?[4] It is at any rate still very much in the spirit of Wagner's title, which foresees not apocalypse, but rather the end of the gods as such and the beginning of a truly human age: a beginning Chéreau captured when in the rubble at the end of the tetralogy—something like the Germany Year Zero of the age—the mortal crowd, momentarily transfixed by the epochal conflagration, slowly turns to face the audience and the human world as the curtain falls.

Still, the question remains whether, even on the occasion of so meaningful and crucial a moment as the opera's ending, Holten's momentous revision is to be considered an interpretation or a witty revision of detail (and it should be clear by now that my whole reading of Regieoper as a historical practice turns on the preservation and persistence of this postmodern ambiguity).

But perhaps, in the spirit of movie reviews ... *die alte Weise* ... we now need to tell the story of Holten's version, which begins with the insolence of restaging the Rhinemaidens as bar girls, and Alberich a lonely and frustrated drinker. Their malicious flirtation— lost in most traditional versions, including Chéreau's, where it is the "special effects" of water, swimming, and so on that focus our attention—is thereby only too painfully underscored, to the point where we begin by feeling sorry for Alberich. The gold, meanwhile, takes the wholly unexpected form of a naked young man swimming in one of those aquatic bar displays for "mermaids" familiar in more touristic American watering holes. Alberich's renunciation of love literally rips the heart out of this libidinal symbol, in what is only the first of any number of shattering climaxes, in a bloody act which sex, desire, envy, gold, and castration are conjugated at the very center of this myth of historical destiny. It is to such excesses as this that the mild experiments of modern dress in Shakespeare

---

4   The temptation to quote Nietzsche again is irresistible: "Siegfried ... overthrows everything traditional, all reverence, *all fear* ... For a long time, Wagner's ship followed *this* course gaily. No doubt, this was where Wagner sought his highest goal. What happened? A misfortune. The ship struck a reef. The reef was Schopenhauer's philosophy; Wagner was stranded on a *contrary* world view," etc. Friedrich Nietzsche, *The Case of Wagner*, in *The Basic Writings of Nietzsche*, ed. and trans. Walter Kaufmann (New York: Modern Library, 2000), pp. 619–20.

have led us! Yet the apparent self-indulgence is hardly gratuitous: it articulates the meaning of the tetralogy—the link between desire and power—in ways only too often obscured by faithfulness to the original Wagnerian instructions. Holten has rather been faithful to the Master's other injunction: *Kinder! Macht Neues!*

There can be no doubt that Holten's more brutal interventions heighten the meaning and the drama of the *Ring* itself, as I will show in a moment. But there is also little doubt that the line between the faithful and the arbitrary or gratuitous is a very fine one indeed, even granting the new postmodern meaning of these words. Perhaps the most perplexing of such novelties is what seems (as in *Tannhäuser*) to be the endowment of the tetralogy with a kind of informational écriture-themed frame: indeed the entire vast series opens in a library in which Brünnhilde seems to be researching the legendary past not only of the curse but presumably of her own lineage; along with the other Valkyries she was conceived during Wotan's "fact-finding" visit to the mysterious earth goddess Erda, after the loss of the ring. Ideally, this framework ought to underscore everything archaic about the *Vorabend, Das Rheingold*, which presumably takes place at least a generation before *Walküre* and brings the ur-races on stage: the gods, giants, and dwarves whose struggle for the ring and the god sets the stage for the human drama of the Trilogy and for the working out of Alberich's curse. I am not at all sure that the ingenious archival frame achieves that, for two reasons: the first is that we spend our time wondering exactly when Brünnhilde is doing her research (that is to say, before or after Siegfried?). The second problem is that *Das Rheingold* has itself been "modernized" so that it has already lost its murky and mythic aura.

As for the gods' royal family, they are living in tents, inasmuch as their grand dwelling has not yet been finished; the young Wotan is a brash and unexperienced entrepreneur surrounded with a predictably frivolous entourage of idlers and in-laws, all of whom are worried in various ways about the contractors' bill, as yet unpaid (the giants—for it is they!—threaten to seize Freia as recompense, along with the golden apples that hold the secret of eternal vigor, as the sequel demonstrates, so that the "end" of this particular family dynasty seems here in fact almost as close as it becomes on the other end of the tetralogy).

As for the giants, they are hard-hats, union organizers negotiating contracts, arriving from their natural heights (they are the race of the mountain-dwellers, as the so-called dwarves are of the under-ground caves) on open construction elevators of the type one finds attached to unfinished high-rises. One is disabled, in a wheelchair; the other, young and more vigorous and impulsive, is clearly enamo-red of Freia, and he is the one who will be killed in the disagreement about the deal to be settled (love or the gold). His death will thus replay Alberich's renunciation (in fact, a kind of self-castration).

The gods meanwhile await their lawyer, for the promised resolu-tion of the contract dispute. But he is not in a hurry to do so, and we are treated to a Loge in the form of a shabbily dressed shyster, dumpy and preoccupied (although as we know he does have an idea, and in the light of what follows we would do well not to underestimate his strategic gifts). Still, with him, the theme of record and informa-tion has worked its way into the central drama of the "preliminary evening" itself, in the form of the little notebook in which Loge assiduously cosigns the relevant details, occasionally augmenting them with photographic documentation, or recording this or that on an extremely archaic and primitive cylinder recorder. Here is yet another stroke of genius: the machine reinscribes the "mythic" note of the drama in an unexpected way (ancient to us in the twenty-first century, rather than in the spirit of the mists of time and the origins of the world), at the same time that it rewrites the final scene in an extraordinary way: the unreceptive Wotan, about to enter his Xanadu, finds himself again beseeched by the Rhinemaidens to restore the gold—but this time from Loge's recording of their origi-nal plea on this ancient wax cylinder. But their first interlocutor is no longer present, for with customary brutality Holten has transformed Loge's banishment by the dissatisfied client who is Wotan (he is re-demoted into his element of fire) by way of a lethal spear-thrust.

As for the descent into Nibelheim—there is no particular attempt to render the respective sizes of dwarves or giants either; Alberich's "deformity" is marked by an extensive facial scar (perhaps the result of a disastrous experiment, as will be understood in a moment), just as Fafner's status was by the wheelchair—here we find ourselves in an experimental laboratory, very much of the Nazi-cum-Frankenstein type, with an Alberich now dressed in the researcher's white jacket, and the terror of the subjugated dwarves appropriately reminiscent of the historical genocides.

The fairy-tale trick achieved, we now witness one of the most fearful of Holten's transliterations: the hapless Alberich, chained and tortured by a Wotan now in his element (Loge having supplied the winning idea), and allowing us to inspect for the first time a ring unlike any other—a band of gold encircling the forearm from its nest in the fingers. To achieve world domination, Wotan simply hacks the arm off.

The *Walküre* is inevitably, in this version, less arresting, as befits a modern bourgeois drama. The house is conventional, the Hunding a classic authoritarian or Nazi type, suspicious of foreigners, and in particular the refugee whom Siegmund clearly is (played, exceptionally, by Stig Anderson, who will also take the role of Siegfried later on; it is a measure of his acting skill that we do not confuse this harried fugitive with the adolescent Anderson is also able to incarnate, in the most convincing Siegfried I have seen). But, of course, the revelations of this first day of the tetralogy will be a new, older and wiser, more disabused, more ironic Wotan (James Johnson), who rivets attention and at once authoritatively assumes the role of protagonist Wagner has intentionally (or inadvertently) assigned him: for the *Ring* is in that sense his drama and not that of Siegfried, who, demigod or not, is little more than a pawn in his master plan.

The other revelation is, of course, Brünnhilde: older, more maternal, she will grow on us throughout the trilogy, and finally, more vulnerable than the classic ones and less majestic, adds shades and subtleties that younger singers could not. Indeed, Holten has in a sense made her the center of the tetralogy, by way of the new ending as well as by her initial appearance in *Rheingold* as the bewildered archivist of the tangled and bloody history. She cannot match the mysterious solemnity of the appearance of Gwyneth Jones's Brünnhilde to the doomed Siegmund (one of the two great uncanny scenes in the *Ring*, the other being Alberich's appearance to Hagen in sleep: Chéreau's version is here far more gripping than that of Holten, who seems uninterested in such effects); yet Holten's Brünnhilde (Irène Theorin) radiates a unique inner joyousness, and the Farewell scene is suitably affecting.

Needless to say, the slaughter of Siegmund is brutal in a very modern spirit, even though here Wotan's contempt for Hunding is so considerable as to let him live (as a messenger to Fricka), quite in defiance of the Master's express wishes.

I have already expressed my admiration for Anderson's Siegfried, which so splendidly captures the adolescent petulance of the character, in his disputes with Mime in the two-story house (in which, like any adolescent, he is able to retreat, pouting, into his upper den). What must be said is that the actor-singer is able to overcome the two greatest challenges written into this impossible role (as Chéreau characterized it): the killing of Mime and the sudden infatuation with Gudrun (in complete and instantaneous oblivion of the eternal love pledged to, and undoubtedly felt for, Brünnhilde). This last, of course, is officially explained by the magic potion; but onstage it risks the comic unless somehow plausibly motivated, which in this production it is, both by Siegfried's youthful inexperience and by the transformation of the traditionally shy and withdrawing Gudrun into an outright vamp and seductress.

As for Mime's death, however, the best that can be done is uncontrollable rage, confusion, regret, and remorse, and all this works onstage to allow the audience to overlook the improbability of an act in which perpetual annoyance and dislike passes over into outright murder, and in which a foster youth kills his guardian of many years. For the most traditional audiences, this premonition of serial killing has always been translated into an ill-disguised anti-Semitism, and it is a triumph of Holten's production to have transformed such reactions into a focus on Siegfried's own mission and destiny.

But the slaying of the dragon merits special attention. I am one of those who expect a real dragon (and even deplore Chéreau's toy-like assemblage); but in this case, Holten has found an altogether worthy and equally awe-inspiring substitute, in the coils of serpentine cable and tubing, ducts, pipes, conduits that crawl out of the manhole to ensnare the unwitting: down below, a crude computer center from which Fafner observes the world from which he has taken refuge. Here too, there is a sad pathos about the way in which the dying giant warns his boy conqueror that I have not observed in other productions. And all this observed from the railing above by Wotan and Alberich together, both vitally interested in the outcome: here Holten's novelty is to add in a silent role the teenage Hagen, who significantly, in parting, mimes a pistol shot at the enemy-to-be.

The older Hagen of the final drama is then appropriately staged as a proto-fascist mafia boss and physical-fitness fanatic (Peter Klaveness), with his paramilitary entourage as sinister as they need to be, replete with Kalashnikovs and balaclavas. The temptation to read Nazism back into the decadent Gibichung stronghold is to be sure a familiar one: what is more unusual is the Gunther of this production (Guido Paevatalu), young and physically vigorous, yet obviously weak and suggestible, and prone to military uniforms of the type associated with banana-republic operettas and small-power fascisms; the very type of the titular ruler born to serve as the cover for takeover of the Hagen type. At home, however, we are treated to a twenties atmosphere of the idle rich, gossiping and sipping cocktails: not only has Holten transformed the pallid Gutrune into an extraordinarily seductive vamp (nothing in Wagner forbids it!), but the brother-sister relationship has begun to echo the Wälsungen incest itself. Finally, unlike most traditional productions, the Gunther-simulacrum who fraudulently woos Brünnhilde the second time around is not played by Siegfried wearing the Tarnhelm, but by this rejuvenated Gunther himself, quite different from the humiliated and exhausted older man of the Chéreau production, to which this whole effort is so monumental and worthy a successor. (Nothing authenticates Wagner's dramatic genius so much as the mysterious first words of this simulacrum, describing the event to her in the third person and in the past tense: *Brünnhilde! Ein Freier kam!*—"a suitor came.")

I have several times here implied that the emphasis on drama releases all those Aristotelian reactions that were repressed in opera proper: or so Joseph Kerman argued years ago in comparing the effects of Shakespeare's and of Verdi's *Othello*[5]—the lyricism of the latter diverting and soaking up all the "pity and terror" of the play. So it is that we rarely feel the extraordinary pathos of the dying Siegfried as he once again recovers the dazzling love for Brünnhilde as though for the first time: "Ach, dieses Auge, ewig nun offen!"

I have saved, for last, my favorite scene from Holten's version: as is fitting, it involves the other great hero of the drama, whose mesmerizing incarnation here I have already underscored: massive self-control and contemptuous irony, the sarcastic hearing accorded the megalomaniac Alberich and the scheming Mime, the repression of his emotion at the defeat by Fricka, the very real bitterness at Brünnhilde's betrayal, the stoic resignation over the failure of the great enterprise itself—significantly, Holten has him break his own spear in two in acknowledgement of Siegfried's supersession (traditionally, it is the young hero who shatters it with Nothung). All these varied reactions powerfully enrich the role and encourage this great actor-singer to exhibit the range of his talents.

---

[5] Joseph Kerman, *Opera as Drama* (New York: Vintage, 1959).

But it is in the final encounter with the earth goddess Erda, the mother of his "illegitimate" children, the Valkyries (Fricka's disdain for Brünnhilde is a nice touch), that we confront the richness of Holten's imagination. For even her first appearance out of the nether realm—she comes to warn Wotan to give up the gold; it is their first meeting—Erda is the prototype of the wealthy career woman, madame or CEO, in furs and hurrying about her multitudinous errands. Now, so many years later, Wotan seeks her out for counsel: an older lover, dying in a lavish hospital room, to whom he has, not disinterestedly, come to pay his respects, his final visit, only to be greeted with a harsh reproach for the way he has treated their daughter. And indeed, her powers are fatally waning in the new regime of the ring, Wotan has made a mistake coming here: it is great theater, and yet more proof that the freedoms of the postmodern do not necessarily trivialize the greatest texts.

Chapter 8

Altman and the National-Popular, or, Misery and Totality

Among the many ways of defining the category of the "nation" and the "national"—geography, language, the state, nationalist aspiration, ethnicity—there is one that has too seldom been evoked; and it is the old French expression which I translate as the national misery, the *misère* of this or that national collectivity. Each nation then knows its own specific misère, its own secret or not so secret burning failure to become a real nation, its own embarrassing neurosis or disability. Nor is this a matter of "culture," whatever that may be, or even historical defeat (as for modern Germany or ancient Serbia): but it certainly includes the explanations and rationalizations of those defeats, as well as the apologetic and seemingly self-deprecating excuses for this or that cultural peculiarity (such as the absence of health care in the United States, for example). And just as the "I," just as first-person narrative, always includes a profound, if deeply hidden and disguised sense of inferiority, so also the national "we," however pridefully deployed, always carries deep shame within itself. Part of all this is of course the result of the dynamic of the Other, who contemplates and judges all this, and to whom we, even if silently, attempt to explain and to justify ourselves. It is played out in cultural envy, and the (quite ill-founded) sense that the Other's is a more joyous and successful collectivity, full of a jouissance precisely denied to us because of our innate miseries. But much is also rooted in the very nature of identity itself, whether individual or collective: identity is always a matter of shame, or of shame successfully repressed or eluded.

So Altman's great film *Short Cuts* (1993) is an epic exhibition of the American misery, whatever else it is. And it makes the national statement by way of artful and strategic exclusions and omissions: a totality in turn constructed by avoiding the inevitable questions about what has been kept out. Black folk, for example, are sent off on vacation at the very beginning of the film: this is not about them; they can write their own literature or make their own films, deal with their own situations and identities. The rich are also left out here: the doctor's villa, overlooking the city, is as close as we come, and we are talking here about the professionally well-off rather than the inherited or dynastic kind; and in any case these people, the well-paid doctor and the fisherman without a job, are fully as miserable as the rest of us. Even more important, for an epic of Los Angeles, is the absence of Hollywood: to be sure, the Robert Downey Jr. character works in makeup, for grade-B horror films, but that gets absorbed into a hobby for this rather repulsive, truly second-rate Iago. The media are here, to be sure, but reduced to the level of professionalization (a TV commentator, a news helicopter pilot), and not yet engaged in that fierce competition for cultural preeminence between the various media first noted by Miriam Hansen and then documented by Kathleen Fitzpatrick in her book *The Anxiety of Obsolescence* (Altman being perhaps too supremely confident in the preeminence both of film and of literature, as we shall see). So this is a truly lower middle class with individual housing: the American dream; no industry either, no representation of work, but rather the service industries with a vengeance (hairdressing, pornography, nightclubs, bakeries, hospitals). A woman's film perhaps (as so often in Altman)? I think it is rather the battle of the sexes, the impossibility of the couple: marriage before, during and after.

But that goes with the house; the couple is what happens inside the house, and this is a film about space, and more specifically about single-family houses. It was what was always meant by the term "private" in that ideological opposition between private and public so often evoked and so rarely useful or meaningful. So perhaps, if *Nashville* (1975) was the public side, and that much neglected third film of the trilogy *A Wedding* (1978) the space between, this one is the private dimension of American life—but it is a private dimension that is no secret to anyone; everyone knows this particular dirty little secret.

What will complicate our discussion is the fact that this film is a literary adaptation. So was his great Chandler film *The Long Goodbye* (1973), whose differences with the novel (and they are very great indeed) are worth study. But let me pause here and say something about film adaptations of literature which is a topic I've written on elsewhere.[1] I summarize my findings: there can really be no parity in value between a novel and the film adaptation it becomes (there have actually been films which were later novelized, but I leave them out of the picture). My sense is that inevitably one or the other, the film or the novel, tends to win out: we are disappointed when we see a mediocre adaptation of a great novel, or when we read a second-rate book which was the source of a truly great film. It is rare that both are truly memorable, and I want very briefly to describe the only situation in which this parity of value is possible, a demonstration for which I use Tarkovsky's film version of Stanisław Lem's novel *Solaris*. Lem was a Voltairean skeptic, and his science fiction novel was designed to demonstrate that even if there were sentient life in the universe (besides ourselves), we would never be able to make genuine contact with it; that sentient life is of course the living ocean called Solaris, and Lem's novel is a catalogue of all the varied failures committed by humans in their attempts to communicate with it. Tarkovsky's film version of this important sci-fi novel is, however, quite different, even though the events of the book are followed quite faithfully: for he is a mystic, and the portrayal of the quest is quasi-religious and well-nigh Proustian in its evocation of the past on Earth and the cosmonaut's long-dead parents, the dacha of his childhood, the vision of time beyond time. So here is my conclusion on film adaptation: it can only work if the two artifacts are radically different in their spirit and in the truth they convey; if each one speaks for itself and in effect is no longer a replica of the other, so that in a sense the very meaning of the term adaptation is completely undermined.

So how do we stand in the present instance? *Short Cuts* is, as is known, an adaptation, not of a single novel, but of a number of short stories by Raymond Carver, which of course complicates our problem still further, since Altman has combined some of these stories, selected bits of others, retained some virtually intact. The object of his adaptation is therefore itself scarcely a text with firm contours and a unified impact as one generally finds with an individual novel.

On the other hand, a great short-story writer often has a world which is even more distinctive than the effect of single novel; and

---

[1]   In Colin MacCabe and Kathleen Murray, eds, *True to the Spirit: Film Adaptation and the Question of Fidelity* (New York: Oxford University Press, 2011).

we have to note that since his death in 1988, Raymond Carver has become one of the single most important writers in the pantheon of contemporary American fiction; and his stories (he never wrote a novel) certainly project a distinctive world, to the point where picture books have been published purporting to illustrate what they call "Carver Country," which is associated with the Northwest of the United States. At the same time his life—poverty, alcoholism, late success, the muse—has become something of a legend.

But we will not grasp his literary significance unless we go back to fundamentals and take note of the tutelary deities presiding over modern American fiction who are Faulkner and Hemingway, now grasped as polar opposites. These two now classical writers have come to stand for the two fundamental tendencies in American literature, maximalism and minimalism respectively, terms we are perhaps more familiar with in music and painting than in literature. But their meaning in this context is clear. Faulkner, coming out of a great Southern rhetorical tradition of orators and preachers, was maximalist in both style and form: the famous long Faulknerian sentence with its breathless piled-up adjectives powering an interlinked series of novels which map out the legend of an imaginary county from earliest times to the present, in which a host of magnificent short stories and novellas are themselves but related episodes.

Hemingway's minimalism meanwhile is the understatement and the charged almost-intolerable silence, the electrifying tension of the withheld and the unvoiced. The feelings and emotions of a great Hemingway story are intolerable, but unspoken, and it is clear that this writer invented a kind of method, a systematic leaving out, a violent omission and an aggressive refusal of speech, that is virtually the opposite of the great flood of Faulknerian evocation. If Faulkner is about History, Hemingway is about personal relations, particularly those of the couple. To which I need to add that at least in my opinion, Hemingway only wrote two good novels, the first ones, both set in Europe, and almost none of the later work is American in its content, especially where the novel is concerned, while the pathbreaking early stories set the standard for a new kind of truly American writing.

It is then scarcely necessary to add that Carver's minimalism places him squarely in the lineage of Hemingway, while that of Faulkner seems to have gone abroad, and found its truest successors in the magic realists of the Latin American boom, in Salman Rushdie, in

Günter Grass, in a whole efflorescence of foreign novels from China to Africa; in America itself the result has been increasing verbiage and pseudo-epic fictional history which has by now more or less dried up.

Now, perhaps, we can get a better idea of what Altman was dealing with here and what he has had the originality to make of his (or Carver's) raw material: the nine stories interwoven into an epic picture of Los Angeles. So from the outset we note one fundamental change, which we may even be willing to call a monumental betrayal. Altman has transposed these vignettes of a suburban Northwest, about lonely men, unhappy marriages, unemployment, drinking, backyards full of rusty cars and weeds, into California at its sunniest and most overpopulated, into one of the biggest cities in North America. I don't want to claim that its inhabitants are any less unhappy than those of the original Carver Country, or any less lonely: but at least they are lonely among lots of people; it is a metaphysical rather than a physical solitude, and the whole mood has changed. Maybe this is a first step on our way towards understanding how Altman's adaptation has made his betrayal more faithful and yet distinctive than a literal reading of Carver could ever have done. But it is only a first step.

Let's begin with the frame itself. In 1981 the state of California (fifth economy in the world and one of the great agricultural producers) was threatened by a devastating invasion of a pest called the medfly. The only solution to the catastrophe was offered by a chemical product called melathion, calculated to render these harmful insects sterile and thus nip the effects of the epidemic in the bud, so to speak. But no one—not the legislature, nor the citizens either—wanted to breathe in this stuff, which had to be transmitted by air. The then governor, who has since acquired the distinction of having been at one and the same time the youngest and now the oldest governor in California's history, took the fateful decision on himself, in what some considered an illegal coup d'état, and ordered the universal spraying of the state.

The film opens with this ominous event, redolent for everyone at the time of the Vietnam war: in the darkness, a fleet of attack helicopters streaming onto the sleeping city, releasing their poison gas on its unsuspecting inhabitants, with the whole panorama of Los Angeles and its night lights spread out below us: the establishing shot of a totality if there ever was one, and of the panic of citizens racing inside to shut their doors and windows, and others registering a kind of nameless fear at the ominous sounds of the aerial vehicles, themselves since Vietnam the very symbols of war and death, of human devastation. (It will be to our purpose at this point to make a first connection with what follows, and to note that one of the first characters we meet, on the following morning, is himself a helicopter pilot, albeit a weatherman quite uninvolved in the assault force of the previous night.)

Such is then the stunning opening of this film by a director whose greatest fame indeed came from the celebrated war movie *MASH* (1970).

But many are the menaces that this ominous opening announces, and Altman needs an ending that will both sum them all up and transcend them: just as he needs to address and transcend his stereotypes of the city (which by the way I think one cannot really map from the locales of the film: Downey, Compton, Watts, Pomona, Glendale) so that in that sense also it includes everything. So naturally enough he will call on the grandest stereotype of all to mimic an ending which turns out not to be the ending of Los Angeles or Southern California, but merely the ending of this film.

It is, of course, the earthquake, which folk wisdom and the popular culture of the area foretell under the slogan of "The Big One," the cataclysm that will topple the towers and send California sliding into the sea. So the breathless expression "Not the Big One!" is the quasi-religious cry of salvation, the happy ending, the unexpected rescue from the brink: it is Altman's last resort for his unquenchable optimism, even in the face of so many dire straits as he has to deal with here, just as the unexpected mass singing of the blues lifts us out of the assassination at the end of *Nashville*, and Elliot Gould's happy-go-lucky skipping into the sunset rescues us from Chandler's soppy sentimentalism at the end of *The Long Goodbye*.

Such is then the frame of *Short Cuts*, and its episodic continuity secured by the interludes of the blues singer character drawn into the series of dramas by way of her daughter in an episode which is not in Carver, but which reasserts the power of music on another scale. The other great form-problem faced by this kind of film is that of its climaxes, particularly in a situation in which we have to do with a writer whose stories by definition have no climaxes in the traditional sense. For one thing, will any single climax predominate and drown the others out? For another, will all the multiple story lines have climaxes? It is a little like the compositional problem faced by composers of the twelve-tone system: as soon as you let repetition back in, however fleetingly and insignificantly, tonal centers threaten to form which unbalance the system as a whole and unsettle what one cannot call its equilibrium but rather its planned and systematic disequilibrium. (And something similar can be said of the star system, in a film without heroes or central figures, all of whose actors are already recognizable stars.)

In short, what to do with storytelling itself in a situation in which it has to be both multiplied and problematized (and I suppose this also leads us back to the ultimate question of adaptation, Altman versus Carver, film versus literature). I think that one very pertinent solution happens midway through the film, when the disreputable father (grandfather of the injured boy Casey) tells his newscaster son the true story of his disappearance and the collapse of the marriage that caused it: this, the Jack Lemmon character, is so badly acted, in true American fashion, that it is absolutely believable and true-to-life, and the embarrassment we feel both about the actor/character and about the stupid anecdote he so badly narrates, that this long monologue (and the son's mute and unreadable reaction to it) somehow seals the whole question of storytelling in an undecidable yet definitive way. Everyone in this film is telling stories, revealing secrets, asking for the truth: this is what happens when you are given airtime and allowed to speak your piece for good; and the audience appropriately cringes. I suppose you could say that it forms a pendant to the telephone sex practiced to make ends meet by another character, but her remark about "virtual reality" is I think one of the few flaws in this otherwise matchless assemblage.

So now to the film itself: I want to discuss it in terms of a few not very theoretical categories. I've mentioned climaxes; I would also suggest that there are rhymes, and there are cognates; and also, in the matter of plotlines, echoes, and what I will call roundabouts as opposed to knots and splittings. Then there is the question of themes, a meaning-concept probably derived from academic literature rather than from painting and iconography; and the whole matter of space itself, obviously a topic imposed on us not merely by the medium of film as such, but by the very existence in the world of such a thing as Los Angeles.

Let's quickly deal with that first of all: for what I have called the frame can also be reexamined in terms of space, the great panoramic shot of the opening and then the subterranean eruptions which call space itself back into question at the close. I will remind you that this is a world of single-family dwellings, and even oppressively so. The great absence here is the Pacific Ocean itself (along with the desert), and it is unexplained and unjustified (we do get a bit of nature in the fishermen's excursion—reached by a three hours' walk—through what?—just as the funeral in Bakersfield is reached through a three- or four-hour drive—through what?—and we also get some nature in the park in which the earthquake becomes visible). Otherwise water is present in the swimming pools, and thereby absorbed back into the infinity of human houses, which form a spatial totality in its own right. But here yet a third force challenges the camera's hegemony over all this closed yet open visual space: it is the chainsaw of the enraged pilot-husband, who systematically trashes his wife's dwelling, only to have it cleaned up and hollowed out into a perfect blank by the unexplained vacuum cleaner salesman, whose intrusion here is something like a brief cameo appearance by God himself: "I have seen everything. I know how to deal with it." Space can be saturated by poison gas, it can be destroyed by seismic undermining, but it can also be hollowed out, like a film set you clear away for a new production.

As for themes and meanings, I guess I want to argue that they are semiotically defused and emptied by being transformed into visuality. Relationship precludes meaning; if you can see it, you don't have to think it. To risk making a statement in film: it is something to be avoided at all costs, here by replacing the clutter of the Bazinian deep shot with the unthinkable multiplicity of the crowded plotlines; and also by adding a visual rhyme to anything you might be tempted to thematize: thus the cellist's body does not mean death, but stands as a cognate to her naked body in the swimming pool.

Let's look briefly at the difference between rhymes and cognates: I wanted some terms to distinguish them because rhymes became a term for the relations between the multiple plotlines, while cognates were closer to individual objects. Now the latter might also be thought to rhyme in a way, but I thought it would be better to use a term—I could also have said homonyms, a single word or sound that means several different things—in order to combine identity and difference in something which is not necessarily a theme or meaning.

Thus we have makeup in the Robert Downey Jr. character's macabre makeup profession, and we have makeup in the clown's

profession; and then we have photographs in the Downey character's registration of his horror faces, but also in the pictures taken
of the girl's drowned body by the fishermen. The latter then loop
back and meet each other in the bizarre "knot"—another made-up
term—in which the two sets of photographs get mixed up, and each
party suspects the other of being a criminal and a pervert. Here,
to be sure, the cognate is transformed into a kind of theme, since
it reproduces the spectator's creative work in combining all these
things into a unified narrative, albeit a false one. So the falsity of
the makeup leads to the question of photographic reproduction and
its truth or falsity, to which one would then be tempted to add that
other technical medium of the telephone itself and the simulacrum
of phone sex and paid telephonic pornography which is so obviously
a striking motif in this film.

But this is the point at which meaning and interpretation again
rear their ugly heads, and I have already suggested that the temptation to interpret and to speculate about some meaning the film is
supposed to have is reinforced by the unfortunate line about virtual
reality so awkwardly attributed to the suburban sex worker. Does this
chain of associations, or of linked or cognate images, mean that the
film is somehow about simulacra or make-believe, about the unreal-
ity of American life, at least in Los Angeles, including that whole
ideology of spectacle society and image or informational society that
is now current in what we call High Theory? I think such a conclusion and such an interpretation of the film are patently false, not
only because the centrality of the media have been excluded here,
but because in that sense interpretation, and interpretation of that
kind, is utterly inappropriate if not to film as such, then at least to
this one. Long ago Susan Sontag write an influential essay entitled
"Against Interpretation," by which she meant the standard academic
readings of literature in terms of what I would call its meanings
and its messages, most of them moral or metaphysical statements
about the human condition: this would be an interpretation of both
Altman and of Carver as portrayals of the frustrations and dissatisfactions of American life today (on such a reading you can see
how the idea of the "meaninglessness of life" itself can become a
"meaning"). I suppose I might be more satisfied with such readings
the more they take on a local and a historical cast: thus, the frustrations of life in California or Washington State, the frustrations of
life in late capitalism, in the 1990s.

Meanwhile, people have suggested that for the most part so-called High Theory has had little usable to offer creative writers as such, with the signal exception of Derrida's concept of difference, enthusiastically adapted by identity-oriented and ethnically based artists. In particular, Altman himself has always had an unconcealed dislike for both kinds of interpretive theory, and his remarks about his own work have mostly limited themselves to technical problems. Thus, he tells us that his main concern with the movement from one plotline to another was the technical one of making sure the audience remembered the characters and the story they were reentering (and that they had been forced to leave behind a few moments earlier). Such technical problems are of the greatest interest, and they recall Umberto Eco's analysis of the problems of the writer of serials, such as Dickens or Eugène Sue in the nineteenth century.[2]

But in fact I cannot accept the division implied here between the technical issues of production of writers and directors and the activities of interpretation, whether theoretical or interpretive, on the part of readers and audiences, or critics and theorists. I believe that there is always a social and historical perspective from which the two kinds of questions come together, and in this case I believe they come together around the problem of genre, from which both technical and interpretive matters derive. A genre has rules which must somehow be creatively navigated, and it is a historical formation which has its social preconditions. This is at least the perspective in which I want to go on examining *Short Cuts*, as the emergence of totality from the short story.

So we were dealing with the matter of cognates: thus, for example, the fish in the borrowed apartment, which signify a kind of class luxury (as well as a kind of aesthetics) and the fish caught by the macho fishermen in their escape from work and family and routine, and then overcooked by the doctor in what was supposed to be a ritual barbecue. It is easy to see how around this common "root" so to speak a number of social stereotypes, most often of a class nature, cluster and are in their specific narrative contexts activated. But now we need to talk about the rhymes which maintain between the segments of the narratives or story lines themselves, rather than

---

[2]   Umberto Eco, *The Limits of Interpretation* (Oxford: Wiley, 1991), Chapter 5: "Interpreting Serials."

between the individual objects or motifs: or better put, the cognates which turn the individual objects into motifs.

Here we will find associations which seem to link the stories thematically: thus, the matter of transportation (in this veritable capital of multiple transportation) in the episodes of the helicopter overflight, the policeman's motorcycle, and the waitress's car that strikes the unlucky child. And obviously enough, we can also tie in the absent travel of the fishermen to their recreational site, as well as the park which marks a kind of rest from such workaday preoccupations. Meanwhile, that initial limousine which is driven by the waitress's errant husband (even though as a narrative it leads nowhere; actually here a Carver story has been omitted by Altman for reasons of length)—this limousine underscores the class character of all this as well, sedans in the wealthier suburbs, jalopies in working-class areas, etc. But I must feel that this is less a thematic expression than the choice of a unifying stereotype: Los Angeles is quintessentially and uniquely the city of highways and private transportation: the great architecture historian Reyner Banham, who wrote one of the fundamental works on this city, confesses that in order to write about it and as it were to speak its syntax, he had to learn to drive (something he had not needed to do in the more traditional cities he grew up in).[3] But is this yet another temptation of interpretation, yet another "meaning" the film might be said to have? I suggest that it is rather yet another element in the construction of a totality. We have seen how the latter required strategic omissions; now we can observe how subliminal themes reassure us as to how all this disparate material somehow belongs together, and is part of a single totality despite all the heterogeneity of its stories.

But there are more insistent echoes as we crosscut from one plot-line to another: for example, the children, who appear in both sides of the policeman's life, and who are equally conspicuous in their absence from the life of the other couples, whose existence reaches one kind of climax in the death of the little boy and another in the unexpected, awkward, painful reemergence of his grandfather; the echo then of the other death, that of a daughter (herself mourning the death of the boy, a neighbor and basketball partner), the discovery that owing to an unexpected visit by one of them, the mother

3 Reyner Banham, *Los Angeles: The Architecture of Four Ecologies* (Berkeley: University of California Press, 2009).

of the two "artistic" sisters is very precisely the waitress now trying to live a henceforth childless (or empty-nesting) life with the limo driver; and so on and so forth. And of course children are at the center of the clown's work, at the same time that nothing in this movie really concerns their experience—they are merely as it were its furniture.

But here too the rhymes threaten to turn into so many thematic echoes on the point of resolving themselves into a meaning or interpretation of some kind. So better to stay with images: compare the body of the dead girl discovered by the fishermen, and the naked body of the young cellist in the neighboring pool, spied on by the frustrated pool cleaner who will eventually, egged on by Iago-Downey, kill the girl in the park in an inexplicable mixture of stupidity and rage. This echo then contains the motifs of three deaths, which themselves echo that other death which is the accidental death of the little boy Casey, but which are none of them oddly climactic in the way in which this last one is. The girl in the stream is an offstage murder; the suicide of the cellist (which includes the story of a dead father) is as muted and enigmatic as her character itself; the violence in the park, a symbolic rape rather than a murder as such, is as meaningless as the earthquake that somehow echoes it, in a parody of the old "pathetic fallacy" of King Lear and the New Critics. But the death of Casey is otherwise central in ways we need to understand, and indeed Altman himself has observed that it is really "the one complete story" and as it were "the main clothes line of the film", "the most intact of all the Carver stories in the film."[4]

If so, however, the primacy of this particular narrative strand is cunningly concealed in the multiplicity of stories and episodes we encounter, where our attention is most often distracted by their overlaps and encounters with each other, which I have here termed roundabouts (the French might say *carrefours*). The one shock I have already mentioned—the discovery that the waitress turns out to be the mother of the two daughters, wives of the doctor and the policeman respectively—is a relatively minor episode in a host of other such discoveries which can lay some claim to being events in this film: but very special kinds of textual events rather than diegetic ones. It is a little like the two levels of the detective story: there

---

[4]   David Thomson, ed., *Altman on Altman* (London: Faber & Faber, 2006), p. 164.

are events that happen in the "real life" of the murder story itself, and then there are events that happen in what we are tempted to think of as the secondary story of the detective's investigation. Both narratives are, to be sure, internal to the work itself, and yet we feel somehow that they belong to different worlds, or at least different levels of textual being. Sometimes such secondary events are wholly external, as in Faulkner's characteristic trick of withholding information from the reader: it makes a mystery of what is often an unmysterious situation in the work, so that we become the detectives and we seem to have discovered something when he finally tells us who his people are and where we are finding them: there is thus a kind of readerly event which is in fact external to the work itself but which we are tempted to include in our memory of it.

Here in Altman such discoveries are different yet again: yes, it is the author/filmmaker who has withheld relationships from us. Nonetheless we experience the fuller account of the characters' background not as explanation but rather as the real encounter between separate plotlines. When the fisherman turns into the clown's husband, and then participates in the social evening of the two couples (and not least, becomes the prototype of Carver's paradigmatic unemployed hero), these are all roundabouts: they are the meeting places for those separate plotlines which we feel to be distinct destinies in the heterogeneous multiplicity of his totality, to put it in a succinct mouthful. This means that each character is a bundle of destinies, or of distinct narratives, and not some unified identity which, like philosophical substance, includes many attributes (in the form of experience). It is a view consistent with the kind of contemporary thought that evokes "multiple subject-positions" and repudiates notions of the centered self; and it makes of Altman's representation of the city something rather different from those earlier works which presented the latter as a combination of coincidences that finally resolve themselves into a unified picture. This is not the old "organic totality" but something closer to Lacan's *pas tout* ("not-all").

The distinction is subtle but significant, I must feel; and the new genre that instantiates it expresses a new historical experience of population, of multiple Others as subjects, of the multitude, if you accept that term, of the phenomenology of globalization, to take it from another angle. This is more than a casual experience of something unique and hitherto unencountered: it amounts to an

expansion of subjectivity itself and perhaps at the limit a modification of its very structure. We may indeed speak here of collectivity,
but then we must take into account the concrete infrastructure of
this representation of collectivity (and as I have observed, it is one
of Altman's most cherished experimental forms, rehearsed most
strikingly in *Nashville* and *A Wedding*, and perhaps less so in *Prêt-
à-Porter* [1994] and *Gosford Park* [2001]): the collective of the film
production itself. If it is so, as George Pierce Baker believed, that the
actors' collectivity itself influenced Shakespeare's forms and practice,
or that, as McGurl has taught us,[5] the very nature of the writing
workshop left its traces in the structure of its alumni's work, then
there is nothing particularly presumptuous about the proposition
that Altman's unique and personal work in handling his technicians
and his actors is the immediate material base for the imagination of
the collective that rages through his filmic practice.

The roundabout is then the most striking signal of that unique
collective multiplicity in which relationships are discovered at the
very moment in which they are constructed. The older simulta-
neities ("meanwhile, at the very same time, in another part of the
forest …") are here transformed into a different kind of temporal
model, one more suitable for the contingent singularities of the
iPhone (which Altman anticipates without imaginatively experiencing the new technology itself). The present creates its own past:
the jealousy sparked by the dinner invitation, the father's offense
revealed in the middle of another crisis thirty years later, the blues
singer's reminiscences, the revulsion and anxiety produced in the
fisherman's wife by the revelation of his delay, the various rhythmic
forgetfulnesses of the alternating sexual fidelities and infidelities:
these are the extraordinary temporalities of the sheer present of
film itself and its "assault on the other temporalities" (as Alexander
Kluge put it), its absorption of everything else into a Now in which
even waiting no longer has anything to do with the future. Waiting
becomes in this sense the fishing and drinking that goes on while
the body remains to be retroactively "discovered."

But there are also the ceremonies, about which the blues interludes remind us, without altogether consummating them, since they
are mostly failures anyway—vacation weekends, dinners, cookouts
and picnics, the coffee break, the children's parties … And besides

---

[5]   See Chapter 13, below.

the externality of the concerts and the music, only one is strangely successful, and with it, in conclusion, we return to the one continuous and sustained narrative line in the film. Why is it so much more successful than Carver's original story?

I guess I must now suggest that in important ways Carver was a failed minimalist. Hemingway's stories after all were most of them driven by something like the rage of Altman's pilot, if not the unreadable, unfathomable reaction of the television commentator to his father's revelation. But Carver had to do, on the one hand, with the alcoholic aimlessness of the unemployed worker passing his life, waking and sleeping, on the couch he never leaves; and otherwise with a kind of emotional explosion the true minimalist would never have set down on paper, like the baker's confession at the end of the story on which we are about to comment:

> Then he began to talk. They listened carefully. Although they were tired and in anguish, they listened to what the baker had to say. They nodded when the baker began to speak of loneliness, and of the sense of doubt and limitation that had come to him in his middle years. He told them what it was like to be childless all these years. To repeat the days with the ovens endlessly full and endlessly empty. The party food, the celebrations he'd worked over. Icing knuckle-deep. The tiny wedding couples stuck into cakes. Hundreds of them, no, thousands by now. Birthdays. Just imagine all those candles burning. He had a necessary trade. He was a baker. He was glad he wasn't a florist. It was better to be feeding people. This was a better smell anytime than flowers.[6]

This is perhaps the moment to mention the scandal associated with Carver's minimalism, which is oddly symmetrical to that of Thomas Wolfe's maximalism: just as the latter had the great good fortune of finding an editor of genius (Maxwell Perkins) who pruned his voluminous outpourings and made them publishable, so also Carver ran into an editor (Gordon Lish) who judiciously transformed his already sparse short stories into truly minimalist achievements, much against Carver's own wishes.[7] The kind of thing he cut out were the sentimental effusions of the kind I have just quoted, which deformed the stories he was unable to touch.

---

[6] Raymond Carver, "A Small, Good Thing," in *Collected Stories* (New York: Library of America, 2009), p. 424.

[7] D. T. Max, "The Carver Chronicles," *New York Times Magazine*, August 9, 1998, p. 131.

For in fact, the essentials of this story take place before the baker begins his tale, but after the coincidental tragedy of the little boy. True to the classical precepts, this story is itself the story of an intersection between two narrative lines (so that in a way, in his film as a whole, Altman has simply amplified this category of intersection and projected it onto the external immensity of the space of his locale). But here, our basic story line intersected several times over: first, by the fact that the driver of the fatal car is known to us and has been identified as the waitress from another story line; then, if you like, by the reappearance in the hospital of the unwanted father and his lengthy monologue; but finally, most of all, by the phone calls from the baker (Altman has changed the child's name to Casey in order to include the nastiest phone call of all), in other words by the impotent frustration just quoted from the written story itself. So far so good, and the story might have ended there, with a powerful and grotesque conclusion having to do with temporality (the boy having died before the cake was baked and delivered), the old-fashioned kind of simultaneity I mentioned earlier.

This is, however, a religious story, the unexpected story of an unexpected communion: the breaking of bread in the midst of tragedy, no wafer and wine but a newly baked muffin, a shared muffin so astonishing and unanticipated that it makes us forget everything else, even death itself (which is I suppose the very meaning of such a ceremony in the first place). And so it is that Altman effectuates a momentous transformation: he makes Carver's infinitely dispirited and depressing stories over into a joyous film: he makes the American misery into festival.

Chapter 9

A Global *Neuromancer*

Neuromancer is now more than thirty years old, a considerable time to remain a classic. Its publication in the Orwellian year will seem ironic and laden with symbolism only for those who think Orwell has remained a classic, or that he had anything to do with science fiction or reflected any serious political thought. But at least in one respect the juxtaposition is useful in showing how dystopia can swing around into the utopian without missing a beat, the way depression can without warning become euphoria. Indeed, I've suggested elsewhere that much of what is called cyberpunk (which begins with *Neuromancer*) is utopian and driven by the "irrational exuberance" of the '90s and a kind of romance of feudal commerce; but I had Bruce Sterling in mind rather than the more sober Gibson, whose postmodern overpopulation ("the sprawl") comes before us rather neutrally, even though its tone is radically different from the older Malthusian warnings of Harrison and Brunner. But *Neuromancer* and the novels that followed it were certainly not utopian in the spirit of the blueprints of More and Bellamy, or Fourier and Callenbach. Indeed, I would argue that the Utopian and still energizing work of the latter, *Ecotopia* (1968), was for the moment the last of its kind. And that, for a fundamental reason that takes us to the heart of our present topic, namely, that since Callenbach, the utopian form has been unable to take onboard the computer, cybernetics or information technology. *Ecotopia* was conceived before the Internet, and whatever utopian fantasies the latter has inspired—and they are many, and often delirious, involving mass communications, democracy, and the like—those fantasies have not been able to take on the constitutive form of the traditional Utopian blueprint. Meanwhile, more recent Utopian work, such as Barbara Goodwin's remarkable *Justice by Lottery* (1992) or Kim Stanley Robinson's monumental

Mars trilogy (1993–1996), however suggestive and influential in their Utopian features, have not seemed to incorporate cyberspace as a radically new dimension of postmodern social life.

And therewith the Gibsonian word is pronounced. Did he invent the word, etc.: such controversies are of literary-historical interest, but probably no one will disagree that he popularized it along with the name for that new genre called cyberpunk, and that these terms are henceforth inseparable from his name. I merely want to remind us that cyberspace is a literary invention and does not really exist, however much time we spend on the computer every day. There is no such space radically different from the empirical, material room we are sitting in, nor do we leave our bodies behind when we enter it, something one rather tends to associate with drugs or the rapture. But it is a literary construction we tend to believe in; and, like the concept of immaterial labor, there are certainly historical reasons for its appearance at the dawn of postmodernity which greatly transcend the technological fact of computer development or the invention of the Internet. Are there any equivalents in the cultural past for such "belief" in the existence of a literary image or figure? Perhaps "courtly love"—that twelfth-century Cathar heresy famously denounced by Denis de Rougement[1]—might serve as an example; might one dare suggest that the idea of evil, as it is transmitted by literary villains and the melodramatic mode itself, constitutes another? But are these not ideologemes—schematic projections of ideological concepts—rather than objective "realities" in which we believe?

I think it behooves us to look more closely at the notion of cyberspace in Gibson, in order to see what it involves: Is it a new kind of concept, for example, reflecting the alleged historical novelty of information technology in general? To what degree does its content then (apart from any formal innovation) somehow reflect this new reality (whether that of the "real foundation" of late capitalism or merely the "neutral" structure of its third-stage productive technology)? And what are its ideological consequences? How does it feed into other contemporary ideologies, and can it be judged to be progressive, or on the contrary somehow reactionary, inasmuch as (whatever the end of history) those possibilities seem to remain ahistorical and eternally with us? Meanwhile if you have a philosophical

---

[1]   Denis de Rougement, *Love in the Western World*, trans. Montgomery Belgion (Princeton: Princeton University Press, 1983 [1940]).

bent, you will want to decide to what degree it has some relation-ship to the popular idea of virtuality, inspired by the work of Gilles Deleuze (which equally reflects and fails to reflect the realities of information technology).

We might begin with the brief entry on the term "cyberspace" provided by Clute and Nichols's estimable *Encyclopedia of Science Fiction*:

> [Gibson, they tell us] takes quite an old SF idea, also much discussed by sci-entists, in imagining a near future era in which the human brain and nervous system (biological) can interface directly with the global information network (electrical) by jacking neurally implanted electrodes directly into a networked computer (or cyberdeck). The network then entered by the human mind is perceived by it, Gibson tells us, as if it were an actual territory, the "consensual hallucination that was the matrix" ... The [term] refers in fact to an imaginary but not wholly impossible special case of *virtual reality*, which is in our con-temporary world a more commonly used term for machine-generated scenarios perceived, in varying degrees, as "real" by those who watch or "enter" them.[2]

That the idea has something profoundly cinematographic about it can then be deduced from effects in the novel like this one. When the protagonists break into the palatial space station at the climax of the novel, for example, they are, as in a cinematic point-of-view, weightless, propelling themselves forward through the door and the corridors:

> [Maelcum] launched himself with another effortless kick. From somewhere ahead, Case made out the familiar chatter of a printer turning out hard copy. It grew louder as he followed Maelcum through another doorway into a swirling mass of tangled printout. Case snatched a length of twisted paper and glanced at it ... Maelcum braced his foot against the white cage of a Swiss exercise machine and shot through the floating maze of paper, batting it away from his face.[3]

But perhaps nowadays novels have to compete with films anyway; and it is not inappropriate to remember that Ken Russell's *Altered*

---

[2] John Clute and Peter Nicholls, *Encyclopedia of Science Fiction* (London: St Martin's Press, 1995).

[3] All page references to *Neuromancer* in the text use the Ace Science Fiction edition (New York, 1984).

States (1980), dealing, it is true, with a rather different kind of virtual reality, came out two years before *Neuromancer*, and that *Tron*, evidently the first film in which characters go inside their computer, dates from 1982 (Gibson says this film already made him nervous). But Kathryn Bigelow's *Strange Days*, a far more vivid prototype in which an individual's sensory experience can be transferred to someone else like a commodity (we will return to it), only appeared in 1995; and the inevitable *Matrix* in 1999. (Fear of television is much older, and can be tracked from *Videodrome* to *Infinite Jest*.) So Gibson did largely anticipate the contemporary cultural craze for simulation, whose concept is elaborated from Debord to Baudrillard; and inasmuch as he allegedly wrote *Neuromancer* on a typewriter, we can readily acknowledge his prophetic powers in this area.

Meanwhile the passage quoted above has some kinship with three-dimensional film—the hole of the corridor burrowing back into the screen, the protagonists floating into this space, kicking themselves along, with the paper finally streaming out of the computer and filling up the empty corridor in front of them. So the notion of space in the term cyberspace is meant to be taken quite literally and is indeed the fundamental metaphor it establishes. But this cinematographic representation is itself a second-degree dimension constructed by the novel's narrative language: something of the converse of an abstraction, as we shall see in a moment.

But first it is worth recalling the plot of *Neuromancer*, if only because it is a dual one whose levels need to be separated from one another. On one of those, this is a heist or caper story, in which a group of characters has been assembled to steal a valuable property (in the event a computer hard drive) from the advanced computer of a powerful transgalactic corporation, whose headquarters is based on a satellite in space. In fact, this ostensible corporate theft turns out to be an elaborate screen for something quite different, namely the junction of the two gigantic computers of these rival corporations, and their unification into the most powerful force in the universe (a story not without its family likeness to Ray Kurzwell's influential fantasy of the post-human "spike," and in fact already filmed in the 1970 *Colossus: The Forbin Project*). But this framework, which can be traced back to the Cold War or analogous geopolitical situations, is only the pretext for the development of a very different narrative development, involving the representation of cyberspace which interests us here.

Still, it is pausing for a moment on the genre of the caper or heist itself, which is certainly not a plot organically related to sci-fi as such, and is far more frequently to be found in crime and gangster films. I want to underscore a utopian impulse at work in this generic paradigm particularly in the light of Ernst Bloch's notion of a secret or unconscious utopian impulse that informs any number of human activities in an obscure investment of which we are not always aware. The analogy is with the Freudian drives, except for the implicit premise that the Freudian drives are ultimately biological in nature. Still, if we see the utopian drive as an impulse of collectivity and the human being as a collective animal, perhaps something of a biological origin might be adduced for it too. At any rate, I will suggest that the heist plot is a distorted expression of the utopian impulse insofar as it realizes a fantasy of non-alienated collective work. Modern collective production is organized as we know on the principle of the division of labor, normally articulated according to the nature of the object—Adam Smith's famous example being the fabrication of the nail. Here, however, in the robbery plot, specializations are certainly present—we need someone to open safes, someone acrobatic enough to get through windows, someone capable of neutralizing the alarm system, someone to drive the car, someone to secure the plans on what is probably going to be an inside job, and finally the brains or the mastermind, who is also the political leader so to speak. But each of these characters will be idiosyncratic: it is a collection of interesting oddballs and misfits, all of them different, and many of them in serious personality conflict with each other. The technological features of the object have thus been humanized and personified if not altogether sublimated: and this new collective mind becomes, like the different instruments of the orchestra, an allegory of the psyche with its inner divisions and contradictions. This utopian projection would then seem to be an allegory of production.

Here I think we face the dilemma of any literary or artistic representation of labor: it is very rare indeed that the content of the industrial product can have any necessity. The production process itself is always interesting: but whether they are producing sausages (*Tout va bien*) or machine parts (*Passion*), or even chamber pots (as famously unrevealed in Henry James's *Ambassadors*), the nature of the object cannot have any real aesthetic necessity without turning into a symbol of some kind. Anything that can produce a profit is equivalent when it comes to generating surplus value; and finally the heist plot expresses this truth as well, and short-circuits the search for a meaningful object by simply positing the cash, the gold, the bearer bonds, or whatever else. So this is, as it were, the negative or critical, the demystifying side of the caper form.

Gibson's novel too is a microcosm of the totality: a hacker, a female ninja, a dead man, a Rastafarian, a holographic illusionist, as well as a crazed army veteran whose schizophrenic mind has been possessed by the Artificial Intelligence who turns out to be the god in this particular complex machine. It is an intensified collection of skills visited on characters who are all maimed or incomplete in one way or another, most notably the dead man whose mind has become the program in the organizing mainframe. They all thus complete each other in one way or another but insofar as their collective (and thereby utopian) act turns out to have been a ruse devised by the two mega-computers in the service of their alliance and transfiguration, this utopian dimension is thereby displaced by a more conjugal if not religious one, and its deeper content repressed (virtually by definition the destiny of any impulse as such).

We might also note in passing that the excitement and euphoria we have attributed to cyberpunk are closely related to what Rem Koolhaas calls the "culture of congestion," the reveling in the overpopulation of a world city in which the center is everywhere and there are no longer any margins (or where the margins have become the center, if you prefer); and this is of course yet another profound expression of the utopian impulse as it celebrates collectivity in general, and not just in particular. It is to be sure also a projection of globalization as such, and another not so remarkable prophetic anticipation of that third stage of capitalism some also call postmodernity.

But it is time to make a closer approach to cyberspace itself as it plays its part in this novel. The protagonist, Case, is a hacker who has been equipped with jacks that give him direct and immediate contact with the space of the new and enlarged Internet. In a sense, this is a quick and easy solution to the mind/body problem which has tormented philosophy for so many years, and yet it is an idealist one. For while serving as this conduit, he must abandon his body which he thinks of as "dead meat," slumped lifeless in front of the computer. It is paradoxical (and rare) for idealism to express itself with such obscenity, and revealing that it must draw on a disgust with the physical as acute as anything in idealistic philosophy from

Plato to Bergson in order to affirm the primacy of the "spirit" or of the realm of the opposite of matter (however that is identified), for it is clear that in cyberspace we face a whole parallel universe of the nonmaterial.

Case will however be able to intervene in the material world by way of his modifications of that of cyberspace: much as the pineal gland allowed Descartes's mind to intervene in that of the physical body. In particular, his task is not only to coordinate the break-in when his team is ready for it; he must initially himself break into the system. What he first finds there is described in Gibson's own mock encyclopedia entry which I quote:

> "The matrix has its roots in primitive arcade games," said the voice-over, "in early graphics programs and military experimentation with cranial jacks". On the Sony, a twodimensional space war faded behind a forest of mathematically generated ferns, demonstrating the spatial possibilities of logarithmic spirals; cold blue military footage burned through lab animals wired into test systems, helmets feeding into fire control circuits of tanks and war planes. "Cyberspace. A consensual hallucination experienced daily by billions of legitimate opera- tors, in every nation, by children being taught mathematical concepts … A graphic representation of data abstracted from the banks of every computer in the human system. Unthinkable complexity. Lines of light ranged in the non- space of the mind, clusters and constellations of data. Like city lights, receding …" (p. 51)

Like city lights, receding … This is the figure we now need to retain, for it not only suggests the spatial landscape into which the mass of interrelated data is somehow projected, but also the manner of that projection. Clearly, quantities of numbers do not yield pictures, unless the picture is simply one of those seemingly encoded columns that run endlessly down the screen. Nor does the cityscape have any particularly privileged symbolic affinity with numbers, except for the fact that both involve masses of relationships. Indeed, even the numbers themselves are clearly a representational transforma- tion of a great many complicated concrete situations: harvests in a poor country, shipping contracts, legal systems and police forces and customs agents, sales on the street, businessmen and organizers, bookkeepers, etc.

What cyberspace promises are then the paths that lead from one moment in the system to another one, and finally to the various nodes and centers which command the operation as a whole; and in our caper story these paths also promise access, how most easily to break in, and to find the object of the question which is of course, like everything else in cyberspace, information as such.

In cyberspace what seems to appear is rather on the order of what sci-fi calls a matrix or a holodeck, so-called because it is a blank analog of three-dimensional space meant to be filled up with holograms. Cyberspace is however more complicated than this, for it does not aim at that kind of illusion or simulacrum, which we do find elsewhere in *Neuromancer*. What furnishes this holodeck is rather different, and comparable only to the axiometric plans and drawings architects use, where three dimensions of a building are drawn on a two-dimensional surface. In cyberspace the imaginary city of data rises like that; it is as it were the architectural plan of a city rather than the city itself; it is already, in other words—and this is the point I have been so laboriously coming to—it is already an abstraction, and as it were the very specific language or code of an abstraction, just as numbers and mathematical symbols are another such code. It is not really visual, to put it another way: this is not the representational mimesis of Renaissance painting (also, with perspective, a kind of language but one which seeks to substitute an illusion of reality for the awareness that it is also a set of signs). Gibson's cyberspace is an abstraction to the second power. The initial metaphor of a city for an information network is a first-level abstraction; then the representation of that city by the abstractions of the architects raises it to a second power. In cyberpunk this second-level abstraction is to be read by being navigated, and the camera eye of the novel moves through them, as we have seen, following their openings and canyons, skirting their barriers, moving ever deeper into the nonexistent space of these new systems:

> Case's virus had bored a window through the library's command ice. He punched himself through and found an infinite blue space ranged with color-coded spheres strung on a tight grid of pale blue neon. In the nonspace of the matrix, the interior of a given data construct possessed unlimited subjective dimension; a child's toy calculator, accessed through Case's Sendai, would have presented limitless gulfs of nothingness hung with a few basic commands. Case began to key the sequence the Finn had purchased from a mid-echelon saraiman with severe drug problems. He began to glide through the spheres as if he were on invisible tracks.

Here. This one.

Punching his way into the sphere, chill blue neon vault above him starless and smooth as frosted glass, he triggered a subprogram that effected certain alterations in the core custodial commands.

Out now. Reversing smoothly, the virus reknitting the fabric of the window.

Done. (p. 63)

What then permits this new narrativization of cyberspace, which was not present in architecture itself—and which could only be dynamized and kinesthetized by Le Corbusier's concept of trajectories—is now the existence of forbidden zones, of blocks and security systems, of the ice. Now we are in the culturally more familiar terrain of the hacker, who is called upon to break into these closed systems, themselves armed with mechanisms a good deal more dangerous than mere passwords. Case is to be sure a prototypical, dare I even say a stereotypical, hacker; but in this new and future cyberworld in which his very body is jacked into cyberspace itself, these powerful blocking mechanisms can reach back into the brain of the hacker and short-circuit it. This is what he first sees:

The unfolding of his distanceless home, his country, transparent 3-D chessboard extending to infinity. Inner eye opening to the stepped scarlet pyramid of the Eastern Seaboard Fission Authority burning beyond the green cubes of Mitsubishi Bank of America, and high and far away he saw the spiral arms of military systems forever beyond his reach. Ice, the great white sealed and glowing cubes on the horizon, these are the figures for those closed systems into which the cyberhero must penetrate, which he must infiltrate with new kinds of viruses, batter through with mechanisms he has brought with him. (p. 52)

This leads us to the first feature of cyberspace as Case experiences or Gibson images it: namely, the peculiar nature of an abstraction to the second degree, which, having accessed the sheets upon sheets of numerical ciphers which are already themselves statistical abstractions of real businesses, real profits, real transactions, now turns all that back into pictures, and pictures on the order of paper architecture at that, two-dimensional representations of three-dimensional models. In principle, it would seem that this second reduction will impoverish Gibson's picture of the information world; but in recent years, in architecture, any number of extraordinary talents have explored the possibility of so-called paper architecture in ways that allowed them to articulate complex, sometimes unbuildable, yet in any case unimaginable spaces by way of just that peculiar visual abstraction which is axiomatic projection. The latter may then be considered as a higher valence than the first-degree mimetic representation which shows us how a room will look, or how the service mechanisms of the building can be organized. Here, on this new level, what can be imagined and mentally grasped is the new dimension of sheer relationship—what Le Corbusier began to theorize as the "trajectories" through space—now intensified to an incalculable degree. What looks here like some stereotypical postmodern lapse into visual representation is on the contrary a complex mapping of the incalculable connections—Spinoza's *rerum concatenatio*—between all the multiple powers and vectors of the real world, that is, the underlying and invisible one, that we cannot see with our normal bodily senses. It is a totality, but a totality in constant movement, evolution, and metamorphosis, and also a mobile autotelic system into which our minds, or at least Case's, can intervene.

How to imagine then this totality, not of things, but of the relationships between things, and indeed of the relationships between those relationships, which are themselves in constant movement and transformation? I propose one of those episodes in surveillance films, in which the phone call from the kidnapper finally comes, but it does not originate in Detroit, as the first tap suggested, nor in Geneva as the terminus of the second; on the contrary, the technicians follow the mysterious trace halfway around the world, from point to point and continent to continent until it is suddenly too late to discover the ultimate point of origin, which may well be just next door or down the street. And all this lights up on a map in which a strange graph zigzags meaninglessly back and forth across the globe, in a cognitive mapping of globalization which is misleading if not deranged, but which somehow nonetheless symptomatizes our impossible efforts to connect incommensurables and to reduce the unrepresentable to the confines of a single unified thought.

I will argue that this unrepresentable totality, which until now only science fiction has uniquely possessed the representational means to designate, is that of finance capital itself, as it constitutes one of the most original dimensions of late capitalism (or of globalization or of postmodernity, depending on the focus you wish to bring to it). This is not the place for a thorough review of the newer literature on finance capitalism today; but in order to situate the new realm of abstraction Gibson has pioneered in his representation of cyberspace, I open a parenthesis on the history of this concept, which plays only a minor part in Marx.

The first serious attempt to theorize finance capitalism as a stage in the development of capitalism as a whole goes back to the period before World War I (the Austrian economist Hilferding, a socialist who was later president of Austria and a victim of Auschwitz): it is a theory which has a family likeness with Lenin's idea of the monopoly stage as the highest and final development of the system; and given capitalism's adventures and its evolution in the century since then, this notion of finance capital has not worn well.

We have had to wait for a remarkable book by Giovanni Arrighi, *The Long Twentieth Century*, for a brand-new theory of finance capitalism which completely rewrites our picture of the stages of capitalism itself. Arrighi begins with a remark of the great world historian Fernand Braudel: "Every capitalist development of this order seems, by reaching the stage of financial expansion, to have in some sense announced its maturity: it is a sign of autumn."[4] The yellow leaves of capitalism are apparent when a specific market has been saturated: production slows down, there is no longer any burning need for refrigerators, automobiles, personal computers, there is no expansion possible in the area of production in general; and at that point financial speculation must begin and profits be made in this higher-level or more abstract fashion, capitalism now as it were profiting from itself and speculating on itself, feeding on itself, by way of the stock market and its allied institutions. Arrighi's insight in fact proposes a three-stage theory of evolution, first a specific market is opened and colonized; then the great moment of production saturates it; and finally, in some third autumnal stage, finance capital sets in and takes over a stagnating economy.

But this account must be supplemented by a geographical one, in which the emergence of capitalism is mapped and charted by a systematic displacement and enlargement of its centers: from Genoa and the Italian city-states to Spain, from Spain to Holland, Holland to England, and thence ultimately to the United States. Each of these stopping points runs through the entire cycle of the three stages before capital, having exhausted its financial moment, takes flight and moves on to greater possibilities elsewhere. We are now, in

---

4   Giovanni Arrighi, *The Long Twentieth Century* (London: Verso, 2010), p. 6.

the United States, obviously in our financial stage, the stage of speculation of all kinds; and we must, with Arrighi, remain uncertain as to what will follow once that stage is exhausted. (But Chinese production and the immense Chinese market cast a suggestive shadow on the longer future.)

This is a theory which sheds new light on all kinds of things; but our immediate interest here lies in what it has to tell us about art and culture. I want to make a correlation between finance capitalism and abstraction generally; but in order to do so I have to argue that this is a very different kind of abstraction from what we are familiar with in the modernist period. The latter, as it moves towards its own kind of non-figurality (which it also called abstraction), was endowed, by the young Worringer, with an influential theory of the process: indeed, in the heyday of vitalism (end of the nineteenth century), this graduate student wrote a classic paper opposing organic to abstract forms, as forces of life versus forces of abstraction and death, from Egypt to emergent cubism.[5] The ideological valorization here is clear, and the social relevance—in an increasingly technological age, and an age increasingly anxious about technology—think of Heidegger, for example, or of the technologies of World War I. But an organic art nouveau disappeared shortly thereafter, and Worringer's famous opposition gradually sank to the level of one between representationality and abstraction, between traditional bourgeois art and modernistic impulses. My argument now posits this: it is no longer a question of any modernistic versions of abstraction of this kind in the postmodern period. The return to representationality in contemporary painting, for example, has nothing to do with nature, and as for ideologies of the organic they are universally denounced and repudiated, insofar as they exist at all.

The new postmodern abstraction is the abstraction of information as such: the way in which the seemingly concrete visual image is already abstract by virtue of its transmission in advertising; it is a visual cliché and no longer merely a conceptual or verbal one. And it is precisely this new kind of abstraction which it was the unique vocation of cyberpunk to convey in literary form.

And what it is to which this artistic form corresponds in globalization is very precisely the historically new abstraction of finance

---

[5] Wilhelm Worringer, *Abstraction and Empathy* (Eastford, CT: Martino Fine, 2014).

capital we have been describing. Since the 1990s we have entered a new phase of capitalism in which it is not production as such which creates profit and surplus value but rather speculation: speculation on land for example, the trading on the gentrified downtowns of older cities, or at least on downtown space to be re-gentrified and rented or sold for new and astronomical profits. Trading and speculation on money itself, where the national currency is bought and sold with a view towards quick turnovers, and rises and falls not in the production for which that currency stands, but rather in what the market will offer for it in just such trading. This is clearly a speculation which can have devastating results for whole populations, whose living standards now depend, in globalization, on the capacity of the local currency in which their wages are paid to buy necessities which are now largely imported. Behind this, currency speculation has disastrous effects on the Debt, into which all these countries have been plunged by the IMF and other international institutions.

My point here is that the money thus speculated on has itself been abstracted and sublimated into the counters and tokens of a higher kind of trading and speculative money which is little more than numbers or figures on a stock market board. Just as physical value, once weighed in gold, was replaced by paper substitutes, so now those physical substitutes, whether paper or not, are replaced by sheer numbers and empty ciphers on a computer, numbers which have no physical substance at all, and very little stability in terms of fixed value. In speculation one may go so far as to argue that the value of a firm and the substance of its material production have little immediate one-to-one relationship with its stock value (although obviously the two cannot be drastically separated for any long period). We thus enter a new era of abstraction and a disembodied state which is indeed that play of signs and signifiers anticipated by the structuralists, and which cyberspace now dramatically embodies in literature and art.

Now it is clear that these axiometric abstractions which exist in cyberspace as buildings and cityscapes greatly enhance the possibilities of the narrativization of this material: Case can thus penetrate this space and explore it, moving from one level to another in search of the weak points in the firewall, the most vulnerable entry points for breakthroughs or strategic redesigns, traps, ambushes, and the like:

Case punched for the Swiss banking sector, feeling a wave of exhilaration as cyberspace shivered, blurred, gelled. The Eastern Seaboard Fission Authority was gone, replaced by the cool geometric intricacy of Zurich commercial banking. He punched again, for Berne.

"Up," the construct said. "It'll be high."

They ascended lattices of light, levels strobing, a blue flicker.

That'll be it, Case thought.

Wintermute was a simple cube of white light, that very simplicity suggesting extreme complexity.

Case punched to within four grid points of the cube. Its blank face, towering above him now, began to seethe with faint internal shadows, as though a thousand dancers whirled behind a vast sheet of frosted glass.

"Knows we're here," the Flatline observed. (pp. 115–16)

My argument has been that in the face of the impasses of modernism, which proved unable to handle the new incommensurabilities of that greatly enlarged and as it were post-anthropomorphic totality which is late or third-stage capitalism, science fiction, and in particular this historically inventive novel of Gibson, offered a new and post-realistic but also post-modernistic way of giving us a picture and a sense of our individual relationships to realities that transcend our phenomenological mapping systems and our cognitive abilities to think them. This is the sense in which literature can serve as a registering apparatus for historical transformations we cannot otherwise empirically intuit, and in which *Neuromancer* stands a precious symptom of our passage into another historical period.

But abstraction is not the only such symptom; and indeed we do not fully appreciate the full value of Gibson's book until we turn to the other feature of the system which it registers and which indeed stands in relationship to this first one as its opposite and its other pole. This is the feature called "simstim" or in other words the simulation of stimulus, and it gives the operator the capacity to inhabit the mind and indeed the body of the agent on the ground, without interfering with her thoughts or movements. This form of vision is in fact implanted in the sensory system of the other character performing the robbery "in reality," in this case the razor-girl Mollie. Thus, when Case switches to simstim, at that point he is inside Mollie's eyes and body as she navigates the real space of the villa, encounters its flesh-and-blood guards, comes up against its material defense mechanisms, and so forth. Case's function is indeed to switch back and forth between these two distinct and very different capabilities: to be in cyberspace, tracking the abstract movement of his "ice-breakers" as they attempt to penetrate the ice of the security system; and then to switch to simstim for an immediate experiential perspective on the empirical operations within one location in the system.

Thus, cyberspace seemed to suggest paper architecture and axiometric design; simstim suggests first-person movies. It was an old idea of Orson Welles (for an unrealized version of *Heart of Darkness*), but Robert Montgomery actually put it into practice in his otherwise undistinguished version of Chandler's *Lady in the Lake* (1946), followed more successfully by the first twenty minutes or so of Delmer Daves's *Dark Passage* (1947). Seeing the world through the eyes of the main character turned out not to be as interesting as the use of the first person in literature (which has its more satisfactory equivalent in the voice-over); but it did come back in an interesting way in Kathryn Bigelow's *Strange Days* (1995), where it becomes an illegal vice, producing transferred footage sold like drugs on the black market. Clearly the various 3-D experiments also contribute to the simstim idea, about which we first need to observe that despite the electrifying immediacy of the experience in *Strange Days*, this kind of projection is an experience of the image of reality rather than of reality itself. In that, it is related to the simulacrum, and rejoins the family of images rather than that of perceptions (save as a perception of the image). This is therefore not a realism, not a recovery of immediacy, not even a demonstration of the validity of the various ideologies of realism as immediacy; but rather—just opposite—another testimony to our unreal life in Guy Debord's society of the spectacle, our life among what Jean Baudrillard calls simulations (a term significantly preserved in the very term simstim). Here then we have a second and different type of abstraction from the real; and indeed what is essential is to see that in Gibson these two abstractions are dialectically related.

Case is the sedentary space for the alternation between two distinct kinds of abstractions of the real: for his own reality—body abandoned in front of the computer—is a wholly impoverished one, which perhaps not so distantly recalls the reality of the reader gazing at this book in the first place. Case is indeed physically called into action at the novel's conclusion, for some welcome and violent real action; but for the most part he is little more than a recording

236 ADAPTATION AS EXPERIMENT IN THE POSTMODERN

apparatus for the axiometric graphs of Internet data on the one hand, and the simulation of real bodily perception on the other.

But the body is absent here; and it is significant that Case refers to his own body as the "meat": what is abandoned when you rise into cyberspace, what he was condemned to in those miserable years in which access to cyberspace was denied him. This is indeed why the simstim pole of the dialectic interests him less:

> Cowboys didn't get into simstim, he thought, because it was basically a meat toy ... simstim ... struck him as a gratuitous multiplication of flesh output ... (p. 55)

As I observed earlier, the very concept and the name of "meat" suggests what in other eras would be an idealistic or a puritanical perspective on the mind/body split. Cyberspace is a sublimation, one might even say a successful, a fully achieved, sublimation; even simstim is secretly a substitute for the body, disguised as bodily perception itself. In the long line of sci-fi visions of future evolution, Gibson's hero rejoins Wells's original Martians as a hypertrophied brain, whose bodies are good for little more than feeding. What is confusing is that we assume punk culture to be somehow more physical than normal bourgeois straightlaced decorum; and also that philosophical idealisms (perhaps with the exception of the rather curious current revivals of Bergson) are today extinct. Even the alleged spiritualisms and religious cults of the present are so grossly materialistic that their founders would scarcely recognize any of them.

Only later on, in a kind of muted love plot, does the body get its due, and find vague feelings revived by his shadow encounter with a dead lover:

> There was a strength that ran in her, something he'd known in Night City and held there, been held by it, held for a while away from time and death, from the relentless Street that hunted them all. It was a place he'd known before; not everyone could take him there, and somehow he always managed to forget it. Something he'd found and lost so many times. It belonged, he knew—he remembered—as she pulled him down, to the meat, the flesh the cowboys mocked. It was a vast thing, beyond knowing, a sea of information coded in spiral and pheromone, infinite intricacy that only the body, in its strong blind way, could ever read. (p. 239)

If *Neuromancer* were a literary novel, we might well want to conclude that it is really "about" precisely this opposition, between the mental experiences of cyberspace and these deeply physical ones of love and desire, of memory. But it is not a novel in that sense, and the very rewriting of this experience of the meat in terms of "a sea of information," in terms of coding and reading, is enough to convey the book's ideological or philosophical bias.

Global versus local? This is indeed the form expressed by the twin presence and opposition between the exploration of cyberspace and the utilization of simstim; but it projects this rather glib contemporary formulation as what it is, namely a contradiction rather than a simple alternation or even a choice of perspectives. The limits of our thinking, of our capacities for cognitive mapping, of our possibilities of imaging and representing, these "our real conditions of existence" are then dramatized by the poverty of the formula as well as by the richness of Gibson's novel. The two poles are two dialectically linked dimensions which structure our daily lives in this society, and confirm the paradoxical proposition that we are both too abstract and too concrete all at once.

The totality of the system determines us in all kinds of imperceptible ways, while we fall prey to the physical illusions of a present constructed out of sheer images. If I called Gibson's novel critical, and an instrument of exploration which is also diagnostic, it is because of the way in which he focuses on the combination of these two dimensions of a dialectic of globalization. The distinction of *Neuromancer* thus lies in the nature of the form itself, as an instrument which registers current realities normally beyond the capacity of the realistic eye to see, which projects dimensions of daily life we cannot consciously experience.

Chapter 10

Realism and Utopia in *The Wire*

Generic classifications are indispensable to mass or commercial culture at the same time that their practice in postmodernity grows more and more complex or hybrid. Is *The Wire* a police procedural, for example? No doubt, but it is also a version of the organized crime story. The majority of its actors and characters are black, which nonetheless does not exactly make it a black film (a film for black audiences). There is a political drama going on here as well, but its nature as local politics reminds us that it is also very much a local series, one framed in Baltimore and very much about Baltimore (something not always to the liking of Baltimore's elites). It is, however, also the case that most detective or crime literature today (as well as its filmic offshoots or inspirations) is local and based on the consumption of a specific landscape (whether a foreign country—Swedish detective stories, Italian ones, even Chinese detective stories—or regional—Montana, Louisiana, Los Angeles, Toronto, etc.). The broadest categories would then be that of the thriller or that of the action film (although there are few chase scenes, no cliff-hangers, few enough mass action or carnage scenes).

Each of the five years of the TV series is a unit in terms of plot and theme; and there are at least a hundred characters deployed in each season, many of whom carry their own independent plotlines. It may be argued that there is a single major protagonist, the Irish-American detective Jimmy McNulty (Dominic West), even though his status fluctuates over the five years of the series and is often eclipsed by other characters. This is to say that a work of this kind challenges and problematizes the distinction between protagonists and "secondary characters" (or stars and "character actors"), in ways most often described, I guess, as "epic" (*War and Peace, Gone with the Wind*)—a characterization that does not help to underscore what may be a historical development in the evolution of this kind of plot (see Alexander Woloch on secondary characters).[1]

The episodes in each series are not separate and freestanding as they were in *Homicide* (David Simon's previous series, also set in Baltimore and using some of the same actors); so this is a real serial, like Dickens, and an inquiry into a specifically televisual aesthetic would want to interrogate the fascination with individual actor-characters (pleasures of recognition and repetition), alongside the development of a distinct plot, where frustration and the week-by-week postponement (even the sense of deliberate retardation and the impossibility of closure)—all of this put back into question by DVD rentals—work in the direction of a difference stamped with a unique temporality, whose rhythm is however then reorganized into a repetition. Repetition enhances the function of the television set as consolation and security: you are not alone when it is on in the house with you, and you are not lonely or isolated when your space is peopled by so many familiar faces and characters. On the other hand, since both these features can function as neurotic denial, television carries with it a permanent possibility of boredom and sterile or neurotic repetition or paralysis. The program must then have available a secondary ideological pretext, the window dressing of a "value": art or quality would be one of those, but also "entertainment" or relaxation-distraction (after a long day at work, for example)—a pseudo-concept if there ever was one. And there is also the alibi of the political or social message, and the "cultural capital" of the cable channel (HBO in this case, which of course claims to be something more than mere television). There could also be an artistic bonus, owing to the fact that each of the episodes is written and/or directed by different people, some of them distinguished visitors (George Pelecanos, Agnieszka Holland).

But initially we approach *The Wire* as a crime story, that is, a struggle between two groups, the police and the crime gangs (for the most part the crime is drug trafficking). Each of these groups has its representational history: it was not terribly long ago in popular culture that the institutional police emerged from the tradition of the private detective; while organized crime gradually became an object of representation during Prohibition (its ethnic identification with

---

[1] Alexander Woloch, *The One vs. the Many* (Princeton: Princeton University Press, 2003).

the "mafia," "Cosa Nostra," etc., comes later on). Mass-cultural representation of this kind is a kind of recognition; it confers something like an institutional status on the group or entity in question; such groups are accorded objective social reality (and so we understand that real-life members of the so-called mafia regularly watched *The Sopranos*; the incidence of police watching procedurals is probably significant, but unrecorded). At any rate such recognition confirms a feeling that society is static and stable; its neighborhoods have long since been mapped out, and if there are shifts or changes in this social geography, they will have been well publicized, so that everyone knows that Lexington Terrace is no longer Polish but black, etc.

But mapping is not so simple: spatial it may be, but it does not inventory objects and substances but rather flows and energies. Yet the essential raw material of any social representation is bound to be that of social types, of stereotypes as well as generic types (like the "protagonist") as well as psychological ones; and *The Wire* is no exception, multiplying its recognizable entities on all these levels. To what degree it is original and innovative will depend on the revisions it is able to bring to these levels, and perhaps even to the new types it is able to invent. A certain modernism was able to deal with the problem of types by dissolving them into individualities and singularities, by approaching them so microscopically that their basis in the general or the universal gradually disappears: yet even this operation must take the familiar type as its starting point, and is menaced by the twin dangers of the emergence of new and more subjective types on the one hand, and of the ironic return to the external social starting point on the other. The word "type" is of course inescapably associated with Georg Lukács's theory of realism, but I think we do his immense culture and theoretical sophistication no service by assuming that this was a conception of pre-given social or class types rather than an attention to their historical emergence.

At any rate, *The Wire* dramatically unsettles our typological expectations and habits by at once drawing us into an epistemological exploration which greatly transcends the usual whodunit formula. To be sure, the series begins with a banal murder whose principal novelty lies in the victim's race (white) and whose solution seems obviously enough related to his forthcoming testimony in another gangland murder trial. But what we are quickly made to understand is that the police themselves are almost wholly ignorant of the structure of the gangs and the very names of the people who control them, let alone the latter's faces and localities. The uniform cops simply know the neighborhoods and the corners on which the drugs are finally sold to customers by teams of juveniles, some of them too young to be prosecuted. But this is as it were simply the *appearance* of the reality, the empirical or sensory form it takes in daily life; it is the most superficial approach to this reality, whose ultimate structure (source, refinement, transportation, sales network, and bulk or wholesale distribution) must remain too abstract for any single observer to experience, although it may be known and studied—and also occasionally sensed in a representational way, as later on in *The Wire* in various forms and probes. But the intermediate reality—the so-called drug lords themselves, here Avon Barksdale (Wood Harris)—are certainly knowable but not yet by the street cops, who learn his name in an early episode and finally manage to get a glimpse of his face and person when he organizes a baseball match with a rival gang. Is this because his rise to power is so recent, or simply because the police have not concentrated on this level of the organization before? Or perhaps, since the drug trade is a business, police observers have not attributed to it the forms and structure of legal businesses before and have therefore not asked the right questions. Whatever the reason, this ignorance of their own city suddenly opens up a space for realism: for seeing things, finding out things, that have not been registered before; and for investigation, for solving problems and tracking down causes as in scientific experiment or classical detective procedures. But here it is not an individual criminal responsible for an enigmatic crime, but rather a whole society which must be opened up to representation and tracked down, identified, explored, mapped like a new dimension or a foreign culture. "Barksdale" is only one component of that whole social complex, which now demands new instruments of detection and registration (just as ever-newer realisms constantly have to be invented to trace new social dynamics).

To what degree is this sociological mystery reducible to the standard plot forms of the detective search or the solving of a puzzle? I tend to think that the deeper motivation of such forms—or it might be better to say, our pleasure in such forms—has something to do with Freud's primal scene (which also underpinned the scientist's passion for unveiling the secrets of Nature). One would want to add that the Freudian-type satisfaction is never complete: just as no desire can ever really be satisfied, so also this one leaves a sense of disappointment. Who cares who killed Roger Ackroyd? famously cried Edmund Wilson in denouncing the detective story as a trivial genre (the reference is to Agatha Christie's ingenious breakthrough novel); and it is certain that there will also be a discrepancy between the passion of the chase and the contingency and triviality of the quarry. But this very discrepancy in the content plays into the form itself—the television serial—for its ultimate satisfactions must never be complete; we must also be motivated to come back for more, in hopes of greater ones. And perhaps the appropriation of these dissatisfactions for high culture or high literature would then consist in affirming that incompleteness: we never do catch the Greek, the ending remains unknown—save that here, that incompleteness simply means the drug trade will rebound, start all over again, continue, no matter who is finally brought to justice. But *The Wire* inscribes this fatal recurrence in social history, when it shows the passionate but superficial Barksdale eventually succeeded by the ruthless and dispassionate Marlo (who finally, however awkwardly, becomes a bourgeois businessman).

There is necessarily a tension here between the mystery and the agon, since we also see things through the villains' eyes and thus know some solutions the police have not yet worked out. Still, what saves the mystery format is that the discoveries are made successively like links in a chain, knots on a cord: they lead us closer and closer, and so some of the suspense is displaced from the Who to the How along with the modalities of legal proof. And here we must remark on the other specificity of *The Wire*.

Not only is the "discovery" or solution a whole milieu, the world of a whole society or subsociety cordoned off from the peace-loving bourgeois civilian public (of whatever color), but the "detective" is also a group and a conspiratorial one at that. The police as a whole is an institution, and as such moves in the direction of a properly political plot (networks, personal relations either of services rendered or of personal animosity, taking credit, passing the buck, ducking blame, etc.), and it is a political dimension which will in the last seasons and episodes come to the surface and be transformed into an official political campaign.

But this is that institutional police which has little capability of identifying its targets since on the one hand it does not even know their names, and on the other it has not yet even grasped the nature of the crimes it is investigating or their interrelationship. The lonely private detective or committed police officer offers a familiar plot that goes back to romantic heroes and rebels (beginning, I suppose, with Milton's Satan). Here, in this increasingly socialized and collective historical space, it slowly becomes clear that genuine revolt and resistance must take the form of a conspiratorial group, of a true collective (Sartre would call it the fused group forming within the serial mass society). Here Jimmy's own rebelliousness (no respect for authority, alcoholism, sexual infidelities along with his ineradicable idealism) meets an unlikely set of comrades and coconspirators— a lesbian police officer, a pair of smart but undependable cops, a lieutenant with a secret in his past but with the hunch that only this unlikely venture can give him advancement, a slow-witted nepotistic appointment who turns out to have a remarkable gift for numbers, various judicial assistants, and finally a quiet and unassuming fixer.

This last—the ultimate hero of *The Wire*—leads us to say something about the title, which rarely means a wire you wear on your body, but in general wiretapping as such. The older movies, seen today, make it clear how the introduction of cell phones radically transformed the constructional problems involved in plotting a mystery or adventure film, as well as in tracing calls and wiretapping as such: complexities which are here explored in detail. But it is the genius of Lester Freamon (Clarke Peters) not only to solve these problems in ingenious ways, but also to displace some of the purely mystery and detective interest onto a fascination with construction and physical or engineering problem solving—that is to say, something much closer to handicraft than to abstract deduction. In fact, when first discovered and invited to join the special investigative unit, Freamon is a virtually unemployed officer who spends his spare time making miniature copies of antique furniture (which he sells): it is a parable of the waste of human productivity and intelligence and its displacement—fortunate in this case—onto more trivial activities that nonetheless absorb his energy and creative powers more productively than crossword puzzles, say. But Lester is also the type of the archivist-scholar capable of spending long hours on minutiae and in dusty files that ultimately crack open financial conspiracies all over the city; and he has deep, unostentatious yet invaluable roots in the community, as when he first uncovers an old photo of the youthful Barksdale in an old boxing hangout not many of his fellow officers would be likely to have any knowledge of: and to many of them he is also an inestimable mentor. This is then the sense in which *The Wire* not only offers a representation of collective dynamics (on both sides) but also one of work and productivity, of praxis. In both instances, then, there is at work a virtual utopianism, a utopian impulse, even though that somewhat different thing, the utopian project or program, has yet to declare itself.

But Lester's creativity may also be said to have a counterpart on the other side. We have not yet mentioned Barksdale's sidekick, Stringer Bell (Idris Elba), who is something like the latter's executive officer or prime minister in the classic political situation: the police themselves also have a degraded version of this dual structure, where the second in command is however by no means as disinterested or as efficient as Bell. Stringer is in fact a real intellectual, and when the police (and the viewers) finally do penetrate his private apartment, they find modernist furniture and a décor of unexpectedly enlightened artistic taste. Yet although this figure may thereby come to seem a positive one, he gives all the most lethal killing orders without a moment of remorse. Still, the interplay with Barksdale, to whom he is absolutely devoted, but who envies his intelligence and sometimes seems to resent it, is characteristic of the extraordinarily dense and minute interpersonal situations through which *The Wire* plays out its larger plot.

Obviously enough, not only do the police not initially even know who Barksdale is, they have no inkling of Stringer's existence, save in those rare moments in which he has to visit the corners and monitor the operation on the street personally. Then one day, Jimmy takes it on himself to follow this so far unidentified figure (it will later on transpire that he is administering a whole expanding real estate investment development for Barksdale, something only gradually revealed by Lester's extraordinarily creative curiosity and know-how). At any rate, the car leads Jimmy to a university, and thence to a classroom, in which, through the window, he can observe the drug kingpin and gangster taking a course in the business school and obediently answering questions and doing his homework. To be sure, the comparison of the mafia with a business enterprise is hardly metaphoric or figurative; although we sometimes omit to think historically and to identify those who actually reorganized the crime gangs in this way, along the lines of profitability (Lucky Luciano, I believe, for the mafia; but see *Gomorrah* [Roberto Saviano] for a vivid contemporary example.) But here, *sur le vif*, we see something of the same well-nigh aesthetic creativity: Stringer will gradually reorganize the

Barksdale mob—he uses words like product, competition, investment; he brings the gangs together in order to eliminate the kind of internecine warfare that is always bad for business (*la douceur du commerce*: its historic taming of feudal savagery). I have deliberately used the word creativity several times in this context: how can this element not be seen as somehow proto-utopian on both sides, in a bureaucratic society for the most part static and content to run in the normal time-honored way, with all the old problems and malfunctions? At this early point already, *The Wire* can be observed to be ceasing to replicate a static reality or to be "realist" in the traditional mimetic and replicative sense. Here society, on micro-levels of various dimensions, is finding itself subject to deliberate processes of transformation, to human projects, to the working out of utopian intentions which are not simply the forces of gravity of habit and tradition.

But I want first to situate this discussion of utopianism within the context of plot construction; and to show that this is not only a purely academic matter (which it also is, of course). I want to situate both these issues within the even larger context of mass culture as a whole. Plot construction is obviously a matter of practical importance in mass culture, as witness all the books and seminars on writing a script or a scenario; but it clearly has a theoretical or philosophical dimension which is not exhausted by these technical recipes and handbooks on the matter.

The philosophical meaning of plot construction has to start from what stands in the way of constructing a plot or story; and that obviously also has its historical side. The literary past—particularly the past of theatrical spectacle, but also the surviving popular literature of various bygone cultures—offers abundant examples of plots that would no longer work for us today. There is, for example, the history of feelings and their expression and evolution: as in Adorno's remarks that the teleology of modernist literature was governed by taboo, by what you could no longer use in an artwork because it had become too sentimental and too familiar, too hackneyed and stereotypical. That teleology no doubt also holds for the history of popular or mass culture, despite the far more central role within it of the pleasures of repetition. For where the modernist novel sought to flee repetition, or at least to translate it into something more lofty and aesthetically worthy, mass culture thrives on what used to be called the formulaic: you want to see over and over again the same situations, the same plots, the same kinds of characters, with enough cosmetic modifications that you can reassure yourself you are no longer seeing the same thing all over again, that interesting twists and variations have freshened your interest. Yet a time comes when the paradigm succumbs under the sheer weight of the cumulative and the fatigue of the overfamiliar.

But I want to look for another kind of explanation for such formal exhaustion: and that is to be found in its raw material. If raw material can be readily adapted to older paradigms, its absence can also modify them in striking ways. We all know the variety of historical and social situations which have provided raw material in the past: country versus city, for one thing; the growth of the new city as a consequence: industrialism, foreign travel and immigration, imperialism, new kinds of wars, colonization, the country house and the urban slum of "lower depths," a "picturesque peasantry" as Henry James called it (indeed his little book on Hawthorne is a founding document on what the unavailability of certain kinds of raw material does to literary and formal possibility—he is promoting the advantages of Europe over America).

But let's turn to a less literary and more conventional mass-cultural genre or sub-genre, the detective story. The absence of sleepy English towns and villages, of cloistered settings and vicarages, has obviously made the (older) practice of the English-type detective story difficult in the United States. But we must also enumerate the shrinkage of motives for that indispensible ingredient, the murder. Not only did there used to exist an interesting variety of motives, they could be investigated by an interesting variety of private detectives, a species which seems to have become extinct. Social respectability—that is, the possibility of scandal and its damages; family structure and dynastic or clan systems; passions and obsessions of all kinds, from hatred and revenge to other complex psychic mechanisms—these are only some of the interesting sources for motivation which have become increasingly irrelevant in the permissiveness of contemporary society, its rootless and restless movement and post-regionalism, its loss of individualism and of bizarre eccentrics and obsessives, in short, its increasing one-dimensionality. Thus today, paradoxically, the multiplication of consumer niches and the differentiation of "lifestyles," goes hand in hand with the reduction of everything to the price tag and the flattening out of motivations to the sheerly financial: money, which used to be interesting in the variety of its pursuits, now becoming supremely boring as the universal source of action. The omnipresence of the word "greed" in all national political vocabularies recently disguises the flatness of this motivation, which has none of the passionate or obsessive quality of older social drives and of that older literature which drew on them as its source. Meanwhile, the psychic realm has also been drastically reduced, perhaps in part as a result of the omnipresence of money as an all-purpose motivation, perhaps also as a result of the familiarities of universal information and communication and the flattening of the individualisms. I have observed elsewhere that that universal communicational equality which Habermas (in *The Theory of Communicative Action*) associates with the spread of a new kind of reason also makes for a widening of the acts we can now understand; what used to be thought of as pathology, as the rarer mental states and acts beyond the pale—all these are now human, all-too-human, in such a way that the very category of evil or absolute otherness has drastically been reduced as well. That the organizers of the Holocaust were mere bureaucrats certainly diminishes their chances of representing absolute evil; that most pathologies are pathetic and provincial rather than frightening is a triumph of reason and liberal tolerance but also a loss for those still clinging to some outmoded ethical binary of good and evil. I have elsewhere argued against this binary system: Nietzsche was perhaps only the most dramatic prophet to have demonstrated that it is little more than an afterimage of that otherness it also seeks to produce: the good is ourselves and the people like us; the evil is other people in their radical difference from us (of whatever type). But society today is a formation from which, for all kinds of reasons (and probably good ones), difference is vanishing, and along with it evil itself.

This means that the melodramatic plot, the staple of mass culture (along with romance), becomes increasingly unsustainable. If there is no evil any longer, then villains become impossible too; and for money to be interesting, it has to happen on some immense scale of robber barons or oligarchs, for whom to be sure there are fewer and fewer dramatic possibilities today, and whose presence in any case recasts traditional plots in political terms, where they are less suitable for a mass culture which seeks to ignore politics. (Or when it turns to politics, then we may begin to wonder whether something has not also happened to politics itself: the reign of Cynical Reason is also the omnipresence of the disabused conviction about the corruption of the political generally, and its complicity with the financial system and its corruptions—so virtually by definition this universal cynical knowledge does not seem to bear any genuine political consequences any longer.)

We therefore have here two converging problems: on the one hand, the repetition of older melodramatic plot forms becomes more and more tiresome, and more difficult to sustain. On the other, the raw material or content for such a practice of form is becoming one-dimensionalized, evil is vanishing socially, villains are few and far between, everybody is alike. The utopian writers already had a problem with the possibility of literature in their perfect world; now we have a problem with it in our imperfect one.

This explains why villainy in mass culture has been reduced to two lone survivors of the category of evil: these two representations of the truly antisocial are on the one hand serial killers and on the other terrorists (mostly of the religious persuasion, as ethnicity has become identified with religion and secular political protagonists like the communists and the anarchists no longer seem to be available). Everything else in sexuality or so-called passional motivation has long since been domesticated; we understand it all, from sadomasochists to homosexuals: pedophilia being a minor exception here, to be classed as a kind of subgroup or subpossibility within the larger category of serial killers (who are generally, but not always, understood as sexually motivated). It is true that with mass murderers of the Columbine type we begin to shade over towards the political and here then terrorism reappears: but the latter for the most part remains firmly organized in terms of the radical otherness of belief and religious fanaticism, since little else remains. If we really grasped terrorism as a purely political strategy, then somehow its frisson also evaporates and we can consign it to debates on Machiavelli, on political strategy and tactics, or on history.

I need not add that these two staples—terrorists and serial killers—have become as boring as the villains driven by "greed." Alas, as with the disappearance of the spy novel after the end of the Cold War, that boredom would seem to betoken an end of melodrama which threatens to become the end of mass culture itself.

It is in the context of these dilemmas of plot construction that we now turn to Season 2 and the first non-virtual appearance of a certain utopianism in *The Wire*. This season deals with the port of Baltimore, with labor unions and corruption, and with a whole outside network of drug suppliers (the Greek!). The magnificent landscape of the increasingly obsolescent port of Baltimore and its container technology perhaps requires a detour through the whole question of place and scene (in Kenneth Burke's sense) in *The Wire*. The place is, to be sure, Baltimore; and anyone's first and quite understandable impulse would be to classify this series as part of the "postmodern" return to regionalism, and not only in "high literature" such as Raymond Carver. I've already mentioned the now constitutive relationship of detective stories and procedurals all over the world to local or regional commitments; meanwhile, "world cinema" makes those commitments virtually by definition, however its works might strike local audiences, since a globalized film-festival culture is organized by national production.

But in *The Wire*, there are some interesting distinctions to be made. For one thing, the regional is always implicitly comparative: not the corrupt old Eastern big cities, but Montana or the South, where we live differently, and so forth, with an emphasis on the small town, or the desert landscape, or even the suburb. Here in *The Wire* nobody knows that other landscapes, other cities, exist: this Baltimore is a complete world in itself; it is not a closed world, but merely conveys the conviction that nothing exists outside it (it is not provincial, no one feels isolated or far from this or that center where things are supposed to be really happening). To be sure, Annapolis (the state capital) is a reference, since it is where budgetary decisions are made (especially for the police force); Philadelphia is a distant reference, since occasionally gang members have to make a drop-off there; New York is the place you have to hire killers from, in very special instances where you need someone unfamiliar from the outside. Where the Greek gets his drugs is absolutely not a matter of conjecture (or of subjective mapping). Even nature (and the shoreline) does not exist, as witness the bewilderment of the one unhappy youngster (Wallace, played by Michael B. Jordan) shipped off to hide out with his grandmother for a while before going back to Baltimore to be killed. Baltimore is the corners; it is the police headquarters, occasionally the courts and City Hall, and this is why the very name of Baltimore is irrelevant (except for local patriotism and the TV viewers), and also why the docks and the port come as a real spatial opening, even though they are fully integrated into the web of interest and corruption as anything else, and even though the distant ports of call of whatever vessels still put in here are also absolutely unrecorded, unimagined and thereby so irrelevant as to be virtually nonexistent.

The labor leader is a Pole, and this is then also the moment to evoke the ethnic in *The Wire*. "Baltimore" is a nonexistent concept, but the ethnic still very much exists here, particularly if you include the police as an ethnic category, both in some figurative or moral sense, and also on account of the Irish tradition still very much in evidence among them. But are black people "ethnic" in any of these senses? We have already seen that the drug scene, run by Barksdale, is not only black, but exists like a foreign city within the official one: it is a whole other world, into which you do not go unless you have business there ("you" here standing for the officially dominant white culture). So here, in absolute geographical propinquity, two whole cultures exist without contact and without interaction, even without any knowledge of each other: like Harlem and the rest of Manhattan, like the West Bank and the Israeli cities which, once part of it, are now still only a few miles away; even like East and West Berlin today, where older East Berliners are still reluctant to travel to the former West, with its opulent shops they have no tradition of, and with a whole capitalist culture alien to them for most of their lives.

Still, this might be considered essentially as a black series; the bulk of its cast is black, drawing on scores not only of underemployed black actors but also on local nonprofessionals as well, Baltimore itself being a predominantly black city. But as has been observed of its predecessor series, *Homicide*, this very preponderance means that you see so many different types of black people (social, professional, even physical) as to utterly dissolve the category. Here there is no longer any such thing as "black" people any longer; and by the same token no such thing as black political or social solidarity. These people can be in the police, they can be criminals or prison inmates, educators, mayors and politicians; *The Wire* is in that sense what is now called postracial (something that might be sure to have its political effect on the US viewing public at large, just as the presence of TV or so many black entertainment celebrities has had its own impact on racial stereotypes and on the unfamiliarity essential to racisms).

But the Poles are still an ethnic group, as witness the ferocious vendetta waged against the labor leader Frank Sobotka by a Polish police major, which is one of the causes of Frank's eventual downfall. His ethnicity is at some distance, however slight, from his role as labor leader; and it is around this last that a certain utopianism begins to gather. For the demise of the port of Baltimore has to do with the postmodern technology of containerization (see M. Levinson, *The Box*) and its impact on the labor movement (many fewer workers needed, leading to the fall of once immensely powerful unions like the Longshoremen), as well as on cities (the post-container development of the port of Newark having suddenly rendered a host of other competing East Coast ports obsolete, very much including Baltimore), the old port now seemingly reserved for police boats, such as the one to which Jimmy has been demoted. This is then an interesting case where the destructive force of globalization has been as it were interiorized along with a more general deindustrialization: it is not only the movement of work to other, cheaper countries that has ruined Baltimore, but rather our own technology (which of course amplifies the impact of globalization generally, as containerization develops foreign ports and modifies industrial production and what can be shipped as well). But this historical story is part of the background of *The Wire*, and not its primary lesson or message.

The message is in part elsewhere, and it lies in the recontextualization of Frank Sobotka's alleged corruption (stereotypically associated with labor unions today, at least since Jimmy Hoffa). It is certain that Frank is deeply implicated in the drug trade and lets the Greek use his container traffic. But Frank is not interested in money (and I suppose you could argue that Stringer Bell is not interested in money either, and maybe beyond that, that the excitement of finance capital itself is not really about money, in its older sense of riches and wealth). Frank uses the money to build up his own contacts, in view of a supreme project, which is the rebuilding and revitalization of the Port of Baltimore. He understands history and knows that the labor movement and the whole society organized around it cannot continue to exist unless the Port comes back. This is then his utopian project, utopian even in the stereotypical sense in which it is impractical and improbable—history never moving backwards in this way—and in fact an idle dream which will eventually destroy him and his family.

But I mean something more than that, and this enlarged conception of utopianism has to do with plot construction. Realism was always somehow a matter of necessity: why it had to happen like that and why reality itself is both the irresistible force and the unmovable obstacle. To include Frank's pipe dream in a purely realistic work, we would have to see it (as Balzac so often did) as a mania, a psychological obsession, a purely subjective drive and character peculiarity. But this dream is not like that; it is not only objective, it draws all of objectivity within itself, such that if the plot of *The Wire* were to show its success, the representation would imply the utopian (or revolutionary) transformation and reconstruction of all of society. Nor is it political pleading, a political program cooked up by *The Wire*'s writers and producers and endorsed by the public as a desirable political and social improvement. It cannot be all that—no viewer will understand this episode in that practical light, because it involves not an individual reform but rather a collective and historical reversal—but it introduces a slight crack or rift into the seamless necessity of *The Wire* and its realism or reality. This episode then adds something to *The Wire* which cannot be found in most other mass-cultural narratives, a plot in which utopian elements are introduced, without fantasy or wish fulfillment, into the construction of the fictive yet utterly realistic events.

Yet Sobotka's utopianism would remain a mere fluke or idiosyncrasy if it did not have its equivalents in later seasons of *The Wire* (we could write it off, for example, by observing that the creators of the show, in their local patriotism, had taken this occasion to add in some more purely local statement). But in fact it does: and at this point I can only enumerate the later incidence of a utopian dimension in succeeding seasons. In Season 3, utopianism is certainly present in Major Colvin's "legalization" of drugs, that is, his creation of an enclave of drug use exempt from police intervention. In Season 4, on education, it is to be found in Pryzbylewski's classroom experiments with computers and his repudiation of the exam evaluation system imposed by state and federal political entities. Finally in Season 5, the most problematical, it is to be located in Jimmy's invention of a secret source for funding real and serious police operations outside the bureaucracy and its budget: and this, despite the artificial crime panic he deliberately fosters, and also somewhat on the margins of what was to have been a series dominated by the newspaper and the media. (For each season of *The Wire*, like Zola's great series, or like Sara Paretsky's Chicago crime novels, is also organized around a specific industry.)

The future and future history have broken open both high and mass-cultural narratives in the form of dystopian science fiction and future catastrophe. But in *The Wire,* exceptionally, it is the utopian future which here and there breaks through, before reality and the present again close it down.

Chapter 11

The Clocks of Dresden

Anyone with a commitment to socialism needs to take an interest in the history and fate of the German Democratic Republic (DDR), up to now the object of systematic neglect by West-of-the-Rhine liberal and radical intellectuals alike, who have scant knowledge of its achievements in painting and film, and assume its economic and political lessons to be exclusively negative. This is yet another instance in which Cold War dismissals in the name of Stalinism and totalitarianism—essentially political judgments—continue to be tacitly accepted by today's Leftists in embarrassed silence. To be sure, the Soviet Union is another matter, and its rise and fall is as respectable a historical topic as the life and death of the Roman Empire; but at the same time it is widely assumed that the evolution of its "satellites" is necessarily a secondary issue.

Yet Germany was the very heartland of Marxism, with the largest party in Europe, its leaders and intellectuals the most enlightened and committed of such formations anywhere, comparable only to the prestige of the Italian Communist Party after World War II. It is not to be assumed that the German survivors who returned from Moscow after the war to found a new socialist state were mere puppets of the Russians (however unattractive we may find Ulbricht's character). On the contrary, there were probably proportionately fewer opportunists among these believers than in the minority parties of the other Eastern states. Meanwhile, as the only socialist country besides Korea to share a border and a language with a capitalist counterpart, and as the object of the most intensive Western strategy of obstruction and sabotage outside Cuba, East Germany—virtually leveled to the ground and its own diminished population drowned in German-speaking refugees from further east—faced problems unparalleled in other socialist experiments since the early years of the Soviet Union itself.

Meanwhile, the disgrace of the wholesale privatization of collective assets after "the fall" was matched only by the crimes of the oligarchs in the soon-to-be ex–Soviet Union. As for culture, after Brecht, only literature in which "dissidence" (a late seventies term) could be detected was of any interest abroad, the daily life of the DDR constituting for the West little more than one long life sentence or waste of time. The absorption of this aberrant entity back into the Bundesrepublik was thereby seen as a simple return to normality, with the exception, to be sure, of economic normality—production, employment, and the like.

This is the situation in which we may well wish to take note of the appearance of what has seemed to some the most considerable work of East German literature, Uwe Tellkamp's massive novel *Der Turm* (*The Tower*).[1] The book appeared in 2008 in what I am still tempted to call West Germany to enormous acclaim, winning all the literary prizes and catapulting its author at once to the summit of the current German pantheon. The scandalous unfamiliarity of this author's name is only partly due to the absence of an English translation until now; probably the lack of interest in the DDR is just as significant, and—despite Susan Sontag's naive questioning of the very existence of a "Second-World literature"—publishers have understood that, after the end of the Cold War, there is little enough public demand here for accounts of everyday socialism. Still, I call this work by a forty-year-old writer who grew up in the DDR an "East German novel" because it is saturated by that daily life, so different from our own, and has an authenticity unavailable even in the finest imaginative descriptions by outsiders, such as Günter Grass's remarkable *Ein weites Feld*, let alone the punk literature of younger Eastern writers who have never lived in the system that formed their elders. Meanwhile, to be sure, Tellkamp's is an extraordinary and demanding art with a sentence-density comparable only to Thomas Mann or Grass himself (in German; in other languages Proust or Faulkner might be distant reference points); while his narrative experimentation, although by no means as complex as that of earlier East German writers such as Uwe Johnson

---

[1]   Frankfurt: Suhrkamp, 2008. Page references in the text designate this edition, and the translations are mine.

or Heiner Müller, has all the maturity of traditional modernist virtuosity.

Even German readers, however, have complained of the length (a thousand pages), of which, as one critic put it, only the last one-fifth—the disintegration of the East German state—has any genuine, if muffled, narrative excitement. And it is certain that the temporal focus of this work, which begins with Marx's centenary (and Brezhnev's death) in 1983 and ends in November 1989, demands a painstaking and detailed laying in place of the daily life of its protagonists in order all the more accurately to show its dissolution.

So the first part of the book is necessarily iterative, in Genette's sense of specifically situated scenes which are, nevertheless, designed to show how it always was, what they always did (Combray on a Saturday or Sunday morning). This makes for an episodic series of sketches of apartment life, school, publishers' meetings, and official encounters with the ideological "central committee" of the region; of parties and of vacations at Party establishments on the Baltic Coast; glimpses of *Haushaltungstag* (when bachelors are given time off to do the cleaning), hospital routines, the brief East-West contact of the Leipziger Buchmesse, and so forth. "Only the exhaustive is truly interesting," said Thomas Mann; and it will be a central question for us whether such loving detail constitutes what is today identified as *Ostalgie*—nostalgia for an "actually existing socialism" that has vanished.

But we must be careful not to grasp Genette's technical concept in any oversimplified way; to be sure, on the one hand, the iterative constitutes a solution to the older way of summarizing past events and their "uneventful" continuities. But it is not necessarily—or at least, not in this novel—the opposite number to the Event, the vivid representation of things finally happening; or to the real time of change and history as we might be tempted to imagine it emerging from the breakdown of a seemingly rather static system. "There is no misfortune other than that of not being alive," cries Christa Wolf at the conclusion of her Stasi-novella *Was bleibt*. "And in the end, no desperation other than that of not having lived." But that is not my impression of living in *Der Turm*; and we will have to wait for its sequel to know what "real life" lies beyond it.

At any rate, events here—and on their presence turns the very status of *Der Turm* as a historical novel—take place offstage; and, in a society as yet uncolonized by the modern media, they are transmitted in gossip and as rumor, as what takes place outside and beyond daily life, but also as what requires no explanation: Bitterfeld 1959, Chernobyl, the meaning of the presence of both German leaders at the reopening of the rebuilt Dresden opera house, Andropov's death, Father Popiełuszko, the Central Committee's suspicions of Gorbachev's new Soviet leadership, etc. Nor are the usual ingredients of the dissident novel present: no mention of the Wall or of the shooting of escapees, no Stasi informants, no secret police visits at three in the morning; only the most distant reminiscences of the suave and smiling villains, familiar since Dostoevsky; no Big Brother; in short, none of the conventional trappings of literary totalitarianism, or of the pity and fear it is designed to arouse. The shortage of consumer goods, which looms so large in Western visions of Eastern unfreedom, is here simply a fact of life, as are the infuriating insolences of a bureaucracy identified by the West as the repressive state.

Of the dissidents themselves, heroically celebrated in the West, little trace is to be found until the final pages, when hitherto unfrequented preachers suddenly begin to attract followings—and to alter their language accordingly; samizdat groups spring up, organized around previously unknown or insignificant figures; massed crowds in the railway stations begin to impede traffic; and the packed trains heading for the Czech and Hungarian borders begin to disrupt the protagonists' daily lives. Christian's hitherto apolitical mother becomes a demonstrator and would obviously be the heroine of an officially dissident novel; here, even the "event" of her political conversion takes place offstage and never becomes part of the novel's narrative representation.

The ordeal of Christian himself—the youngest of the three protagonists and the one of whom it can be said that *Der Turm* is at least his Bildungsroman—thus remains the principal exhibit for a political —that is to say, an anti-communist—interpretation of this novel, which is certainly no apologia for socialism either. The regimentation of his military service (in this country, for all practical purposes it lasts six years!), his moment of revolt (at the accidental death of a fellow draftee) and his condemnation to hard labor—these experiences, which seem to have been at least partially autobiographical, are ambiguous to the degree to which they can also be accounted for by his rebellious temperament; not necessarily the best argument for political heroism. In any case, the oppressiveness of military service is no more unpleasant than what one finds in Western war novels, though no less, either; while Christian's labor in the mines (he will in fact eventually be reinstated in the army) gives the novelist a brief opportunity to convey the true proletarian underside of what remains an essentially bourgeois existence and indeed a privileged one at that.

Indeed, the very title of *Der Turm* designated a relatively affluent section of Dresden, whose spatial disposition and distinctive buildings—on an elevation reached by way of an antiquated funicular—play no small part in Tellkamp's story. The old saw, that this or that (generally non-Western) city is really a small world in which everyone—that is to say, the intelligentsia—knows everyone else, is certainly true of *Der Turm* and its narrative. (The inhabitants of the most important apartment houses are listed inside the back cover.) The novel is organized around three such inhabitants, related, but dwelling in different buildings: the teenager Christian; his father Richard, a hand surgeon with a short fuse but many high-placed contacts; and Christian's Uncle Meno, in some respects the central protagonist. A zoologist by training, he now occupies a significant position in a prestigious publishing house; which is to say that he is also professionally part of the state censorship system, even when he resists it.

Richard's dilemmas are the most familiar: he has to deal, in secret, with a second family (there is occasional halfhearted talk about "fleeing" to the West). His position in the hospital is a vantage point from which we can observe the process of promotion in this system, as well as the ways in which hierarchy is felt in collegiality and in treatment. Richard's bluster is also capable of expressing itself in all kinds of aberrant adventures, from stealing a Christmas tree in a state-protected forest to the rebuilding in secret of a rare Hispano-Suiza car. These amount to a pushing of the envelope without serious consequences, since allowance has already been made for his character in his evaluation by the system. On the other hand, a series of futile attempts to appeal or at least to reduce his son's sentence testifies to the limits of influence of even so highly placed and valued a skilled professional. At least he escapes the fate of his superior, Dr. Müller, a Party member and disciplinarian whom we first observe at Richard's birthday party, warning his colleagues (and Christian) against telling jokes against the regime. But Müller—head of the entire hospital system—has indulged himself privately in amassing an impressive (and expensive) collection of glass sculptures and art-works; on the day after his retirement he receives a summons to the police station and notification of a house search and confiscation of unlawful property. Müller destroys the collection before committing suicide, leaving a note whose final sentence reads: "This is not the socialism we dreamed of."

Richard is not, to be sure, unlike his brother-in-law, a Party member; but it may still not be inappropriate to range him among a kind of cultural *Nomenklatura* (the Germans say *Bildungsbürgertum*, to distinguish them from the more secular garden-variety petty bour-geoisie); and to observe that, as is the case in so much of Lukács's "critical realist" tradition, there is not much proletarian presence in this particular realism either. Still, one must note that as a hand surgeon, Richard's activity does lay a kind of manual labor in place; and his hobby of carpentry underscores a utopian handicraft tradi-tion, explicitly related to the construction of *Dichtung*: "As in the operating room here also [in his workshop] there reigned, not the speech of words, but rather that of the hands—a speech familiar to him, in which he felt at home." In one of those lyric digressions which so frequently enrich and interrupt this lengthy novel, to our delight or annoyance, the hand itself is celebrated (the occasion is an operation on his own wife, injured after a domestic accident—or argument):

> He loved hands. Hands belonged to those living forms that gave him joy. He had studied hands: the lily-like femininity of Botticelli's women's fingers (and did these fingers not make up the hands themselves?); hands stubbornly con-vinced of something; hands in despair both about their failure to grow and their emergence from childhood; hands creamed and uncreamed; cooing hands, as unfathomable as moss; lady gardeners' tanned by the sap of plants, and male stokers' so devoured by coal dust as to be unwashable … *Reading* hands had already given him satisfaction in his internship, challenges that might have seemed chafing or bothersome to others for him were sources of excitement, that you approached carefully and willingly, shyly, fearful of a nakedness that was however there, throbbing softly, in the lust to be known.

Richard's fascinations are here the very locus of a central ambiguity in praxis as such: they can express Sohn-Rethel's sense of the emer-gence of ideology from the split between manual and intellectual labor; or a phenomenon akin to those discoveries by Michael Fried of the embodied autoreferentiality of the act of painting itself in the presence of the hand in a Menzel or a Caravaggio. And in fact this celebration of the "hand" in *Der Turm* means both and faces both ways: as the shadow of a fundamental production process in this socialist state, in which it has slowly begun to deteriorate; and as the mirage of art and its objects and traditions, by which so many of its protagonists are mesmerized and, as it were, immobilized, under a timeless spell.

As for Christian, we have already observed that this otherwise unremarkable protagonist of the Bildungsroman—a shy, musically gifted boy, attentive to his uncle's lessons and experiencing the first bewildering approaches of love and sexuality, as well as the confusion of the unpolitical soul (this side inherited from his maternal uncle), reacting to the approach of the political with rebellious anger (his inheritance from his father)—this story is the place to which the representation of the peculiar oppressions of the DDR is centrally consigned.

But it is important to note that Christian's transgression is one of language, and that indeed, in this elitist version of DDR life and politics, it is language which is, from literature to politics, the crucial space in which the relationship to the state is tested: "The problem is not what you did but what you said," explains the interrogator to Christian. "You damaged trust. This is not a matter of comrade junior officer Burre's death, which is of course regrettable. We will naturally investigate that, it goes without saying. But that's not the debate at present! That's a wholly different case. No, Hoffman, you and your buddy Kretschmar, whom we know very well, you made observations. You slandered us. You openly attacked our state."

Our own first lesson in language sensitivity is in fact administered by the very same unhappy Dr. Müller, who observes, at Richard's birthday party, "Not a very good joke, gentlemen … we have responsibilities, gentlemen; and it is easy to take part in cheap denigrations of our country …" (the alternation between the words *Land* and *Staat* is a crucial clue; Müller here uses the former). Only the Nomenklatura, whose fidelity to the state can for the most part be taken for granted, are allowed to permit themselves the occasional political pleasantry, as we shall see. But as far as Christian is concerned, his lessons began much earlier, and in a rather surprising form:

Erik Orré [an actor] had been a patient of Richard and wanted to show his thanks in an unusual way, namely to demonstrate the art of effective and professional lying to the boys, Richard estimating that this was something Christian in particular needed to learn; so the mime ... practiced enthusiastic expressions of praise and flattery with them in front of a mirror, corrected their gestures, showed them how one could blush and grow pale at will, and how one could toady with dignity, emit stupidities with a straight face, using these as a mask over one's true thoughts, thresh out empty and yet intelligently flattering compliments, dissipate distrust in others and even in a pinch recognize other liars. (p. 332)

It is obviously not a lesson Christian has assimilated, despite his Uncle Meno's maxim: "A wise man walks with his head down, almost invisible, like dust."

Meno Rohde is by far the most interesting character in *Der Turm*, as well as being the most reserved; and despite the political ambiguity that has led a number of (West) German reviewers to charge him with the kind of apathy and submissiveness which not only kept the regime in power, but can even be read as a form of active support, by virtue of its very passivity. As the reader for Hermes-Verlag and its prestige series of classic authors, he is part and parcel of the censorship apparatus, as we have noted, however often he seems to argue against its decisions; and we may well wonder why it is always to his chapters that one looks forward and with his reticences and withdrawals that one feels sympathy. One of those rare people for whom silence is not shyness, nor indifference either, but rather some genuine distance from things, an almost Buddhist disengagement from personal action, coupled with an equally genuine passion and detached curiosity for observing it in others, Meno is a genuine intellectual—even though mostly patronized by the novel's official intellectuals, inasmuch as he is not a professional writer (save for his book reports and a private diary of which only the reader is given installments).

Yet there exists a more positive way of celebrating Meno's passivity and that is as scientific observation. His formation was in zoology, and it is this active detailing of the outside world and, in particular, of its life forms that Christian learns from his uncle, "and is not troubled by Meno's demands, not angry when Meno in a friendly but implacable fashion gives him to understand that he had observed poorly and had not couched his impressions precisely enough in his language." For it is also a training in *le mot juste*, in the fashion in which Flaubert corrected the descriptions and observations of the young Maupassant; and much of the ensuing discussion (in the passage just quoted) turns on the characterization of the kind of green to be identified on the wings of the Urania moth. (Veronese green? They finally settle on "powder-green," which elicits not enthusiasm but the slightest nod of assent from his teacher.)

The professional hunt for bad punctuation and incorrect grammar in his authors' manuscripts therefore has its creative dimension in such observations, which are verbal as well as visual (let's also remember Nabokov's lepidopterology); but perhaps its social equivalent is something rather different. Meno himself observes a young writer, Judith Schevola, scrutinizing her fellows like "a researcher on insects": "her face distorted and twisted ... only the eyes belonging to her ... seeming to register everything with hostile curiosity." But that drive is the motor impulse of great satire, as in Proust's portraits; and as for the smaller details, Meno's characterization might well come from the Thomas Mann of *Doctor Faustus*: "These are the orchestral parts to which the composer devoted his most painstaking labour, even though the public will scarcely hear them ..."

It is to Meno then that we owe the most painstaking reconstruction of this seemingly timeless world, its antique objects rescued and stored up in the apartments of this once-prosperous quarter, the memory of the goods of yesteryear, marked with forgotten brand names ("a Fortuna typewriter as bulky as an old 'Konsum' cash register," etc.). Sometimes indeed it seems as though the life-world of these characters were little more than one immense collection of prewar objects and furniture, with the proviso that they are threatened at every moment by the coal dust that also saturates this novel, by its odor when not by smears and coatings, or its literal omnipresence in Christian's life in the mines.

But it is to Meno also that we owe the extraordinary and well-nigh zoological tableau of the intellectual flora and fauna of the late DDR, in portraits in which German scholars and historians have identified historical DDR celebrities (not always known in the West). I will say a little about those portraits before returning in conclusion to the issue of temporality (or timelessness) of the Dresden of this novel. Nothing here is indeed quite so delicious as these portraits, whose mimicry—as in Proust—expresses malice and sympathy in equal parts. Here we truly have a kind of intellectual and artistic Nomenklatura of the regime, at one and the same time believers and cynics; and the central proving ground for *Der Turm*'s insistent foregrounding of language. Stalinist dandies, with their theatrical delight in outright affirmation: "I was and remain an avowed defender of Stalin's order and have never concealed it … The murders were necessary, on the whole. Urgent times cannot have recourse to less-than-urgent measures. Desperate times cannot have recourse to less-than-desperate measures. The Soviet Union was surrounded, what else was he supposed to do?" Others are more resigned: "We are a part of the Soviet Union, without it we couldn't exist [*wären nicht lebensfähig*]." There are hatreds and passionate exchanges in the official meetings, particularly when exclusions are debated (that of Judith Schevola in particular); but the regional boss (Hans Modrow) deals with such decisions and the people they affect in a jovial yet matter-of-fact way. What goes without saying on this level—what the writers ought not to say in the first place—is rather different from the more standard ideological arguments of the everyday; as in the defense of the demands on professionals by Christian's girlfriend: "This country gives you a free education and free health care, isn't that something? Don't you think we have to give something back?"

Characteristically, the sons of both Nomenklatura speakers above violently disagree with their fathers' positions, from the Right and the Left, respectively; thereby underscoring the generational dynamics that also run through this novel. (Indeed, in my opinion, this theme is allegorical of socialism's most fundamental political problem, which is that of generational succession, or if you prefer the technical term, of social reproduction.) Still, it is important to realize that the apparent cynicism of this cultural Nomenklatura, at least in East Germany, in fact expresses a more complex psychological and political disposition, namely the tension between a believer's commitment to socialism and an insider's embarrassed distance from the Party's public decisions and rules (whose political necessity—the presence and support of the USSR—these intellectuals fully grasp). Irony is the expression of that embarrassment, and it is quite different from the cynicism of the characteristic West German talking points. I cannot resist quoting virtually the only sample of the latter (since these characters have so little contact with the West or indeed interest in it): this one we owe to a West German publisher visiting the Leipzig book fair, who in feigned astonishment at the continuing participation of the DDR writers in their state, places the following "devastating" question: "Would you be capable of killing a dolphin?"

Meno's presence in the novel then also affords an opening onto the question of temporality in what is, at least from one perspective, a lovingly detailed recreation of the space and objects, the daily life, of the DDR, with an intensity of feeling that might well be identified as nostalgia, or even *Ostalgie*—were it not for the obviously critical stance on the political administration of these realities, summed up in Christian's rash outburst after his accident: "*So was ist nur in diesem Scheissstaat möglich!*" To the degree to which the "timelessness" of this moment of DDR history is identified as stagnation (*zastol*, in the Russian characterization of the Brezhnev years), and attributed to late (or so-called "actually existing") socialism in general, the two perspectives are paradoxically one and the same.

On one level, to be sure, that of the *Bildungsroman,* the nostalgia is most easily explained as Christian's vision of his own childhood, brought abruptly to an end by military service. For Meno, the past is Dresden itself, virtually destroyed in the notorious firebombing of February 15, 1945: its geography, scarcely disguised by the cosmetic substitution of street names, the recognizable monuments and surviving buildings; even the very objects themselves which—as we have said and in the absence of investments in the production of consumer goods—resemble the artifacts in an immense museum of a past in which prewar Weimar and Wilhelminian Germany are virtually indistinguishable. Indeed, in this sense nostalgia is an unstable contagion, an existential contamination whose objects are interminably substitutable. So it is that the writing of a novel about the nostalgia of the people of the 1980s for some older world before the war becomes itself effortlessly transferable to the later years of the DDR in which that nostalgia was experienced.

Still, the seemingly timeless atmosphere of the first part of the novel—a timelessness which the title of Alexei Yurchak's study of the comparable period of Soviet history formulates as "Everything was Forever until it was No More"—demands closer attention. The matter of consumer goods clearly enough marks a crucial objective misunderstanding and interference with Western perspectives on the situation, as when we experience traffic in Cuba as a delightful return to 1950s America, when it is in fact the result of the half-century-long blockade of the Communist island. Here, the seeming transformation of commodities into antiques may itself be taken as an allegory of a non-commodity-producing society, in which books, artworks, and musical instruments are cherished, and each rare item—the von Arbogasts' *Granatapfelsaft* from the Black Sea—is the object of heightened perception and intensified appreciation, as though the modernist "make it new, make it strange" had been reversed in the direction of the past.

Meno's own peculiar "ten-minute clock" might well be an example of this heightened perception, were it not for the fact that Richard's father had been an actual clock manufacturer, thus suggesting an older and more archaic state of production which we ourselves are tempted to confuse with handicraft work; and, above all, the fact that the novel is punctuated insistently by the tolling of bells, whose irreversible temporality itself foretells the impending intrusion of History into this seemingly arrested, timeless world. Yet timelessness is also a political issue in a different sense, and we may pause to observe the way in which so much of Left politics today—unlike Marx's own passionate commitment to a streamlined technological future—seems to have adopted as its slogan Benjamin's odd idea that revolution means pulling the emergency brake on the runaway train of History, as though an admittedly runaway capitalism itself had the monopoly on change and futurity. It may well be that it is the gradual supersession of time by space in postmodernity which has released the very concept of temporality to a bewildering variety of speculative forms today. Thus Freud's notion of *Nachträglichkeit* (retroaction), in which the effect precedes the cause—a paradoxical, subordinate, and pathological concept in its own period, governed by a now old-fashioned chronological time scheme—has become one of the dominant contenders for theoretical hegemony (in Lacan, Derrida, and Deleuze alike); while older forms of succession associated with Hegel are dismissed as teleological.

But perhaps here too, in this experience of the East, some new lessons on time are available to us by way of the temporalities of *Der Turm*. Heiner Müller has characterized time in the DDR as a kind of waiting-room situation, in which the train is announced but never arrives—a novel version of the locomotive of History.[2] As Charity

---

[2] Quoted in Charity Scribner, "From the Collective to the Collection," *New Left Review* I/237 (September–October 1999), p. 147:

There would be an announcement: "The train will arrive at 18.15 and depart at 18.20"—and

Scribner noted in 1999: "While the delays in the East allowed people to accumulate experience, Müller claims, the imperative to travel forward destroyed any such potential in the West."[3] This is another version of Benjamin's critique of progress, but perhaps it suggests some new possibilities for imagining what a different present of time and of history might look like.

At any rate, the temporality with which *Der Turm* concludes, and with which it represents the dissolution of the DDR, is not at all a heroic narrative of resistance and freedom. This is not, in other words, a political narrative at all: what we glimpse here is the breakdown of the infrastructure itself, rather than that of the political system. It is foreshadowed in Richard's experience of the power blackout in the hospital, and the desperate measures with which the staff attempt to keep the patients alive; in the heating crises, as well, in which the bitter cold of the German winter demands all kinds of black-market ingenuities; in the breakdown of the little funicular, which normally lifts the privileged inhabitants of the *Turm* suburb to their quaint dwellings; in the stalled railway stations of the city, finally, in which the whole transportation system of the region comes to a halt. This is, in other words, "the material base" on which super-structural collapse is predicated; and appropriately it breaks into the characters' existential experience with all the intermittent confusion of unconscious causation generally, whether physical or mental.

Meanwhile, in an odd and somehow impersonal montage, these events and experiences in the late DDR present are juxtaposed and punctuated with what appear to be long extracts from a seemingly autobiographical narrative of World War II and atrocities on the Eastern Front (presumably the work of the writer here named Altberg, but who seems to represent Franz Fühmann; on this interesting figure, see Benjamin Robinson's 2009 *The Skin of the System*). We have had very little information about the past of any of these characters—Richard's experience of the Dresden firebombing, for example, or Meno's involuntary change of profession. Now, suddenly, this historical disaster, as it were an East German Year Zero,

---

it never did arrive at 18.15. Then came the next announcement: "The train will arrive at 20.10." And so on. You went on sitting there in the waiting room, thinking, "It's bound to come at 21.05." That was the situation. Basically a state of Messianic anticipation. There are constant announcements of the Messiah's impending arrival, and you know perfectly well that he won't be coming. And yet somehow, it's good to hear him announced all over again.

3   Ibid.

seems to summon up overwhelming memories of the older one, in a flash flood of returning temporality. *Der Turm*, however, ends, as befits a novel whose main character is much concerned with punctuation, with a colon, leaving the whole matter of political futures very much open. The author has projected a sequel, about the year 1990, entitled *Lava*. Perhaps, as 1983 took five hundred pages of the present work, it will not be necessary to repeat that tour de force for this next even more interesting year. But one is certainly curious to learn the reactions to it of intellectuals and inner Party circles, as well as of Meno himself and his family.

Chapter 12

Counterfactual Socialisms

In general, in the novel, youth is riding for a fall; something in the very form of the novel itself warns us obscurely that things will not turn out, indeed, in the very nature of "things" that they can never turn out. So it is refreshing to come upon a novel in which youth and its hopes and excitements are preserved as in a time capsule, forever enthusiastic even in its minor disappointments, as under a spell, indeed as in a fairy tale (as the author tells us). And this, in a historical novel—one of those new so-called postmodern historical novels that are springing up all around us—in which we all know very pertinently indeed that the experiment did not turn out, indeed, that twice over it did not turn out.

This youth, in which the world was new, and very bliss it was, is the youth of the Soviet Union: but not the 1920s, not the world of revolutionary hopes, but rather the youth of Khrushchev's 1960s, the youth of a whole new generation of Soviets who have put Stalin and the war, deprivation and the secret police, behind them, indeed, who have never known any of those things, whose emblem is Sputnik and education, and whose hope is "red plenty" in a distinctly different sense than in the consumerism of the American postwar. Spufford has done well, first to stock and bury his time capsule, and then to dig it up and open it for us: he has his own lessons to draw from its contents, but there may also be others he has not thought of.

But what a wonderfully and formally unusual novel: the docudramas on TV to which it presumably corresponds generically are really nothing like this, and not only because they keep encouraging us to compare the actors with the originals. Nor is this exactly a historical novel, even though it deals with a specific historical period—the Soviet 1960s—and includes real people as characters, most notably Nikita Khrushchev himself, alongside fictional characters, as well as "fictionalized" characters who "stand roughly where real people stood" (p. xiii).[1] Why this is not, then, simply a historical novel is an important theoretical question, which transcends the merely technical and classificatory one of genre.

It can be sharpened, however, by a few more classificatory questions of that kind: Why is it not a nonfiction novel, for example (in some more meaningful sense than the fact that that generic category no longer exists or never really caught on in the first place)? And what about what might be called the new "narrative journalism"— big books which purport to tell the story of a given crisis? I quote the beginning of one, perhaps the "biggest" and best, certainly the most famous, Andrew Sorkin's *Too Big to Fail*:

> The morning air was frigid in Greenwich, Connecticut. At 5:00 a.m. on March 17, 2008, it was still dark, save for the headlights of the black Mercedes idling in the driveway, the beams illuminating patches of slush that were scattered across the lawns of the twelve-acre estate. The driver heard the stones of the walkway crackle as Richard S. Fuld Jr shuffled out the front door and into the backseat of the car.[2] (p. 9)

Now every detail of this paragraph could be true and probably was and that would not make it any less fictional: Barthes called this kind of writing "novelistic," I believe, without thereby implying that it had to be part of a novel, only to give off the signals that a novel is supposed to give in order to instruct its readers to shift into the novel-reading mode (or gear, in this case).

Red Plenty is not like that either, despite its equally novelistic opening sentence: "A tram was coming, squealing metal against metal, throwing blue-white sparks into the winter dark" (p. 8). It includes, for example, fifty pages of footnotes, many of which are long and readable explanatory prose (Sorkin has forty pages of online references, plus the "five hundred hours of interviews" he was able to draw on). To be sure, novels have included footnotes before (as in *Finnegans Wake* or *Infinite Jest*), but not for reference purposes (and both Sorkin and Spufford include lengthy bibliographies). Thus, both books are based on research, but what is the (generic)

---

[1]   All page references in the text are to Frances Spufford, *Red Plenty* (Minneapolis: Graywolf, 2012).

[2]   Andrew Ross Sorkin, *Too Big to Fail* (London: Penguin, 2010), p. 9.

difference between journalism and history? Neither is supposed to include fictional characters, after all.

Spufford tries to clarify all this, and the uniqueness of his own text, by framing it as a fairy tale. I will say later on what I think this means and why it is not wrong. For the moment I think we need to return to the uniqueness, not of the form, but of the content, and to the strangeness of the fresh start, the new age, the new beginnings. This is not exactly "the sixties," which is a period concept rather than a date, and which happens at different times in different countries (Spain's *Movida* begins after Franco's death, or better still, after the failed coup; perhaps Russia's does as well; China's starts in the 1980s, etc.). Nor is it exactly the same as "the Thaw" or "perestroika," let alone the Cultural Revolution; but it is certainly a generational event and a youth movement, which breaks with the attitudes (both moral and political) and the authority of an older generation and a ruling class ("antibourgeois" captures something of this revolt even where we are dealing with non-bourgeois societies).

But the Soviet '60s dealt with here is not that kind of period; for one thing, the young still believe in socialism (as do their elders): for another, the objective situation has itself changed, not merely by the disappearance of something (Stalin and his programs and methods) but with the emergence of something new, which is not only the new technologies of the dawning computer age but also the release of older heavy industry to produce consumers' goods for the first time (this is the first and as it were literal meaning of the title). So we might call this new age "the postwar," as it happened in non-Soviet reconstruction as well (the Labour Party's national health service, the US highway system, MacArthur's agrarian reform in Japan, decolonization in Africa). In that case, *Red Plenty* can be seen as an analysis, not of reconstruction itself so much as of its ideology. In the Soviet case, however, the ideology of reconstruction, the ethos of the "new beginning" and the "fresh start," is not framed, as in the West, as the invention of something new and the call for a whole new mentality, but as a continuation or rather a restoration: the restoration of the original Soviet revolution, the starting up again of the original aims of Soviet communism, as they were before foreign intervention and the Hitlerian war. As for the Cold War itself, Khrushchev's trip to the United States (whose story is again told here) is enough to dispel the anti-Soviet fears aroused by Truman (and then again by Reagan after the chronological end of this book).

The characters are mostly scientists, young and old, real and invented; and the principal new beginning staged here is a scientific one (or to be even more precise about it, an informational one, involving the use of computer technology). But we are given enough of a sampling of daily life to understand that the scientific excitement and enthusiasms of the students are representative (allegorical) of a much more general feeling: the visit to the US pavilion, the life of peasants and racketeers, natural childbirth, popular crooners, the factories and their suppliers and contracts—even though all of this does not seem to follow a laundry list of the topics any thorough sociologist might want to cover in a totalizing picture of everyday life in a modern or modernizing society. Indeed, what would such a list look like? Yet we somehow feel that the novel has covered enough of its subject, and that its nontechnological or nonpolitical sections are not mere examples of something, nor relief from the more serious historiographic parts (which can, as I will show, be taken as steps in an argument), but that their variety ends up giving a fairly complete picture. (This is to be sure a miserable capitulation on my part inasmuch as the account of how and why a work of art feels complete and seems to stand as a totality is probably the first and most difficult task any critic has to confront.)

To put it another way, Spufford's artistry lies in his ability to make us forget (while we are reading his novel) all the things that have been left out: the areas in Soviet life in which people do not have renewed hope, the realities that do not fit into the fairy tale. But papering over the necessary exclusions is also part of the writer's métier.

Yet it is not fair to mention exclusions without commenting on some of the more surprising inclusions, starting with the footnotes, where we find information on open-air markets (pp. 372–3), viscose production (pp. 397–8), Soviet cars (p. 404), the psychology of middlemen (p. 400), types of apartments furnished to officials according to rank (p. 388), popular music (p. 418), and much more. To be sure, all this information is referred back to (probably nonprimary) sources, but the point is not only that it functions like local color in the old-fashioned costumbrista or exotic historical novels, but also that the novel as a form is today in competition with popular nonfictional genres (such as economic or sociological texts, popular biography, and the like). These genres scarcely existed in the nineteenth century, where novelists like Balzac functioned as experts and sourcebooks of the various social strata and their life customs. Indeed, the naturalists understood their vocation precisely as the supplying of just such information: Zola's notebooks and fieldwork testify to how seriously he took the responsibility of reporting on the structure of mines, for example, or the functioning of the stock market (something that occasionally returns today in bestsellers—a generic term—about airports [Arthur Hailey] or architecture [Ayn Rand]; where however this knowledge also has a secondary novelistic or ideological function). But that is precisely the point about the naturalists' descriptions: they could not, in the framework of the novel or of literature in general, consist in the communication of technical information for its own sake. All the objective material had also to be endowed with a symbolic or metaphorical function (Zola's mine thus *devours* human beings). It is not until the collapse of the aesthetic systems of the modern that postmodern works such as this one can again shamelessly include information as such and again briefly function like textbooks. Whether this is the result of the aestheticization of information in an informational society or on the other hand the informationalization of aesthetics in a specular or image-saturated one I do not decide, except to underscore the ideological significance of the answer settled on; and on the availability of yet a third solution, which is the dedifferentiation of specialized fields in the postmodern. This is a kind of response to the problem of historical information as such in *Red Plenty*, and it is a kind of return to Brecht's defense of the didactic—learning facts and functions or skills is a pleasure in itself, which the work of art need never renounce.

Still, this is supposed to be a fairy tale, and at its very center is set a real utopia (or "paradise," if you follow the Persian etymology of a walled or gated garden): this is Akademgorodok, founded by Khrushchev in 1958, and gathering together all kinds of scientists and academicians, including graduate students and even some artists, musicians, and the like:

> the path she was following turned in among a denser group of trees, and delivered her, only a hundred meters on, into forest hush. Suddenly the path beneath her feet was carpeted with dry pine needles; suddenly, the world was roofed with a speckled canopy of leaf and sky through which the sinking sun filtered only as a focus of greater brightness. Sounds were filtered too. Now and again she could still hear the grinding of construction machinery, but it had become

as tiny and unimportant as the buzz of the occasional bees that cruised beneath
the tree trunks. The wood was a mix of pine and silver birch … (pp. 153–4)

The love of nature also comes with national characteristics, and
this whole settlement is a collective dacha in the industrializing
Siberian waste. It is a dacha for Russian intellectuals and mushroom
hunters; and we may well recall the charmed surprise of Europeans
on encountering American college campuses for the first time.
Something of that, and even something of the American freshmen
arriving on campus for the first time in their family-sheltered lives, is
captured here in Zoya Vaynshteyn's (Raissa Berg's) disembarkment
in this socialist campus, which, like the other kind, will combine the
excitement of learning and discovery with the toxins of academic
politics.

This is then the moment to admit that *Red Plenty* is essentially
about intellectuals, however wide it seems to cast its net. In fact, the
"totality" of Soviet life it presents is a totality seen from the point
of view of intellectuals: even the political crisis it will face will be
a kind of academic crisis; and this is no doubt what will make the
novel so attractive for a certain kind of reader. It is not a historical
novel about the Thaw: these people have for the most part not even
known Stalin, any more than students today know the Jim Crow
laws or the anti-communist witch hunts. It is not a novel about
"hope" in the sense in which great revolutionary periods live that
out and determine genuine collective struggle, as in the China of the
1950s or the Spain of the early years of the Spanish Civil War. No, it
is rather a novel about activity, having a chance not only to do things
but to do new things, in fields that have never existed before. No one
here is passive, suffering a kind of forced objective paralysis or the
onslaught of terrible waves of subjectivity: neither unemployment
or depression. Even Khrushchev's first thought, when deposed, is:
"Nobody needs me now … What am I going to do without work?
How am I going to live?" (p. 282) Defeat here means, not existential anguish, but the melancholy of the unemployed: and it is a pity
that more Western writers do not better understand what they are
tempted to denounce as greed—the lust for power and ambition
also having as its secret driving force the delight in activity.

Yet as the very event of Khrushchev's fall testifies, this lively
period (and *Red Plenty* itself) must come to its end in something
it would be too hasty to call disillusionment. (It is significant, in

its hindsight, that the Brezhnev years were universally characterized as "the period of stagnation.") Many theories have been advanced to explain the collapse of the Soviet Union, including the failure to implement computer technology, to which I will return in a moment. But many have also agreed that the Khrushchev moment was the last one in which any genuine rebirth of socialism in the USSR was possible. Spufford has his own theory, and this novel is in that sense a thesis novel, which has a point to make. The author's own (genuine) "disillusionment" (as distinct from his characters') may be detected in his remark about Galina's painful experience of "natural childbirth" (the Lamaze method itself, of course, came from the Soviet Union): "another piece of mangled Soviet idealism, another genuinely promising idea ruined by the magic combination of compulsion and neglect" (p. 410).

The word magic nonetheless inconspicuously underscores something unique about this situation, something like the Strugatsky brothers' mixture of spaceships and Baba Yaga which is alluded to in the footnotes. It is time then to come back to this whimsical, seemingly generic question of fairy tales, and their relevance for what is assuredly a seriously researched and scholarly historical novel. Spufford's thesis has to do with that age-old Left question of the market and market socialism, a topic seemingly rendered extinct by the triumph of "free market" ideology, despite the contradictory evidence that in our situation free market means, not competition, but rather monopoly, and on a world scale. Yet funny-money theories, and the abolition of markets altogether, the elimination of the commodity form, and so on and so forth—these heady visions, along with their often disastrous consequences, do now seem a thing of the past: consumer society is not a propitious environment in which to dream of the abolition of money, however easy it may be to dream of the abolition of financial markets, which is not the issue here.

But the novel's hero—its world-historical figure, mostly glimpsed in the distance by the book's more "average" protagonists (in Lukács's sense)—is a real-life mathematical economist, Leonid Vitaliyevich Kantorovich, whose revolutionary discoveries of the late 1930s—in their isolation—mirror and anticipate the intellectual excitement of this generation of the dawning 1960s. Exceptionally, in the darkest days of Stalinism, his aloofness from every form of political consideration and the specialized character of his field meant that Leonid Vitaliyevich prospered, his theories were put into practice, and, far from suffering the by now stereotypical fate of all Soviet innovators (or of all Soviet Jewish innovators), reached the heights of Soviet academic glory (and also won the only Soviet Nobel Prize).

This mathematical analysis of production—it seems to be a kind of Taylorization of industrial production processes, as opposed to Taylor's own analysis of the industrial exploitation of human labor—then feeds directly into the exploration of cybernetics and information technology by the generation of the '60s, in Akademgorodok and elsewhere. The idea that computers can solve the dilemmas of a planned society, and that a computerized information system can serve as the material foundation for some future socialism, is not a new one: we find it in both of Ursula Le Guin's utopias, *The Dispossessed* and *Always Coming Home*, as well as in all kinds of theoretical projects. Yet the very sensitivity of the topic is also reflected negatively in the fact that there are no great utopian texts after the widespread introduction of computers (the last was Ernest Callenbach's *Ecotopia* of 1968, where computers are not yet in service). Instead, we have the free market deliria of cyberpunk, which assumes that capitalism is itself a kind of utopia of difference and variety. I think this failure of imagination on the Left can be attributed to the assumption that computers "take care" of totalization: that the well-nigh infinite complexities of production on a global scale, which the mind can scarcely accommodate, are mysteriously (Spufford might say, magically) resolvable inside the computer's black box and thus no longer need to be dealt with conceptually or representationally.

The term "market socialism" is carefully avoided by the Soviet economists, probably because it is generally thought to be the first step on the road back to capitalism (Spufford points to some who argue strenuously against such a presupposition, and to others whose language prudently veils their ultimate opinions on the topic). But perhaps the matter can be sorted out by distinguishing the perspectives of production and consumption. From the latter standpoint, that of consumer society, everyone wants the same thing—the standardized product, labeled by whatever different brand name you may prefer—and it is a question of polling those desires and then making sure there are enough items to go around, and in the proper places (how advertising intervenes into consumers' unconscious is yet another factor, which can presumably itself be measured). For the Soviet economists it is rather a question of computerizing the costs of production, and the sources of its various ingredients: totalization is here a matter, not only of the networks of raw materials, but of the way in which each source itself becomes a new center whose restructuration by the outflow of such basic ingredients then must be recomputed in its turn. Notoriously, the managers defend their own production sites against any attempt to integrate them into a larger system, which is of course just what the computer people want to do.

At any rate, it is a question of returning politics to the primacy of economics and putting the actual costs back into the plans, which only now begin to show mathematical accuracy. The intellectuals are predictably jubilant when these new ideas are adopted by their superiors and then by the state itself: for them, this is the climax of the new era, the moment in which "actually existing socialism" (a later expression) is on the point of rising to the level of its own concept, as Hegel would have put it.

But the moment in which costs are adequately reflected in their mathematical formulations is also the moment in which prices are made to rise: prices are indeed the cost of the concept, and the result are bread riots and the one (relatively unintentional) massacre of the Khrushchev era, the little-known repression of Novocherkassk on June 3, 1962. As in the ironies of misrecognition in the Victorian novel, our protagonists evidently know nothing of this carefully censored event, and are thus astonished to find, in the much-heralded Kosygin reforms of 1965, that everything but the essential corresponds to their own recommendations and calculations. In the same way, the Great Innovator himself is presumably astonished when he is quietly packed off into retirement in a grade-B limousine. All downhill from there!

This fairy tale is then in reality the novelistic working out of a rather different genre, which the historians know under the term counterfactuality, whose simplest exercise has to do with the turning of a crucial battle in warfare, or the unexpected death of a leader: thus, Arnold Toynbee speculated that had Alexander the Great not died at the Christological age of thirty-three, a world empire of lasting peace would have emerged. So also a Philip K. Dick allows us to glimpse a world in which the Germans and the Japanese won World War II; while Niall Ferguson adumbrates the blessings (no Soviet revolution!) that would have accrued to mankind had Germany won World War I.

Spufford's fairy-tale counterfactuality does not undertake to represent his alternate universe with science-fictional speculation; but the point of his wonderful novel is certainly to flex the mind's long-numb faculty of wondering "What if?" and to restore the freshness of an era in which for a long moment still, everything was possible.

As for the future of this past which scarcely existed, it is worth concluding with the author's somber reflections on it, typically consigned to a footnote:

> On the face of it, one of the great historical mysteries of the twentieth century should be the question of why the Soviet reformers of the 1980s didn't even consider following the pragmatic Chinese path, and dismantling the economic structure of state socialism while keeping its political framework intact. Instead, the Soviet government dismantled the Leninist political structure while trying with increasing desperation to make the planned economy work. But the mystery resolves rather easily if it is posited that Gorbachev and the intellectuals around him, all children of the 1930s and young adults under Khrushchev, might strange to say have been really and truly socialists, guarding a loyal glimmer of belief right through the Brezhnevite "years of stagnation," and seizing the chance after two decades of delay to return to their generational project of making a socialism that was prosperous, humane, and intelligent. With disastrous results. This whole book is, in fact, a prehistory of perestroika. (p. 413)

Chapter 13

Dirty Little Secret

The secret Mark McGurl discloses is the degree to which the rich-ness of postwar American culture (we will here stick to the novel, for reasons to be explained) is the product of the university system, and worse than that, of the creative writing program as an institu-tional and institutionalized part of that system. This is not simply a matter of historical research and documentation, although one finds a solid dose of that in *The Program Era*:[1] it is a matter of shame, and modern American writers have always wanted to think of themselves as being innocent of that artificial supplement to real life which is college education to begin with, but which is, above all, the creative writing course. Those who can, do; those who can't, teach. Think of the encomia of European intellectuals like Sartre and Beauvoir to the great American writers who didn't teach, didn't go to school, but worked as truck drivers, bartenders, night watchmen, stevedores, anything but intellectuals, as they recorded "the constant flow of men across a whole continent, the exodus of an entire village to the orchards of California,"[2] and so on.

There is the real, and then there is the university; and of course in one sense (the best sense) the university is that great vacation which precedes the real life of earning your living, having a family, finding yourself inextricably fixed in society and its institutions. The campus is somehow extraterritorial (McGurl identifies that relatively new genre, the "campus novel"; and he also compares the enclave experi-ence of the university to that now ubiquitous cultural activity, which has itself become an economic industry, called tourism); and the life

---

[1] Mark McGurl, *The Program Era* (Cambridge, MA: Harvard University Press, 2011). All page references in the text are to this edition.
[2] Jean-Paul Sartre, "American Novelists in French Eyes," *Atlantic Monthly*, August 1946.

of the student, when he or she does not have to sacrifice it in finding the tuition fees (the cost of living that life, the at first imperceptible setting in place of the lifelong Debt), is one of freedom: freedom from ideology (class interests have not yet come down like an iron cage), the freedom of discovery—sexuality, culture, ideas—and in a more subtle sense, perhaps, the freedom from nationality, from the guilt of class and of being an American. What the "real" writer wants to write about is not that kind of free-floating freedom, but rather the realities of constraint (the campus novel has the vocation of reintroducing that constraint back into the apparent freedoms of university life). So somehow the shame of being "taught to be a writer" (itself a kind of insult) is bound up with the guilt of a freedom your subjects (the "real people" in your novels) are not able to share.

There is more. Those European writers envying earlier American writers who, like Hemingway, were not university students and very far from any thought of writing courses and learning technique— those writers were citizens of societies in which universities were part of the state, and in which attending school was a social activity, sanctioned by society and classified among the official social roles it distributed. But of course in those systems there were no creative writing classes, an invention with which McGurl credits the United States. What the European university produced was not writers but intellectuals, and here we hit on the deeper reason for the American writers' shame at the country's institutional dirty little secret: American anti-intellectualism.

It is a very old tradition here, which is however not to be explained by some cultural characteristic or peculiarity, since in fact it expresses that most permanent dynamic of all societies—namely, class consciousness. Left intellectuals have the most trouble understanding this, insofar as they expect the content of their ideologies to shield them from the resentment of those with whom they identify. But anti-intellectualism is a form of populism, and it is the privileged position of intellectuals that is targeted and not their thoughts. Universities are part of that target as well, and the writers who feel guilt about their academic associations are also at least symbolically attempting to pass over to the other side, to dissociate themselves from idealism as well as privilege. Indeed, so omnipresent is symbolic class struggle in these matters that we find it at work in all the binary systems that run through McGurl's magisterial book, even though the class identifications shift position according to the concrete local situation. Thus the ubiquitous realism/modernism debate is coded and recoded perpetually, depending on whether realism is identified with bourgeois positions (as in Europe) or with the European colonizer (as in African and many other postcolonial societies). Gender itself is recoded over and over again, depending on whether it stamps literature as feminized and passive (as for the first modernists) or identifies feminism as a militant and oppressed position (as tends to be more the case in many countries today):

> Like the high/low binary to which it is often attached, but even more pervasive and various in its uses, the male/female binary floats throughout the system of higher education, the creative writing program and postwar fiction alike: one can point to the division between the (hard) sciences and the (soft) humanities, or to the division between the low-status "schoolmarm" and the high-status "professor," or, perhaps most interestingly, to the distinction between feminized "caring" institutions (e.g., the hospital) and masculinized "disciplinary" ones (e.g., the army). The school is neither a "feminine" nor a "masculine" institution per se but is rather the scene of countless micro-struggles between "maternal" love and punitive "paternal" judgment as two different forms of institutional authority. This reflects at long distance the advent of large-scale coeducation in the postwar period, and the related entry of (some) women into the professional-managerial stratum of the corporate workforce. (p. 44)

The unavoidable class opposition even recurs within the university; thus McGurl lets us understand that his restriction of the topic of American writing to the novel is itself a vehicle of class meaning. The poets have a nobler calling, and tend to look down on their lowly storytelling cousins; even theater dissociates itself from this humbler and more proletarianized vocation, while yet a fourth alternative—journalism—offers the would-be writer an escape from literature and its connotations altogether. The judgments of each of these "specializations" on each other are no less harsh than that of "ordinary Americans" on the university system in general. (To which we must add the stifling presence of the university itself as an institutional actor, within an already ominously bureaucratized and institutionalized society.)

The point is not so much to argue the "pros and cons" of these social connotations (which McGurl would like to avoid as much as possible), but rather to see how for the writers, in their new postwar situation as inevitable dependents of the university's largesse, the problem of escaping such coding and such identification is a profoundly formal one, which offers several alternative and seemingly contradictory solutions. It is these solutions and their systemic relationship to each other which *The Program Era* proposes to explore, succeeding triumphantly. It is a complex and dialectical book that practices what McGurl himself identifies as historical materialism and that makes unique demands on the reader, demands which are neither those of traditional literary history (even though the story wends its way from Thomas Wolfe through Nabokov and John Barth, Philip Roth and Joyce Carol Oates, all the way to Raymond Carver), nor those of traditional aesthetics and literary criticism, which raise issues of value and try to define true art as this rather than that.

The dialectical problems come in the reversals of class coding I have already mentioned. Whatever we think of Wolfe today, he not only invented an influential solution to the dilemmas McGurl lays out, but was once (by Faulkner, for example) considered the greatest American writer of his time; and there are reasons for that evaluation which have considerable historical and structural interest for us still. As for the theoretical problems the book poses for the reader, they result from what I will call the practice of transcoding implicit in McGurl's remarkably capacious topic. Transcoding presupposes an allegorical structure, a system of levels, in which we find ourselves obliged to translate from one to the other, inasmuch as each of these levels speaks a different language and is decipherable only in terms of a specific code. So it is that even in these opening paragraphs we have found ourselves moving from the economic situation of the writer to his or her aesthetic, from the status of the university— enormously enlarged since World War II and the very symbol of a new and enlarged democratic populace—to its class meaning for the immigrants and racial and gender underclasses who find themselves excluded from it, or on the contrary obliged to use it as a class ladder. We have had to invoke anti-intellectualism (and even to suggest the issue of the difference between America and Europe, and perhaps even, in globalization, between America and the rest of the world).

McGurl's argument makes its way sinuously among a number of different discourses: the history of writing programs and the mentality of their teachers, the way in which these professional developments are related to the evolution of late capitalism, the meaning of multiculturalism, the reevaluation of the central role of New Criticism after the war, the "hidden injuries of class" and the meaning and function of the Jamesian "point of view" (now rebaptized "focalization"), and so on. The text is itself experimental writing, and we have to learn how to shift gears and yet keep the thread, how to remain equal to its demands and to appreciate the originality of its historical judgments and the new system of American literature it proposes, as well as the originality of its method and form.

The book sets out a system in which two triads are coordinated (it will be their interrelationship which poses the most interesting problems for theory). The first of these tripartite systems is that of the teachings and doctrine of the creative writing programs introduced after the war. It can naturally enough be assumed that these literary and formal injunctions reflect significant changes in American subjectivity as well as modifications in the class relationships it reflects. They are quickly summarized: write what you know, find your voice, show don't tell.

In their form, these injunctions constitute an attempt to resolve a dilemma, or better still a contradiction: how can that very personal and individual practice that is writing, and in particular the writing of the novel, be taught? Remember that the novel, for Bakhtin and Lukács and so many others, is the very expression of modernity as such, and thereby transcends and annuls all the older fixed forms which presumably in one way or another could be taught: epic, drama, the various forms of the lyric, etc. The novel is in that sense always "lawless," as Gide liked to say, and we may have to raise some questions when someone like Henry James comes along and offers to codify its new "laws" in doctrines like "point of view." Even though he is virtually absent from this book, for reasons I will come to, Faulkner offered his own useful tripartite formula for what the novelist's practice presupposed: experience, imagination, observation—any two of which will suffice in a pinch (only Wolfe had all three). Maybe observation can be taught, as Flaubert tried to do with Maupassant; unfortunately, the other two are not available in the classroom.

McGurl's three injunctions try to address this difficult problem in a historically new way. (1) Write what you know. This emphasizes experience, in a way that tends to bracket "imagination" and to turn the writer's attention to the autobiographical, if not the confessional. It will be focused and intensified by the next injunction: (2) Find your voice, which perhaps begins with the premium placed by modernism on the invention of a personal "style," and develops into a virtuoso practice of the first person as performance. This seems at odds with the final injunction: (3) Show don't tell, which is the obvious legacy of James's theorization of point of view, and most directly reintroduces "craft" or technique, a set of rules (drawn mostly from drama) that would seem to be more teachable in the context of a writing program than the two other (negative and positive) recommendations.

The attention to craft is the trickiest of these formulas, as its ultimate tendency is the despised return to genre and subgenre (and the loss of any claim to genuinely "literary" prestige, unless the genre is handled reflexively, as pastiche). But it is clearly also the disciplinary component, without which all the excesses of narcissism and verbiage are potentially released. Thus, in a way, "craft" tends to connote not merely discipline and self-discipline, but a kind of restraint that will eventually be identified as minimalism in another thematic opposition, never theorized directly, which runs centrally through McGurl's book. From this perspective, maximalism is rhetoric and self-expression, and its most distressingly monumental prophet is Thomas Wolfe, while in the contemporary moment the extraordinary productivity of Joyce Carol Oates will come to embody a different but no less troubling and potentially non-canonizable excess. The maximalist impulse will then tend to find ideological confirmation in the (relatively modern) notion of genius, which

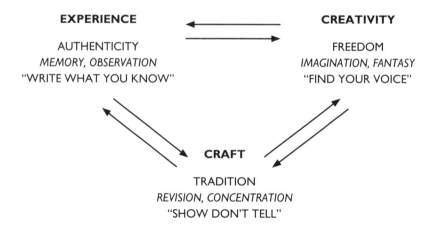

Kant saw as the eruption of the natural into the human, while its most congenial plot formation will be the novel of the artist.

This is not to suggest that minimalism finds its realization in the repudiation of the category of expression as such. On the contrary, the inaugural model of minimalism, Ernest Hemingway, simply opened up another alternative path to expression, one characterized by the radical exclusion of rhetoric and theatricality, for which, however, that very exclusion and its tense silences and omissions was precisely the technique for conveying heightened emotional intensity (particularly in the marital situation). Hemingway's avatar Raymond Carver then learned to mobilize the minimalist technique of "leaving out" in the service of a rather different and more specifically American sense of desolation and depression—of emotional unemployment, so to speak.

This is the point at which Faulkner's near-absence may be illuminated, for Faulkner is the very locus, one would think, of a maximalism that runs from the full-throated deployment of an expressive outpouring of language to the overweening ambition of the creation of a world extending from a tragic Southern past to a degraded commercial present. The Faulknerian long sentence is then the paradigm of a maximalism that remains high art, but it certainly cannot offer the craft and the tools for pedagogy available in minimalist discipline. I think that leaving Faulkner out of the picture (it is true that, virtually alone among modern American writers, he never had anything to do with writing programs)[3] allows McGurl to avoid embarrassing questions of value that risk disrupting the magnificent and unique theoretical construction he has achieved in *The Program Era*.

I have been emphasizing the subjective turn in postwar American aesthetics which the writing program's theory and practice symptomatizes and reinforces at the same time as it reveals and satisfies profound changes in the American psyche after World War II. The three injunctions are thus a precious clue for exploration both of the new postwar society and economy, and of the evolution of that subjectivity so often loosely identified as individualism. McGurl offers a few sociological references (Wright Mills, Pine and Gilmore, Thomas Frank), and even a few socioeconomic ones (Ulrich Beck,

---

3   Towards the end of his life, Faulkner taught for several semesters at the University of Virginia. See F. L. Gwynn, ed., *Faulkner in the University* (Charlottesville, VA: University of Virginia Press, 1995).

Anthony Giddens). The point is, however, not necessarily to endorse these (many are standard culture critiques), but rather to indicate the direction in which literary theory opens onto other disciplines. Class analysis is meanwhile omnipresent, and plagued as usual by the sometimes involuntary, sometimes intentional and strategic American habit of calling everything "middle class," so that what might once have been called the working class is now some form of lower middle class along with the others. But perhaps it is characteristic of American society today in late capitalism, and of the literature that expresses its realities and its ideologies alike, that working-class realities somehow reach classification only via stories told in terms of race and gender, rather than in terms of work, outsourced and famously transformed into so many "service industries." Still, the transformations of subjectivity in this postwar period are necessarily dependent for their inspection on the kinds of narrative available, which McGurl codifies according to class terms.

There is one further observation to be made here: the increasingly self-centered and obsessively reflexive cast of this literary production, which seems to be implied in McGurl's injunctions (write what you know, find your voice), is not to be understood in an exclusively negative or critical way. "Write what you know" and "find your voice" can also be understood as the exploration and opening up of wholly new areas of experience: a naming of new findings, as with the model of the body so influentially pioneered by Foucault, which can now, for good or ill, be adapted to a kind of generalized colonization of subjectivity, its transformation into new experience(s). This process is radically different from the psychic "discoveries" and inventions we associate with the late nineteenth century, with Dostoevsky and James, George Eliot and Pontoppidan; those drew on the openings and possibilities of a competitive capitalism, in which robber barons and monopolies signified an expansion of individual and collective power. This American version, in the late twentieth century, signifies instead the constricted spaces and constraints of an already bureaucratized society, in which the "individualism" of the now lower middle classes is increasingly, as in Carver, the experience of impotence and vulnerability.

In fact, one of the more productive developments of the "post-individual" lies in its gradual allegorical transformation into group identities. This begins with the dialectic of the outsider and the rebel, who gradually—as McGurl demonstrates, relying on a notion of Walter Ong's—become the insiders of new collectivities, the small groups and new ethnicities of multicultural late capitalism. Meanwhile, the emphasis on the individual voice now slowly develops into militant ideologies of difference (which, as McGurl remarks, moves an otherwise distant High Theory such as Derrida's back into closer contact with, and increases its usefulness for, literature and creative writing).

So it is that what initially looked like a "culture of narcissism" now unexpectedly begins to generate new social formations and a new kind of non-introspective literature to express them. Thus McGurl's other tripartite system, which maps the literary forms of the novel into which contemporary production falls.

Once again, it is important to remember that while arising as responses to a common situation and a common dilemma, the three tendencies or modes are also antithetical to one another aesthetically, experientially, and in their class connotations: it is here, indeed, that the antagonisms of high and low literature, of the realism/modernism opposition, of art versus life, are played out. But our deeper

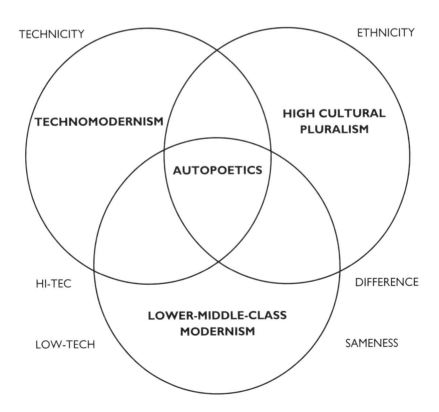

theoretical question has to do with the relationship between this second tripartite schema and the three writing program injunctions I have laid out. Here it is better to quote McGurl himself:

> Venturing to map the totality of postwar American fiction, I will describe it as breaking down into three relatively discrete but in practice overlapping aesthetic formations. The first, "technomodernism," is best understood as a tweaking of the term "postmodernism" in that it emphasizes the all-important engagement of postmodern literature with information technology; the second, "high cultural pluralism," will describe a body of fiction that joins the high literary values of modernism with a fascination with the experience of cultural difference and the authenticity of the ethnic voice; the third, "lower-middle-class modernism," will be used to describe the large body of work—some would say it is the most characteristic product of the writing program—that most often takes the form of the minimalist short story, and is preoccupied more than anything else with economic and other forms of insecurity and cultural anomie. (p. 32)

In the first triad, it was easier to see what united the three injunctions than what divided them; here it is the reverse, and unless we somehow identify the aesthetic of production all three classifications share (their "autopoiesis"), the system, however useful or satisfying it may be, will risk breaking down into a series of empirical traits and characteristics.

One has to begin with their differences. Thus so-called "high cultural pluralism" turns out to comprise various kinds of ethnic literature, which unite the particularity of their races, genders, and ethnicities with the universality of a literary modernism which has come in our time to stand for Literature itself (Toni Morrison becomes the exhibit here, whose *Beloved* McGurl ingeniously converts into a kind of schoolroom drama). But now the universalism of these multicultures is rather startlingly contrasted with a "lower-middle-class modernism" (I would have preferred the word "realism"), which is white and thus in this case not only unmarked but also particular rather than universal. This is the textuality and the world of Carver's loners and losers, and it is also the place in which regionalism is suddenly activated as a term: the presumably Northwest regionalism of Carver Country, marked by subalternity and economic marginality, is confronted with the transcendental regionalism of a now truly universal South (indeed, a fascinating part of McGurl's research details the struggle for form and universality between Midwest and South in the early University of Iowa writers' workshops).

There is therefore a struggle for literary status or universality or class prestige involved in these antagonisms (I have already identified such struggles as symbolic class struggle), but in this case what seems to be excluded is "technomodernism." One can once again quibble about the terminology, but much as I would like to I will limit myself to its translation into the single popular term "reflexivity," in particular as it concerns communication, information theory, and language, along with its cybernetic extensions and protensions. At stake here, perhaps, is the distinction between modernism and postmodernism, insofar as the reflexivity of the modern tends to turn merely on writing as such (as in *Pale Fire*), while the postmodern kind (as in the expression "postmodern novel," which seems by now to have become a genre) involves informational technologies that lie beyond old-fashioned language.

Indeed, this distinction can clarify the presence of the idea of the modern in the adjacent category, "high cultural pluralism," where "high cultural" can be supposed to mean not a periodization but simply an ensemble of now codified and socially accepted techniques that did not exist in the realist era. These techniques can now be used for a range of materials, such as race, which used to be class-marked and thereby automatically registered in the realist category (where they scarcely fit, as with Jean Toomer or Zora Neale Hurston); and now are transmogrified into Literature as such (another sign of this process being the authorization from High Theory to translate race and ethnicity into the concept of "difference").

If we then assume that the two sets of circles are "the same" in the sense of forming a homology, and that it is the implementation of the three writing injunctions which, according to emphasis, projects each of the respective literary areas or categories, we would presumably be reasoning as follows. Writing what you know becomes, reflexively, writing itself, in its multiple and reflexive technologies and communicational manifestations. It probably also means emitting a scent of origins (much like Barth's *Giles Goat-Boy*), in this case the university, making the campus novel (beginning with Nabokov) a favored vehicle. But by now the campus has become the world:

John Barth began to write *Giles Goat-Boy* at Pennsylvania State University, a land-grant institution where, as he later explained, "in an English department of nearly one hundred members" he taught his classes "not far from an experimental nuclear reactor, a water tunnel for testing the hull forms of missile submarines, laboratories for ice cream research and mushroom development, a lavishly produced football program ... a barn-size computer with elaborate cooling systems ... and the literal and splendid barns of the animal husbandry departments." Massively infused with federal funding for the support of Cold War weapons technology and other scientific research, but still catering to a regional and state economy (and its large football fan base), the secular university has become, for Barth, comically expanded and diversified in its worldly pursuits, nothing like the pious gentleman's college of yore. (p. 40)

As for high cultural pluralism (sometimes called multiculturalism), it too has acquired the status of universality or of Literature (technomodernism already had that, by definition) by way of a category henceforth excluded by the technology of writing or of High Communication: namely, the humble voice, establishing itself in the no-man's-land between "show don't tell," where telling is bad, and "find your voice," where the voice now stands not only for difference but also and above all for storytelling, and for a new modernist first person, perhaps harkening back to Mark Twain but now authorizing new kinds of transformation, such as the one that lifts Philip Roth's voice out of a narrow ethnic or Jewish literary category into Literature.

I have neglected until now the supplementary complication resulting from yet a third framework of McGurl's presentation, a chronology authorized more by the history of writing programs than the history—yet to be constructed—of American literature itself. The three historical periods are 1890–1960, covering the founding of the programs, especially the 47 Workshop, Iowa, and Stanford; their institutionalization (1960–75); and their omnipresence today in what remains our contemporary scene of literary production (1975 onward). Fair enough, and there is rich material here, particularly on the anecdotal and biographical level (Wallace Stegner and Paul Engle being particularly significant figures). But the consequence of this necessary and even indispensable supplementary framework (which endows a structural system prone to static and ahistorical cross sections with a dynamic of metamorphosis and continuity/change which it was not, according to the critiques of structuralism, supposed to have) is the illusion that what we have here is a literary history, and in a sense we do have a literary history, or at least a mapping bound to modify traditional literary histories. For we do move from Wolfe to Carver, we take in Barth and Kesey, Oates and Morrison along the way, and a host of minor writers from yesterday and today. Unfortunately, this quickly and unconsciously translates back into a canon and questions of value; and at this point, quite apart from the absence of the poets, sets off all kinds of idiotic questions about inclusion, principally the one I have asked throughout: where is Faulkner?

But now we approach an even more momentous problem, and it lies in McGurl's tripartite schema. For it is the fate of any third term to linger precariously on the margins, disabused of any ambition to become the synthesis between the two already in place, and thus condemned to struggle to displace one or other of its opposite numbers to find its own proper place in the binary system. What McGurl has called "lower-middle-class modernism" is always on the edge of proletarianization, slipping back down into mass culture and the genres still available in the form of pastiche to Literature in its nobler modes of technomodernism and high cultural pluralism.

The lower-middle-class mode cannot hope for that distinction, and so in it the two great tendencies of minimalism and maximalism fight it out to exhaustion, the former producing Carver, the latter Oates. Of the two, it may be said that minimalism carries the palm by way of a genuine high-literary invention—the rebirth of that quintessential writing-program form, the short story.

Meanwhile, both continue to exude the American misery, and more authentically than any of the competition convey the shame and pride of the human condition as lived by white America. It is a case of winner loses: the closer it is to real life in America, the less it can aspire to the distinction of Literature. At this point, the shame of the writing program joins the shame of America itself, which the other two modes have so successfully disguised.

Unfortunately, every triadic structure tends to fall into a pseudo-Hegelian pattern, and labors mightily to produce a synthesis. McGurl's triad cannot really do that, and so the burden of the operation falls back on the opposition between maximalism and minimalism. McGurl here produces, in the guise of Bharati Mukherjee's concept of "miniaturism," a seemingly satisfying place to stop. Probably the most famous deployment of this term, however, appears in that perverse and dramatic moment when Nietzsche, attacking the Wagnerian "sickness," pronounced Wagner to be a great miniaturist. That startling event should give us pause. Indeed, I want to suggest, following Nietzsche, that only a great maximalist can be a miniaturist (think of Mahler, Proust, even Faulkner); minimalism has no place for the obsessive perfectionism of the miniaturist. So the synthesis won't work (I hesitate before adding my own idiosyncratic feeling that four is better than three, and that we are missing a fourth term, which I would locate beyond the boundaries of the Program Era somewhere in poetry and in individual words).

Is *The Program Era* limited to the United States? It's true that Pascale Casanova's *World Republic of Letters* is evoked, but only so as to adapt it to the "inner globalization" of the multiplicity of literary modes and forms of distinction surveyed throughout this complex history. But American literature and the English language can scarcely be assumed to stop at our borders: for Casanova, consecration by Paris was a crucial stage in the world reception of non-French writers (to that we must also add translation into English, for world recognition today consists in securing this particular green card). Meanwhile, some of our literary positions have also been outsourced; much of what takes place outside can probably be assigned to the lower-middle-class waiting room, and peremptorily classified as mere "realism." Reflexive experimentation has probably long since been played out abroad, but there is one category in which Americans have begun to flag, and that is Faulknerian maximalism, whose interminable voices no longer seem tolerable without their Southern framework. Now, translated into something called "magic realism," this American specialty—whether adopted by Günter Grass or Salman Rushdie or the authors of the Latin American boom—has been promoted into a genuinely global genre, and we glimpse, outside the confines of an American Program Era, the outlines of some wholly different world system of letters coming into being.

Index